Augsburg College
Lindell Library
Minneapolis, MN 55454

WITHDRAWN

D1780831

Adjudicative Competence
The MacArthur Studies

Perspectives in
Law & Psychology

Sponsored by the American Psychology-Law Society / Division 41 of the American Psychological Association

Series Editor: Ronald Roesch, *Simon Fraser University, Burnaby, British Columbia, Canada*

Editorial Board: Jane Goodman-Delahunty, Thomas Grisso, Stephen D. Hart, Marsha Liss, Edward P. Mulvey, James R. P. Ogloff, Norman G. Poythress, Jr., Don Read, Regina Schuller, and Patricia Zapf

Volume 2	THE TRIAL PROCESS Edited by Bruce Dennis Sales	
Volume 3	JUVENILES' WAIVER OF RIGHTS: Legal and Psychological Complications Thomas Grisso	
Volume 4	MENTAL HEALTH LAW: Major Issues David B. Wexler	
Volume 5	HANDBOOK OF SCALES FOR RESEARCH IN CRIME AND DELINQUENCY Stanley L. Brodsky and H. O'Neal Smitherman	
Volume 6	MENTALLY DISORDERED OFFENDERS: Perspectives from Law and Social Science Edited by John Monahan and Henry J. Steadman	
Volume 7	EVALUATING COMPETENCIES: Forensic Assessments and Instruments Thomas Grisso	
Volume 8	INSANITY ON TRIAL Norman J. Finkel	
Volume 9	AFTER THE CRIME: Victim Decision Making Martin S. Greenberg and R. Barry Ruback	
Volume 10	PSYCHOLOGY AND LAW: The State of the Discipline Edited by Ronald Roesch, Stephen D. Hart, and James R. P. Ogloff	
Volume 11	JUDICIAL DECISION MAKING: Is Psychology Relevant? Lawrence S. Wrightsman	
Volume 12	PRINCIPLES OF FORENSIC MENTAL HEALTH ASSESSMENT Kirk Heilbrun	
Volume 13	DANGEROUS ADOLESCENTS, MODEL ADOLESCENTS: Shaping the Role and Promise of Education Roger J. R. Levesque	
Volume 14	TAKING PSYCHOLOGY AND LAW INTO THE TWENTY-FIRST CENTURY Edited by James R. P. Ogloff	
Volume 15	ADJUDICATIVE COMPETENCE: The MacArthur Studies Norman G. Poythress, Richard J. Bonnie, John Monahan, Randy Otto, and Steven K. Hoge	

Adjudicative Competence
The MacArthur Studies

Norman G. Poythress
University of South Florida
Tampa, Florida

Richard J. Bonnie and John Monahan
University of Virginia
Charlottesville, Virginia

Randy Otto
University of South Florida
Tampa, Florida

and

Steven K. Hoge
Private Consultant
Charlottesville, Virginia

Augsburg College
Lindell Library
Minneapolis, MN 55454

KLUWER ACADEMIC / PLENUM PUBLISHERS
NEW YORK / BOSTON / DORDRECHT / LONDON / MOSCOW

ISBN 0-306-46790-9

©2002 Kluwer Academic / Plenum Publishers, New York
233 Spring Street, New York, New York 10013

http://www.wkap.nl/

10 9 8 7 6 5 4 3 2 1

A C.I.P. record for this book is available from the Library of Congress

All rights reserved

No part of this book may be reproduced, stored in a retrieval system, or transmitted in
any form or by any means, electronic, mechanical, photocopying, microfilming,
recording, or otherwise, without written permission from the Publisher, with the
exception of any material supplied specifically for the purpose of being entered and
executed on a computer system, for exclusive use by the purchaser of the work

Printed in the United States of America

To the memory of our friend and colleague
Robert A. Nicholson

Preface

With the publication of Robey's (1965) "checklist for psychiatrists," Competence to Stand Trial became a topic of serious study among legal and forensic mental health researchers. Over the next quarter century substantial contributions were made by investigators from a variety of disciplines, prominent among them being the work of psychiatrist A. L. McGarry and colleagues at the Harvard Laboratory of Community Psychiatry (1973) that resulted in the development of two clinical measures for assessing defendants' competence, sociologist Henry Steadman's extensive follow-up of dispositions and outcomes for defendants adjudicated incompetent to stand trial in New York (Steadman, 1979), and the comprehensive text by psychologists Ronald Roesch and Stephen Golding (1980).

Despite the advances made by these and other investigators, there were significant gaps in our knowledge and limitations in the clinical measures for assessing adjudicative competence as the decade of the 1980s drew to a close. In two significant papers published in the early 1990s, Grisso (1991, 1992) noted:

> After two decades of research to improve CST [competence to stand trial] evaluations, CST examiners are still without any instrument offering standardized administration and scoring (as contrasted with CST interview guides and subjective ratings) to assess the domain of CST-related abilities for the general population of defendants who are referred for CST-evaluations. (1992, p. 366)
>
> We know very little empirically about the relationships between ratings/scores on these instruments and defendants' diagnostic features or characteristics... Further, current research offers almost no normative data for performance on these instruments by various special populations. (1991, p. 56)
>
> Without an objective measure of the legally relevant abilities, development of a research foundation for the field of CST assessment will continue to be limited. (1992, p. 367)

In the last decade of the 20th century, a significant research effort was mounted to close some of these gaps in knowledge and clinical instrumentation through studies conducted by the MacArthur Foundation

Research Network on Mental Health and the Law (John Monahan, Network Director) and other studies funded by National Institute of Mental Health grant R01 MH54517-O1A1 (Norman Poythress, P.I.). We bring together in this volume the fruits of this research effort including: the first epidemiological studies of attorney-client decision making (Chapter 1); advances in the conceptualization (Chapter 2) and measurement of adjudicative competence (Chapter 3); research findings regarding the relationships among psychiatric diagnosis and discrete psycholegal abilities relevant to competence (Chapter 4); the development of a standardized and norm-referenced clinical measure of diverse competence-related abilities, the MacArthur Competence Assessment Tool-Criminal Adjudication (MacCAT-CA, Chapter 5); and emerging research on adjudicative competence (Chapter 6).

Acknowledgments

We would like to acknowledge the generous and unwavering support of the staff of the John D. and Catherine T. MacArthur Foundation, including Laurie Garduque, Denis Prager, Robert Rose, Idy Gitelson, and Ruth Runeborg, and the guidance, insights, and expertise of the other members of the Network who stood outside the adjudicative competence working group—Shirley S. Abrahamson, Paul S. Appelbaum, Thomas Grisso, Pamela S. Hyde, Edward P. Mulvey, Stephen J. Morse, Loren Roth, Paul Slovic, Henry J. Steadman, and David Wexler. We would also like to acknowledge the contributions of other collaborators of the Network's adjudicative competence working group—Marlene Eisenberg, Thomas Feucht-Haviar, and Lois Oberlander; Network consultants Kirk Heilbrun, Robert Nicholson, Ronald Roesch; and other members of the NIMH study research team—Robert Nicholson and John Edens. Finally, there is a host of judges, public defenders, forensic hospital administrators and staff, jail administrators, and research assistants across nearly a dozen states without whose efforts this nine year program of research could not have been completed. Our thanks go out to all whose efforts made this work possible.

We are also thankful to the editors of the journals and works listed below for permission to use text and tables from the following previously published materials:

Chapter 1: Hoge, S., Bonnie, R., Poythress, N., & Monahan, J. (1992). Attorney–client decision making in criminal cases: Client competence and participation as perceived by their attorneys. *Behavioral Sciences and Law*, 10, 385–394; Poythress, N., Bonnie, R.J., Hoge, S.K., Monahan, J., & Oberlander, L.B. (1994). Client abilities to assist counsel and make decisions in criminal cases: Findings from three studies. *Law and Human Behavior*, 18, 435–450; Bonnie, R.J., Poythress, N.G., Hoge, S.K., Monahan, H. & Eisenberg, M.M. (1996). Decision making in criminal defense: An empirical study of insanity pleas and the impact of doubted client competence. *Journal of Criminal Law and Criminology, 87,* 48–62.

Chapter 2: Bonnie, R.J., & Grisso, T. (2000). Adjudicative competence and youthful offenders. In T. Grisso & R.G. Schwartz (Eds.), *Youth on trial: A developmental perspective on juvenile justice* (pp. 73–103). Chicago: University of Chicago Press.

Chapter 3: Hoge, S.K., Poythress, N., Bonnie, R., Eisenberg, M., Monahan, J., Feucht-Haviar, T., & Oberlander, L. (1996). Mentally ill and non-mentally ill defendants' abilities to understand information relevant to adjudication: A preliminary study. *Bulletin of the American Academy of Psychiatry and the Law, 24,* 187–197; Hoge, S.K., Bonnie, R.J., Poythress, N.G., Monahan, J., & Eisenberg, M. (1997). The MacArthur Adjudicative Competence Study: Development and validation of a research instrument. *Law and Human Behavior, 21,* 141–179; Poythress, N.G., Hoge, S.K., Bonnie, R.J., Monahan, J., Eisenberg, M., & Feucht-Haviar, T. (1998). The competence-related abilities of women criminal defendants. *Journal of the American Academy of Psychiatry and the Law, 26,* 215–222.

Chapter 4: Bonnie, R., Hoge, S., Monahan, J., Poythress, N., Eisenberg, M., & Feucht-Haviar, T. (1997). The MacArthur Adjudicative Competence Study: A comparison of criteria for assessing the competence of criminal defendants. *Journal of the American Academy of Psychiatry and the Law, 25,* 249–259; Hoge, S.K., Poythress, N., Bonnie, R., Monahan, J., Eisenberg, M., & Feucht-Haviar, T. (1997). The MacArthur Adjudicative Competence Study: Diagnosis, psychopathology, and adjudicative competence-related abilities. *Behavioral Sciences and the Law, 15,* 329–345.

Chapter 5: Otto, R.K., Poythress, N.G., Nicholson, R.A., Edens, J.F., Monahan, J., Bonnie, R.J., Hoge, S.K., & Eisenberg, M. (1998). Psychometric properties of the MacArthur Competence Assessment Tool-Criminal Adjudication. *Psychological Assessment, 10,* 435–443; Poythress, N.G., Nicholson, R.A., Otto, R.K., Edens, J.F., Bonnie, R.J., Monahan, J., & Hoge, S.K. (1999). Manual for the MacArthur Competence Assessment Tool-Criminal Adjudication. Odessa, FL: Psychological Assessment Resources, Inc.

Contents

CHAPTER 1: THE NATURE OF COMPETENCE TO PARTICIPATE
IN ADJUDICATION 1
    Study 1.. 3
        Method.. 3
        Results 5
        Discussion of Study 1 9
    Study 2.. 12
        Method.. 12
        Results 13
    Study 3.. 16
        Method.. 16
        Results 16
    Study 4.. 20
        Method.. 20
        Results 20
        Discussion of Studies 2, 3, and 4 23
    Study 5.. 26
        Method.. 26
        Results 28
        Discussion of Study 5 33
    Conclusion.. 37

CHAPTER 2: ADJUDICATIVE COMPETENCE IN LEGAL THEORY
AND PRACTICE.. 39
    Toward a Theory-Based Understanding.................... 41
    Values Served by the Competence Requirement 43
        Dignity.. 43
        Accuracy 44
        Autonomy 45

Components of Adjudicative Competence................. 46
  Competence to Assist Counsel........................ 46
  Decisional Competence............................... 47
Limits of the Unitary View............................ 49
Competence Adjudication in Practice................... 49

CHAPTER 3: DEVELOPMENT OF AN ADJUDICATIVE COMPETENCE
RESEARCH MEASURE: THE NETWORK'S ADJUDICATIVE
COMPETENCE RESEARCH AGENDA............................ 53
  The Limitations of First Generation Measures of Adjudicative
    Competence.. 53
  The Research Agenda.................................. 56
  Design and Development of the MacSAC-CD.............. 57
    General Design Features of the MacSAC-CD........... 57
    Component Measures of the MacSAC-CD................ 59
    Measures of Competence to Assist Counsel........... 61
    Measures of Decisional Competence.................. 65
    Basic Findings from the Adjudicative Competence
      Pilot Study...................................... 67
  The MacArthur Adjudicative Competence Field Studies.. 68
    Overview and Hypotheses for the Field Studies...... 68
    Research Objectives................................ 69
  Method... 72
    Participants....................................... 72
    Measures... 73
    Procedure.. 74
  Results I—Main Field Study (Male Defendants)......... 74
    Sample Description................................. 74
    Psychometric Properties of the MacSAC-CD........... 77
    Construct Validity of the MacSAC-CD................ 78
  Results II—Female Defendants......................... 83
    Sample Description................................. 83
    Psychometric Properties............................ 84
    Construct Validity................................. 85
  Discussion... 87
    General Findings and Conclusions................... 87
    Limitations.. 89

CHAPTER 4: RESEARCH ISSUES IN ADJUDICATIVE COMPETENCE.... 91
  Study 1: Diagnosis, Mental Status, and Legal Capacity...... 91
    Demographic and Criminal Justice Features of Diagnostic
      Groups... 92

MacSAC-CD Performance by Diagnosis................ 93
Mental Status and MacSAC-CD Performance within
    Diagnostic Groups................................... 96
Discussion 98
Study 2: A Comparison of Criteria for Adjudicative
    Competence... 99
    Assumption 1 99
    Assumption 2 100
    Assumption 3 100
    Refining Experimental Groups: Groups HI(C) and JS...... 100
Results 101
    Hypothesis 1 102
    Hypothesis 2 102
    Hypothesis 3 102
Discussion 103
Study 3: Comparison of Adjudicative Competence and Civil
    Competence... 104
    Abilities for Criminal Defendants with Schizophrenia 104
Results 107
    Criminal Defendants' Performance on Civil Competence
        Measures 107
    Comparisons of Performance Across Criminal and Civil
        Standards...................................... 108
Discussion 109

CHAPTER 5: DEVELOPMENT OF THE MACARTHUR COMPETENCE
ASSESSMENT TOOL-CRIMINAL ADJUDICATION (THE MACCAT-CA)..... 111
    The MacCAT-CA....................................... 112
    The NIMH Norming Study 113
    Method 114
        Selection of Study Sites........................ 114
        Selection of Participants 115
        Selection of Measures 118
        Procedures 119
    Results 120
        Sample Characteristics 120
        Psychometric Properties of the MacCAT-CA 123
        Interpretive Norms for the MacCAT-CA............ 131
        Prediction/Classification Performance Characteristics 137
        Patterns of Impairment Across Domains of Psycholegal
            Ability..................................... 138
    Discussion 141

Clinical Utility of the MacCAT-CA	141
Cautions in the Use of the MacCAT-CA to Assess "Competence"	143
CHAPTER 6: NEW RESEARCH ON ADJUDICATIVE COMPETENCE	145
The Competence-Related Abilities of Youth in Juvenile Court	146
The Competence-Related Abilities of Youth in Criminal Court	150
The MacCAT-CA and Defendants with Mental Retardation	151
Competence Assessment in Other Countries	152
Conclusion	154
REFERENCES	155
INDEX	161

1

The Nature of Competence to Participate in Adjudication

The requirement that criminal defendants be competent to participate in the adjudication of their cases is deeply rooted in Anglo-American law. Scholars generally agree that the underlying goal has been to promote fairness in the criminal justice system (Melton, Petrila, Poythress, & Slobogin, 1997). Subsidiary to the promotion of fairness, competent participation of defendants has several distinct purposes: to enhance the accuracy of factual determinations; to preserve the dignity of the criminal process; and to promote the defendant's exercise of self-determination in making important decisions in his defense (Bonnie, 1990).

The authoritative definition of competence for criminal defendants was provided by the Supreme Court in *Dusky v. United States* (1960): "the test will be whether [the defendant] has sufficient present ability to consult with his lawyer with a reasonable degree of rational understanding—and whether he has a rational as well as factual understanding of the proceedings against him." Although the legal standards for competence to stand trial differ from jurisdiction to jurisdiction in precise wording, all follow *Dusky* and have similar conceptual content.

In *Godinez v. Moran* (1993), the Supreme Court declared that decision-making abilities are encompassed within the construct of competence to stand trial, and that a defendant's trial competence and competence to plead guilty should be assessed under a single standard. Although the Court's decision in *Godinez* has clarified some aspects of the law governing the adjudicative competence of criminal defendants, the Court's silence regarding the criteria for decision-making capacity invites further conceptual development and continuing controversy.

While legal standards provide guidelines for judicial determinations, competence to stand trial—like competence to consent to treatment or to execute a will—is fundamentally a normative judgment. As applied, such normative judgments inevitably are highly contextual, depending heavily on the circumstances of the particular case and the impact of the defendant's perceived impairments—if any—on the values mentioned earlier. What is curious—particularly in view of the importance of competence determinations—is how little input practicing attorneys have had in the articulation of norms interpreting the legal standard. For the most part, content has been given to the construct of competence to stand trial by forensic researchers from the mental health disciplines who have attempted to operationalize the judicial and statutory standards in order to facilitate assessments (Grisso, 1986; Roesch & Golding, 1987). Defense attorneys have been consulted in these efforts, if at all, at the initial stages of instrument development.

The literature in the forensic field reflects the scant attention paid to the actual experiences of defense attorneys. Research and clinical assessment guidelines have focused primarily on the assessment of defendants' ability to function adequately in a trial setting, notwithstanding the fact that more than 90% of defendants plead guilty (Grisso, 1986; Roesch & Golding, 1987). Comparatively little attention has been devoted to the capacities of defendants to understand and make commonly occurring decisions, such as whether or not to accept a plea bargain or waive a jury trial. Little is known about the actual demands placed on criminal defendants in the criminal process, the problems faced by attorneys in their interactions with defendants, and which problems attorneys attribute to incompetent participation by their clients (Grisso, 1986; Steadman & Hartstone, 1983; Steadman, 1979). As Steadman and Hartstone (1983) noted, "The research that has been done both on incompetent defendants and on the processes for determining competency begins at the point the defendant is brought in for screening for competency...The whole set of interactions from the point of arrest to admission for initial competency evaluation is an empirical void" (p. 54).

In contrast, norms regarding competence to consent to treatment have emerged primarily from the experiences and practices of front-line practitioners—in this context, psychiatrists and psychologists (Grisso & Appelbaum, 1995). The practical problems and realities of providing professional service have been kept in the fore. Perhaps as a result, the construct of competence in this area is richly informed by context, particularly the seriousness of the consequences of the decision. And informal norms arising from grass-roots practice have often become formalized: the values and judgments of the responsible clinicians have dramatically influenced how appellate decisions are interpreted in routine cases and, ultimately, how legal decisionmakers think about competence to consent to treatment (President's Commission, 1982). While much is known about the norms operating to shape the practices of mental health clinicians in treating possibly incompetent patients, a comparable body of data does not exist regarding the norms applied by attorneys in their representation of criminal defendants. In this chapter, we describe five studies that have attempted to uncover and articulate professional norms regarding adjudicative competence.

STUDY 1

The first study was undertaken as an exploratory effort to examine the perceptions of defense attorneys regarding their clients' competence and participation in decision-making. In the only previous study in this area, Berman and Osborne (1987) surveyed 20 attorneys about clients whose competence they had questioned and found that attorneys reported a broader range of problematic behaviors than did clinicians. However, little is known about how frequently attorneys doubt their clients' competence, the nature and severity of the problems encountered in the process of conducting a criminal defense, or attorneys' approaches to clients whose competence is doubted.

METHOD

A structured interview was administered to attorneys working in the Public Defenders Office (PDO) in Tuscaloosa, Alabama. The PDO represents approximately 80% of indigent defendants charged in Tuscaloosa and the surrounding areas. (Indigent defendants comprise approximately two-thirds of all criminal defendants.) All six PDO attorneys gave their informed consent and participated in the study. The attorneys were told that their responses were confidential, and that neither they nor their clients would be identifiable in the aggregate reporting of the study. A sample of 122 of the 202 non-dismissed felony cases that reached final disposition between November 15, 1989 and June 30, 1990, was randomly selected.

Data on offenses were classified according to Alabama's criminal code. Class A felonies consist of the most serious and violent crimes, e.g., murder and first-degree rape. Class B felonies were less serious, e.g., second-degree kidnapping and arson. Class C, the least serious felony offenses, consists of residual felonies, such as property crimes.

Individual attorneys were interviewed monthly concerning cases that had been closed since the previous interview. Research assistants (RAs) used a structured interview designed by the research team to gather information about the nature of the defendant's assistance to the defense effort, including his or her participation in the case, contribution to the development of factual information, and participation in making decisions in the course of the defense. Attorneys were also questioned about their perceptions of the competence of their clients. Because the focus of interest was on the attorneys' perceptions rather than on whether their clients met the formal legal definition of incompetence, cases were identified for group inclusion on the basis of responses to the question, "Did you ever have any doubts about your client's mental capacity to participate in defense of the case?" Defendants for whom the attorneys responded positively were designated the DC (doubted competence) group; defendants whose competence was not doubted by the attorneys constituted the PC (presumed competent) comparison group.

The interview took approximately 20 minutes, on average, to complete and was branching in nature; depending on the attorneys' responses, between 25 and 58 questions were asked. When quantitative responses were required, the RA verbally presented the appropriate scale. Questions which called for categorical answers (e.g., the reasons for clients' unhelpfulness) were open-ended. Categories of responses had been established in advance for each of these questions. Attorneys' initial responses were recorded as clearly one of these pre-determined responses, or, alternatively, were recorded as "other." The list of possible responses was then read to the attorneys and they were given the opportunity to endorse each one.

When an attorney identified a client as of doubtful competence, additional questions were asked to determine the particular mental capacities that were thought to be impaired and the steps taken by the attorney to address these concerns about competence. When a formal evaluation of competence to stand trial was sought, additional questions focused on the conclusions reached by the mental health professional and the court. In every case, attorneys also provided information regarding demographics, criminal charges, case outcome, and sentences.

Results

Sample

The defendants were predominantly male (82%, $n = 100$) and somewhat more than half were black (58%, $n = 71$). The average age was 29 years ($SD = 8.2$). Overwhelmingly, cases were terminated by guilty pleas (95%, $n = 116$); fewer than 5% ($n = 6$) of selected cases went to trial. In the six cases that went to trial, three defendants were convicted, two were acquitted and one was found not guilty by reason of insanity.[1]

Class A felonies comprised 13% ($n = 16$) of the sample; Class B, 19% ($n = 23$); and Class C, 68% ($n = 83$). Among the convicted defendants, the sentences varied, as expected, with the seriousness of the offense. Of those convicted of Class A felonies, 63% ($n = 10$) received sentences with maximum lengths greater than 5 years; Class B, 44% ($n = 10$); and Class C, 15% ($n = 12$).

Attorneys reported spending a mean of 8 hours meeting with, or in telephone conversation with, their clients ($SD = 7.9$). The range of time spent varied from 1 hour to 55 hours. Attorneys reported significant doubts about their clients' competence in 14.8% ($n = 18$) of the cases. Defendants whose competence was doubted did not differ from the remainder of the sample in age, race, gender, or number of meetings with attorneys. These defendants, when compared with the defendants whose competence was not doubted, however, were charged with more serious felony offenses, $\chi^2 (2) = 25.7, p < 0.0001$.

Functional Abilities in the Criminal Process

Attorneys were questioned about the degree and adequacy of their clients' functioning as it related to: (1) the development of facts necessary to the defense, (2) participation in decision-making, and (3) overall participation in the defense. Findings are summarized in Table 1.1.

Defendants' Assistance in Developing Facts

Most defendants were viewed by their attorneys as being "very" or "somewhat" helpful in developing facts. Defendants of doubtful competence evidenced no comparative disadvantage in this functional domain. Stated

---

[1] The single insanity acquittal, a third-degree burglary case, was actually arranged by stipulation. It is noteworthy that this was the only (NGRI) acquittal in the total universe of 210 felony cases, including dismissals, from which our sample was drawn. These Tuscaloosa data thus provide additional evidence of the infrequency of insanity verdicts in felony prosecutions and the uncontested nature of most insanity dispositions (Callahan, Steadman, McGreevy, & Robbins, 1991).

TABLE 1.1. ATTORNEYS' VIEWS OF CLIENT FUNCTIONING

	Competence Doubted		Competence Not Doubted	
	%	N	%	N
Client Assistance in Developing Facts				
Very helpful	38.9	7	45.2	47
Somewhat helpful	38.9	7	41.3	43
Not helpful	22.2	4	13.5	14
Client's decision-making role				
Active	44.4	8	73.1	76
Passive	55.6	10	26.9	28
Overall client participation				
Unusually active	5.6	1	18.3	19
Somewhat active	38.9	7	63.5	66
Pretty passive	55.6	10	15.4	16
Very passive	0.0	0	1.9	2
Not involved	0.0	0	1.0	1

another way: attorneys' doubts about client competence were not related to their assessments of the degree of client "helpfulness" in developing the facts of the case.

While the two groups did not differ on the degree of help provided, their attorneys' reported reasons for the lack of helpfulness paint divergent portraits of the members of each group. In the PC group, 71.4% ($n = 10$) of the unhelpful defendants were thought to be lying to the attorney; in comparison, only one of the four unhelpful defendants in the DC group was thought to be lying. Instead, the unhelpful members of the suspected incompetent group all were seen as having "personality" problems ($n = 4$) and "mental confusion" ($n = 4$); in comparison, in the competent group, 23.0% ($n = 3$) of the unhelpful clients were seen as suffering "personality" problems, 7.7% ($n = 1$) as experiencing "mental confusion."

In sum, while the degree of help provided may not distinguish the two groups, attorneys perceived a significant qualitative difference: defendants of dubious competence were unable to provide information, while presumed competent defendants chose not to be helpful. We note, however, that the sample size of unhelpful defendants is small and precludes drawing definitive conclusions.

Defendants' Participation in Decision-Making

In order to allow statistical comparison, participation in decision-making was dichotomized as active (including rejection of advice) versus passive/

not involved. The suspected incompetent defendants were twice as likely as their counterparts to be described as passive/not involved in decision-making (55.6%, $n = 10$, of the DC group, versus 26.9%, $n = 28$, of the PC group; χ^2 (1) = 5.9, $p < 0.02$).

Attorneys were also questioned about the specific decisions that arose in the context of litigating each case. Only two decisions arose with sufficient frequency to permit statistical analysis: which witnesses to interview in the course of developing a defense ($n = 70$), and the decision to plead guilty ($n = 116$).[2] There were no differences between the two groups on participation in either of these decisions.

No bright-line ethical or legal principle requires attorneys to elicit their clients' participation in decisions about which witness to interview. The degree of defendant involvement is likely largely a function of the attorneys' inclinations rather than the defendants' capacities. Thus, it is not surprising that about 50% of each group of defendants were either passively involved or completely uninvolved in this decision.

The decision to plead guilty is a different matter; law clearly places the decision in the hands of defendants. And, unsurprisingly, attorneys reported that nearly 80% of each group were actively involved in deciding to plead guilty. The puzzle is why attorneys reported such active client involvement in this fundamental decision among the DC group while characterizing their overall decision-making role as passive. Two explanations can be offered. It is possible that defendants in the DC group are passive or uninvolved in decision-making as a whole, but when the crucial plea decision comes up, their involvement is greater, either through the efforts of others or because the importance of the decision elicits greater motivation. Alternatively, the attorneys may be exaggerating their clients' involvement in the plea decisions in light of the legal norm requiring client autonomy in this context.

Overall Participation of Defendants

A sizable minority of all criminal defendants were considered to be relatively uninvolved in the defense of their cases. According to their attorneys, about one-fourth of all defendants were at best "passive"

---

[2] Other decisions that were made in some of the cases were the decision to seek a mental health evaluation (8 cases), not to seek a mental health evaluation (10 cases), and to waive a preliminary hearing (2 cases). Aside from the stipulated NGRI verdict, 5 cases went to trial. In the tried cases, the decisions that were made were: which witnesses to call (5 cases), to testify (4 cases), not to testify (1 case), not to waive a jury (3 cases), the basic theory of the defense (5 cases), and not to raise an insanity defense (1 case). Of the 3 cases in which post-trial decisions were made, in two cases the decision was made to appeal, and in one case not to appeal.

participants in their cases. When this variable is dichotomized to allow statistical comparison, members of the DC group are significantly more passive than the comparison group, χ^2 (1) = 11.8, $p < 0.001$.

Dimensions of the Dusky Standard

Attorneys were questioned about the performance of members of the DC group on various functional dimensions of competence. While the numbers are small, it is interesting to note that among the 18 defendants whose competence was questioned by their attorneys, no defendant was described as being unable to understand the charges, the nature and purpose of criminal prosecution, or the roles of prosecutors, attorneys, and judges; these are the dimensions of competence which form the core of current conceptualizations and instrumentation of competence to stand trial (see Chapter 3). Clearly, the attorneys' doubts or concerns regarding their clients' competence pertain to capacities other than basic understanding of the criminal process.

Attorneys' Approaches to Defendants' with Doubtful Competence

Attorneys took a variety of steps when they suspected that their clients were not competent to participate in their own defense. In 52.6% ($n = 10$) of the DC cases, attorneys obtained formal evaluations by forensic mental health professionals.[3] However, in the remaining eight DC cases the attorneys responded in other ways. In three cases, attorneys reported that they made special efforts to communicate with clients whose ability to participate was perceived to be impaired by youthfulness, lack of education, or neurological impairment. One attorney consulted with an intimate of the defendant. (It is not clear how this consultation resolved the problem— that is, it might have resulted in a change in approach or understanding that altered the attorney's perception of competence; or it might have served as a substitute for competent defendant involvement.) One attorney was reassured by discussions with the probation officer and colleagues on the public defender officer staff. One case resulted in a plea of insanity, apparently without the competent involvement of the defendant. One attorney did nothing; and the efforts made in another case seemed to have been superficial. Attorneys also reported that significant others were more often involved in decision-making in DC cases (38.9%, $n = 7$) than in cases involving PC clients (13.5%, $n = 14$), χ^2 (1) = 7.0, $p < .01$.

---

[3] In only one case was the defendant found incompetent to stand trial. This was the same defendant who was adjudicated not guilty by reason of insanity.

Outcome

There was no difference between the two groups on whether or not a guilty plea was entered; nearly all cases were disposed of in this manner. However, it should be noted there were no cases of suspected incompetence among the five defendants whose cases actually went to trial. Two of the five were acquitted. All members of the DC group except one pleaded guilty; in the remaining DC case, the defense and prosecution stipulated to a finding of not guilty by reason of insanity.

Even though defendants the DC group were charged with more serious crimes, there was a trend for the DC group to be more likely (16.7% versus 5.1%) to receive probation as a sentence, χ^2 (1) = 3.17, $p < .08$.

Discussion of Study 1

Prevalence of Questionable Competence

The rate of referral for evaluation of competence has not been rigorously studied. Estimates of the proportion of felony defendants referred for evaluation of competence to stand trial, based on aggregate state data, are in the range of 2–4% (Institute of Law, Psychiatry and Public Policy, unpublished manuscript). We found about double this rate. And the rate at which clinicians supported a finding of incompetency, 1 in 10 cases referred, is somewhat lower than the 30% rate average across studies (Nicholson & Kugler, 1991). These deviations from reported rates are relatively insignificant and may be accounted for by our methodology—which is unlikely to miss referred cases—or by the small number of cases referred for clinical evaluation and local differences in assessments of competency. What may be more significant is that attorneys in our study doubted the competence of their clients in a much higher proportion of cases (14.8%) than is reflected in the rate of referral (8.2%). This finding, if substantiated, indicates that, at present, the magnitude of the problem of impaired defendant participation has not been appreciated and nor received sufficient attention in the professional literature. Before confronting these broader problems, two issues need to be addressed: (1) the factors influencing attorneys' judgments of client competence, and (2) the norms expressed by these judgments.

Factors Influencing Attorneys' Judgments

Authorities in the field have reported a number of factors which have led defense attorneys to refer their clients for competence assessments inappropriately, including ignorance of legal standards and strategic use of referral—to gather information, to delay the proceedings, or to avoid being criticized for failing to obtain an assessment (Melton et al., 1997). Our data suggest that attorneys who expressed doubts about their clients' competence seemed to have a real behavioral basis for being concerned. The DC clients were felt to be impaired in ways likely to threaten significant areas of defense preparation: they were seen as uninvolved in decision-making and passive participants in their own defense. And attorneys referred about half of the defendants whose competence they doubted; in most other cases, they sought other means to address their concerns. Finally, the family members of the DC defendants were more likely to become involved in the defense decision-making. These findings all suggest that attorneys were responding appropriately to signs of impairment of their clients' ability to contribute to their own defense. Of course, because our data were obtained solely from defense attorneys, we cannot exclude the possibility that the findings were affected by self-serving responses. And it is plausible that attorneys referred clients because they were concerned about their competence *and* because they sought to gain strategic advantage (Roesch & Golding, 1987).

Attorneys' Norms

From the findings in this study, one can begin to describe a coherent set of informal norms that shape attorney behavior in the shadow of the formal legal prohibition against convicting incompetent defendants. These norms are remarkably similar to the ones applied by physicians in treatment settings.

First, the data suggest that attorneys do not have a fixed notion of competent participation. Rather, attorneys' concerns about competence varied with the charges: as the charges increased in seriousness, defendants' competence was more likely to be doubted. This suggests that attorneys either had higher expectations of their clients when more was at stake, or that a greater degree of certainty about competence was sought in these circumstances, or both. Such an approach is remarkably similar to the "sliding-scale" of competence applied by clinicians in treatment settings which has been endorsed by the President's Commission for the Study of Ethical Problems in Medicine and Biomedical and Behavioral Research. In brief, as the consequences of a particular decision or procedure increase in seriousness, the higher the standard of competence applied (President's Commission, 1982).

Second, attorneys were not satisfied with a minimal level of understanding; they seemed to place significant weight on defendants' ability to participate in making important decisions. While authorities have noted the importance of decisional competence in theory and in selected circumstances (Bonnie, 1990), our findings suggest that this is a pervasive concern of attorneys. This is an under-appreciated aspect of competence in criminal cases.

Attorneys also resembled medical and mental health professionals in their approaches to clients perceived as having impaired competence (President's Commission, 1982). Formal means of resolving doubts about client competence were not invariably pursued. Instead, attorneys—like clinicians—sometimes involved family members in decision-making and modified their approaches in an effort to minimize the impact of client impairment. In one case, an attorney sought the advice of another attorney, much as a physician might seek advice from a peer about the proper course to follow.

Forensic Mental Health Referrals

Our findings suggest that the clinical assessment of competence might be improved in several ways. Currently, forensic clinicians often conduct assessments without significant defense attorney input about the complexity of the case or the attorney's expectations of the defendant. Authorities in the field of forensic assessment have recommended routine involvement of the defendant's attorney (Melton et al., 1997; Grisso, 1986). The evaluating clinician is usually not in a position to appreciate the quality of attorney-defendant interactions. In the absence of contextual information, forensic clinicians tend to apply a flat, unvarying yardstick of competence to all cases. Finally, forensic clinicians' assessments tend to give little, if any, attention to decisional competence. Routine involvement of the defense attorney in the assessment process may be helpful in correcting these problems. And forensic assessments more closely attuned to the concerns of defense attorneys may increase the utility, and perhaps the rate, of referral of those whose competence is doubted.

Defense attorneys may also benefit from easier access to assessments of competence. While the views of their colleagues may suffice in many instances, a second opinion from a mental health clinician has independent significance. As in the medical setting, it seems reasonable for attorneys to look for greater assurance of higher levels of competence as the stakes increase. Referral for evaluation may serve similar purposes to obtaining a consultant's opinion about the adequacy of informed consent for a risky procedure.

Although Study 1 yielded interesting results, it was exploratory and of limited scope. Cases were obtained from a single public defender office and included only defendants with felony charges. Little was learned about attorney-client decision-making in tried cases because so few cases ($n = 5$) went to trial. Thus, the generalizability of the findings is open to question. Further, our data were gathered exclusively from the perspective of the attorney and could potentially be influenced by attorneys' inclinations to report behavior in a manner consistent with legal norms (e.g., that otherwise passive defendants are actively involved in important decisions, such as whether to plead guilty). We therefore conducted three additional studies in cooperation with the Public Defender Office (PDO) in Tampa, Florida[4] that attempted to address these limitations. Study 2 was intended to replicate our previous work, but with a larger sample that included both felony and misdemeanor cases. Study 3 was designed to focus on those important but relatively rare cases that are resolved by trial rather than by a negotiated plea. Study 4 allowed us to compare attorneys' perceptions with the perceptions of their clients, the defendants themselves. Finally, Study 5, conducted in cooperation with Michigan's Center for Forensic Psychiatry, examined perceived impairments in a population of defendants with a clinically-supported claim of insanity.

STUDY 2

METHOD

Sample

This study involved debriefing attorneys regarding their interactions with their clients in a sample of 200 cases, identified prospectively from February 15, 1991, which were resolved by any means (e.g., trial, plea, dismissal). Consecutive cases were selected for debriefing without stratification on any variables except level of offense (felony versus misdemeanor); the sample was selected to preserve the approximate proportion of felony (45%) and misdemeanor (55%) cases handled by the PDO. Cases excluded from this study included traffic violations, juvenile cases, and mental health (probate commitment) cases. Twenty-two of the PDO's 35 felony division attorneys were debriefed on from 1 to 8 cases each, and 11 of the 16 misdemeanor division attorneys were debriefed on from 1 to 18 cases each.

Procedure

A structured interview similar to the one used in Study 1 was employed to debrief attorneys about individual cases that had recently been closed.

---

[4] In 1991 the PDO was assigned 7,467 cases, 42% of the total number of cases opened by the County Clerk's office; the remaining 58% of cases were assigned to private attorneys.

The interview, which took approximately 20 minutes to conduct, explored attorneys' perceptions of their clients' competence and helpfulness in providing factual information, and of their clients' overall participation in the defense and, in particular, decisions that arose in the case.

The interviews were conducted at the PDO by psychology graduate students and law students who served as research assistants. All attorneys approached for the study agreed, following an oral informed consent procedure, to participate in the debriefing interviews. The attorneys were told that their responses were confidential and that neither they nor their clients would be identifiable in the aggregate reporting of the data.

"Doubted competence," as used here, is not synonymous with a belief on the attorney's part that the client was incompetent to stand trial or even with a "good faith doubt" regarding the client's competence (which might give rise to a legal duty to raise the issue). Instead, a lower threshold of doubt was utilized: the attorneys were asked, "Did you ever have any doubts about your client's mental capacity to participate in the defense of the case?" A low threshold was set to discourage attorneys from excluding cases at the outset based on judgments of degree that would be explored later in the interviews.

Results

Sample Characteristics

Most of the defendants (78%, $n = 155$) were male. Forty-nine percent ($n = 98$) were African-American, 45% ($n = 90$) were white, and 6% ($n = 12$) had other ethnic backgrounds. The average age was 28.6 years. Attorneys reported that they had doubts about their clients' competence in only 5% ($n = 10$) of the cases. Attorneys doubted the competence of 8% ($n = 7$) of the clients charged with felonies, but only 3% ($n = 3$) of clients charged with misdemeanors. The average age of the doubted competence (DC) group was 25.7 years, not significantly different from that of the presumed competent (PC) group, 28.7 years. The average age of felony defendants (27.4 years) was not significantly different from that of persons charged with misdemeanor offenses (29.5 years).

Case Resolution and Attorney Work Intensity

A substantial proportion of cases ($n = 185$, 92.5%) was resolved by the defendant entering a plea of guilty ($n = 75$, 37.5%) or *nolo contendere* ($n = 110$, 55%), the functional equivalent of a guilty plea. There was a significant relationship between the type of case (felony versus misdemeanor) and type of plea entered (guilty versus *nolo contendere*), χ^2 (1, N = 179) = 127.32, p < .001. Eighty-five percent of defendants facing felony charges entered a guilty plea, while 94% of defendants charged with misdemeanors entered *nolo* pleas. Attorneys reported that the misdemeanor courts at the Florida site somewhat routinely resolved cases by *nolo* plea as a matter of expediency, in return for "time served" sentences. For convenience of reference, we will refer to all of these as "guilty pleas." Of the remaining 15 cases, 10 were dismissed, and 5 were resolved by verdict at trial (3 bench trials, 2 jury trials).

All 10 of the DC defendants were convicted—9 pleaded guilty and the other was found guilty at trial; 7 of the DC defendants were convicted of the most serious original charge, while 3 were convicted of a less serious offense. Ninety-two percent (n = 175) of the PC group were convicted. Among the PC defendants who were convicted, 89% (n = 155) were convicted of the most serious original charge, while only 11% (n = 201) were convicted of reduced charges or probation violation.

Attorneys reported spending significantly more total time on felony cases (M = 8.9 hours) than on misdemeanor cases (M = 1.0 hours), F (1, 199) = 134.61, p < .001. Attorneys spent significantly more total time on cases involving clients whose competence was doubted (M = 15.7 hours) than on those of clients presumed competent (M = 3.9 hours), F (1,199) = 8.04, p < .001.

The attorneys were questioned about time spent directly with the client, including face-to-face or telephone consultation. They reported spending significantly more time with the clients charged with felonies (M = 2.5 hours) than with those charged with misdemeanors (M = .4 hours), F (1, 199) = 126.15, p < .001. Attorneys also reported spending more time with DC clients (M = 3.2 hours) than with PC clients (M = 1.3 hours), F (1, 199) = 3.63, p < .001. The sample of DC clients was not sufficiently large to allow a statistical comparison controlling for felony-misdemeanor offense.

Functional Abilities in the Criminal Process

The small number of cases in the DC group (n = 10) precludes statistical analysis in some of the comparisons of interest. However, trends can be suggested by inspecting the raw data in some instances.

ASSISTANCE IN DEVELOPING FACTS. Attorneys rated their clients as "very helpful," "somewhat helpful," or "not helpful" in developing the facts of the case. Among PC clients, most (90%) were perceived as either very helpful (42%, n = 79) or somewhat helpful (48%, n = 92); in contrast, attorneys rated 60% (n = 6) of the DC clients as not helpful in developing the facts of the case. Attorneys were also asked to comment on why their clients had not been more helpful. Regarding the DC defendants, attorneys referenced factors that may have limited the clients' ability, such as low intellectual functioning, in most cases (67%). In contrast, attorneys' explanations about the unhelpfulness of PC defendants more often suggested unwillingness rather than inability; in 49% of the cases unhelpfulness was attributed to client indifference, lying, unwillingness, or distrust of the attorney.

ACCEPTING ADVICE OF COUNSEL. Attorneys also rated their clients in terms of willingness to accept advice given by the attorney, using categories of "always," "usually," "sometimes," "rarely," or "never." Approximately 80% of both PC and DC groups were described as always or usually having accepted the attorney's advice; however, 20% of the DC group ($n = 2$) were described as rarely or never accepting advice, compared to 4% ($n = 8$) of the PC group.

CLIENT PARTICIPATION. DC clients were perceived as less actively involved in terms of overall participation in the case. Ratings on this issue were clustered in three rating categories – "active," "neutral," or "extremely passive/not involved." While 40% ($n = 4$) of the DC group were rated as extremely passive/not involved, only 7.4% ($n = 14$) of the PC group were so perceived. DC clients were also perceived to be less actively involved in decision-making than were PC clients. DC clients were approximately half as likely to be rated by their attorneys as actively involved in decision-making (30% versus 58%), and much more frequently rated as not involved or extremely passive (40% versus 7%).

Among specific decisions, the key decision explored was the decision to plead guilty. Data regarding client involvement are available for 88% ($n = 66$) of the cases in which defendants pled guilty and 50% ($n = 55$) of the cases in which defendants pled *nolo contendere*. As previously indicated, all these are referred to as guilty pleas in the text. Because only 5 cases went to trial, decisions regarding whether to waive a jury and whether or not to testify did not arise with sufficient frequency to be analyzed.

Despite the data above suggesting non-trivial levels of client passivity/uninvolvement in decision-making *generally*, attorneys described almost all of their clients, including DC clients, as actively involved in the decision to plead guilty. In guilty plea cases for which data were available, 100% of DC clients ($n = 7$) and 96% of PC clients ($n = 114$) were described as actively involved in the decision.

Response to Doubted Competence

In the 10 cases in which client competence was doubted, attorneys were questioned about the performance of DC defendants on various functional dimensions of competence. Attorneys noted client difficulties in the following areas: capacity to understand charges ($n = 4$), the role of defense counsel ($n = 6$) or the nature and purpose of criminal prosecution ($n = 4$); capacity to recognize and relate relevant factual information ($n = 7$); capacity to trust counsel ($n = 8$); capacity to understand decisions that the client was called upon to make ($n = 5$) or to make rational decisions ($n = 8$); and capacity to pay attention in court ($n = 7$) or avoid disruptive behavior in court ($n = 5$).

Although 10 defendants were of doubtful competence, only 2 were referred for a formal competence evaluation by mental health professionals. Of these, one was adjudicated incompetent. As alternatives to formal evaluation, attorneys consulted with another attorney in five cases. Relatives (or significant others) of the client were involved in decision-making in 70% ($n = 7$) of the DC cases (compared to only 15% of the PC cases).

STUDY 3

METHOD

Sample

Study 3 was designed to provide data regarding attorneys' perceptions of their clients and the attorney-client interactions in cases resolved *by trial*. Working back from February 12, 1991, a retrospective sample of 200 consecutive cases that had been resolved in the prior year by bench or jury trial was selected. Cases were selected in an identical fashion as in Study 2. Twenty-five of the PDO's 35 felony division attorneys were debriefed on from 1 to 11 cases each, and 13 of the 16 misdemeanor division attorneys were debriefed on from 5 to 13 cases each.

Procedure

The procedures used in this study were identical to those used in Study 2.

RESULTS

Sample Characteristics

Most of the defendants were male (76%, $n = 152$); 52% ($n = 104$) were African-American, 45% ($n = 91$) were white, and 3% ($n = 5$) were of other ethnicity. The average age was 31 years. Attorneys reported that they had doubts about their clients' legal competence in 11% ($n = 22$) of the cases. Attorneys doubted the competence of 14.7% ($n = 14$) of the 95 clients charged with felonies, and 7.6% ($n = 8$) of the 105 clients charged with misdemeanors. The relationship between type of offense and perceived competence did not reach statistical significance. The average age of the doubted competence (DC) group was 37.1 years, not significantly different from that of the presumed competent (PC) group, 30.3 years. The average age of felony defendants (30.9 years, $n = 95$) was not significantly different from that of persons charged with misdemeanor offenses (31.1 years, $n = 105$).

Case Resolution and Attorney Work Intensity

Most cases (66%, $n = 132$) were resolved by bench trial; 33.5% ($n = 67$) were resolved by jury verdict, and one case was dismissed after trial had begun. Of the 94 felony cases that went to trial, 60.6% ($n = 57$) that went to verdict were tried before a jury and 39.4% ($n = 37$) were bench trials; in contrast, 90.5% ($n = 95$) of misdemeanor cases were heard before a judge and 9.5% ($n = 10$) were jury trials. This relationship between the type of case and type of trial was statistically significant, $\chi^2 (1, 199) = 55.76, p < .0001$.

Perceived client competence was not associated with conviction rates; conviction rates for DC clients and PC clients were 54% and 56%, respectively. Both groups were convicted of the most serious offense charged in 45% of the cases. Misdemeanor charges resulted in conviction in 44% ($n = 46$) of the cases; the conviction rate in felony trials was 72% ($n = 68$). The relationship between offense type and rate of conviction was significant, $\chi^2 (1, N = 200) = 14.57, p < .0001$.

The attorneys reported spending significantly more total time on felony cases ($M = 34.9$ hours) than on misdemeanor cases ($M = 4.0$ hours), $F (1,199) = 81.64, p < .001$. Attorneys reported spending significantly more total time on cases involving clients whose competence was doubted ($M = 65.0$ hours) than on those of clients perceived as competent ($M = 12.9$ hours), $F (1,199) = 10.32, p < .001$. Again, due to the small sample of DC subjects, it was not possible to control for offense in making this comparison.

The mean time spent with the client (including face-to-face and telephone consultation) in felony cases ($M = 5.4$ hours) was significantly greater than the mean time consulting with clients in misdemeanor cases ($M = 1.2$ hours), $F (1, 199) = 82.3, p < .001$. The mean time spent consulting specifically with DC clients ($M = 5.9$ hours) was higher than that spent with clients perceived as competent ($M = 2.9$ hours), but this difference was not statistically significant, $F (1, 199) = 1.01, ns$.

Functional Abilities in the Criminal Process

As in Study 1, the small number of cases in the DC group ($n = 22$) precludes statistical analysis in some of the comparisons of interest. However, trends can be suggested by inspecting the raw data in some instances.

ASSISTANCE IN DEVELOPING FACTS. Attorneys rated their clients as "very helpful," "somewhat helpful," or "not helpful" in developing the facts of the case. Among PC clients, most (88%) were perceived as either very helpful (51%, $n = 91$) or somewhat helpful (37%, $n = 65$); only 12% were rated as not helpful. In contrast, attorneys rated only 69% of the DC clients as very helpful (14%, $n = 3$) or somewhat helpful (55%, $n = 12$), while 32% ($n = 7$) of the DC clients were rated as not helpful in developing the facts of the case. The relationship between perceived competence and helpfulness was statistically significant, χ^2 (2, $N = 200$) = 12.62, $p < .002$.

Attorneys were also asked to comment on why their clients had not been more helpful. As in the previous studies, attorneys' more often attributed the unhelpfulness of DC clients to disability, such as low intellectual functioning or mental confusion (63.2%) rather than intentional unwillingness (19.5%). In contrast, the attorneys more often ascribed the unhelpfulness of PC clients to indifference, lying, unwillingness, or distrust of the attorney (65.7%) than to factors related to impaired ability (26.4%).

ACCEPTING ADVICE OF COUNSEL. Attorneys also rated their clients' willingness to accept advice provided by them, using categories of "always," "usually," "sometimes," "rarely," or "never." Approximately 70% of both PC and DC groups were rated as always or usually accepting the attorney's advice; however, 22.7% of the DC group ($n = 5$) were described as rarely or never accepting advice, compared to 7.3% ($n = 13$) of the PC group.

CLIENT PARTICIPATION. Attorneys reported that DC clients were less actively involved in terms of overall participation in the case. Ratings on this issue were clustered in three rating categories—"active," "neutral," and "extremely passive/not involved." Fewer than half (45.5%, $n = 10$) of the DC clients were perceived as actively involved in their cases; 22.7% ($n = 5$) were rated as neutral and 31.8% ($n = 7$) were perceived as extremely passive/not involved. In contrast, 59.6% ($n = 106$) of the PC clients were perceived as active, 29.8% ($n = 53$) were rated as neutral, and only 10.7% ($n = 19$) were rated as extremely passive/not involved.

Despite these data suggesting non-trivial numbers of clients as passive/uninvolved participants in their cases *generally*, attorneys described their clients as quite actively involved in those important case decisions for which the legal system demands personal client involvement. In this study of tried cases, three discrete decisions of considerable importance arose in attorney-client discussions in most of the cases. Whether or not to plead guilty was explicitly discussed with 86% ($n = 19$) of the DC clients and with 92.7% ($n = 165$) of the PC clients. Whether to waive a jury and request a bench trial was discussed with 81.8% ($n = 18$) of DC clients and 87.6% ($n = 156$) of PC clients. Whether the client should testify at trial was discussed with 90.9% ($n = 20$) of DC clients and 82% ($n = 146$) of PC clients.

Attorneys rated the large majority of their clients as actively involved in these important trial decisions. In discussions regarding whether to plead guilty, 100% of the DC clients and 97.6% of the PC clients were rated as active; on the issue of requesting a bench trial 77.8% of DC clients and 85.9% of PC clients were rated as active; on the issue of testifying, 80% of DC clients and 95.9% of PC clients were rated as actively involved.

Response to Doubted Competence

In the 22 cases in which client competence was doubted, attorneys were questioned about the performance of DC defendants on various functional dimensions of competence. Attorneys noted client difficulties in the following areas: capacity to understand charges ($n = 7$), role of defense counsel ($n = 7$) or nature and purpose of criminal prosecution ($n = 7$); capacity to recognize and relate relevant factual information ($n = 16$); capacity to trust counsel ($n = 10$); capacity to understand decisions that the client was called upon to make ($n = 15$) or to make rational decisions ($n = 15$); and capacity to pay attention in court ($n = 15$) or avoid disruptive behavior in court ($n = 14$).

Although attorneys expressed doubts about the competence of 22 defendants, they referred only 10 clients for formal competency evaluation by mental health professionals. In these 10 cases the clinical examiners opined that the defendants were competent in 5 cases, incompetent in 2 cases, and the opinions of the two court-appointed examiners diverged in the 3 remaining cases. A formal adjudication was made in 6 of these 10 cases, and one defendant was adjudicated incompetent. Other actions taken by the attorneys to deal with problems posed by DC clients included consultation with another attorney (12 cases) and involvement of relatives (or significant others) of the client (8 cases).

STUDY 4

Method

One limitation of the first three studies is that the attorneys were the only source of data regarding client behavior and attorney-client interactions. Accordingly, these studies may be criticized on the grounds that attorneys may not accurately characterize these interactions; for example, they may overestimate the amount of time spent with clients, or inflate reports of defendants' involvement in key decisions in order to report behavior consistent with legal norms. To respond to this concern we conducted a fourth study in which we debriefed both attorneys and clients at the conclusions of cases in order to compare their perceptions regarding client participation.

Sample

Thirty-five felony cases closed after January 15, 1992 and were randomly selected for study. Each of the PDO's seven felony division chiefs identified five cases. The eventual sample contained 21 pled and 14 tried cases.

Procedure

Instrumentation and procedures for interviewing the attorneys were identical to those used in the previous studies. A second interview was constructed for use with defendants. Although the content paralleled that of the attorney interview, items and rating scales were reworded to reflect the client's point of view and the language was simplified. Defendants who had been acquitted or who were released on bond pending sentencing were interviewed in the community. Defendants who had been detained following conviction were interviewed in the county jail. The defendants were assured that participation in the study was voluntary and that their responses would be confidential. They were offered a $10.00 incentive to complete the interview, which took approximately 20 minutes.

Results

Sample Characteristics

The defendant sample was 76.5% male; 57.6% were African-American, 39.4% were white, and 3% were of other ethnic origin. The mean age of the defendants was 30 years.

Time Spent with Client

Clients and attorneys were asked to estimate the amount of time spent with each other (in person or on the telephone) discussing the case. Their paired estimates were within 2 hours of each other in 74% ($n = 26$) of the cases. In the remaining 9 cases, the clients' estimates were higher than the attorneys' in 5 cases and the attorneys' estimates were higher than the clients' in 4 cases.

Functional Abilities in the Criminal Process

ASSISTANCE IN DEVELOPING FACTS. In 80% of the cases, the attorneys and clients agreed that the client had been either "very helpful" or "somewhat helpful" in developing the facts of the case. In the remaining 20% of cases ($n = 7$) the attorneys and clients disagreed about the clients' helpfulness, but the responses did not differ in a particular direction. Attorneys reported that the clients had been "unhelpful" when clients described themselves as having been helpful about as often ($n = 4$) as the reverse ($n = 3$).

ACCEPTING ADVICE OF COUNSEL. Clients and attorneys indicated the frequency with which the client accepted the attorney's advice using a 4-point scale (*always, usually, sometimes, rarely*). In 80% of the cases the attorneys and clients were in close or exact agreement (within one scale point). For example, when clients reported that they "always" accepted the attorney's advice ($n = 16$), the attorneys reported that the clients always ($n = 6$) or usually ($n = 8$) did so in 88% of the cases. Similarly, in 70% of the cases where the attorneys reported that the clients always or usually followed their advice ($n = 27$), the clients reported that they always ($n = 14$) or usually ($n = 5$) followed their advice. In only 6% of the cases ($n = 2$) were the attorneys' and clients' perceptions of client acceptance of attorney advice in complete disagreement; in both of these cases the clients reported that they rarely took their attorneys' advice, while the attorneys reported that the clients always did so.

CLIENT PARTICIPATION. As noted earlier, attorneys and clients rated the client's overall level of participation on a 5-point scale, ranging from extremely passive to extremely active. Again, the paired responses were in close (within one scale point) or exact agreement in the substantial majority (71%) of cases and were in complete disagreement (more than two points apart) in only a small portion (11%, $n = 4$) of the cases. For example, in each of the 11 cases in which the attorney rated the client participation as a "4" (5 = *extremely active*), the client rated his/her own within one point of the attorney's rating (i.e., 7 rated a "5", 2 rated a "4", and 2 rated a "3"). In all four cases involving complete disagreement, the attorneys described the clients as extremely active while the clients described themselves as very passive (1 or 2 on the scale).

PARTICIPATION IN SPECIFIC DECISIONS. Clients were asked whether particular issues or decisions were discussed in the course of representation. In the pretrial stage of representation, one key issue is which witnesses to interview, and the level of agreement as to whether such discussions occurred was relatively high ($n = 33$, kappa = .63).

Fourteen of these cases went to trial; nine were jury trials and five were bench trials. The client testified in 10 of these cases. Attorneys and clients reported general agreement on whether certain key decisions were discussed: whether to waive a jury ($n = 8$, kappa = .71), whether the defendant should testify ($n = 13$, kappa = .41), whether other witnesses should testify ($n = 13$, kappa = .84), and whether the defendant should make a statement at sentencing ($n = 8$, kappa = .71). The attorney-client reports were in complete accord in connection with several infrequently occurring decisions: the probability of raising an insanity plea was discussed in only one case but was not raised; the possibility of waiving a preliminary hearing was discussed in two cases, and the hearing was not waived; and the possibility of appealing a conviction was discussed in only one case, and a decision was made to appeal. Interestingly, the possibility of a mental health evaluation was discussed in three cases according to the attorneys, but only one client recalled such a discussion (and an evaluation was obtained in this case).

Attorneys and clients were also asked to rate the client's level of participation in the specific decisions that were eventually made. In order to conduct statistical analysis of the level of agreement, the attorneys' and clients' reports were rated as in agreement if they both reported active participation in decision-making by the client or if they both reported passive participation by the client. The most important issue concerns the decision to plead guilty or go to trial. For decisions to plead guilty, the attorneys and clients both reported active client participation in 75% ($n = 12$) of the cases ($n = 16$) in which matched responses were obtained. In the remaining 25% ($n = 4$), the attorney reported active participation and the client reported passive participation. For decisions not to plead guilty, the attorneys and clients both reported active client participation in 80% ($n = 4$) of the five cases in which matched responses were obtained.

Among tried cases, the attorneys and clients substantially agreed regarding the level of client involvement in deciding that the client should testify (agreed in 6 of 8 cases), that the client should not testify (agreed in

2 of 3 cases), and that jury trial should be waived (agreed in 2 of 2 cases), but were not in accord regarding the level of client involvement in deciding whether other witnesses should testify (agreed in only 1 of 5 cases).

Perceptions of Client Competence

Attorneys reported that they had some doubts about their clients' competence in 11% of the 35 cases ($n = 4$), and a mental health evaluation was obtained in one case (the evaluator(s) regarded the client as competent). In none of these four cases did the attorneys report any concerns about the clients' capacity to understand the charges, the role of the attorney, the nature of a criminal prosecution, or their capacity to recognize and relate relevant facts. Instead, the basis of the attorneys' concern in all four cases was the clients' ability to make rational decisions. (Three of these were tried.) Interestingly, none of these four defendants doubted his or her own competence, but three other defendants did express doubts about their own competence.

DISCUSSION OF STUDIES 2, 3, AND 4

These studies replicate, extend, and clarify the results of our previous exploratory study. In Studies 2 and 3 we gathered data on substantially larger samples ($Ns = 200$ versus $N = 122$ in Study 1), and we included both felony and misdemeanors, whereas Study 1 examined only felony cases. In addition Study 3 extends the investigation into the small proportion of unusual cases (<10%) that go to trial. Finally, Study 4 provided information on attorney-client decision-making from the perspectives of both the lawyer and the defendant.

Reliability of Attorneys' Reports

These studies are the first in the literature to provide data on such questions as the amount of time attorneys spend with their clients, defendants' level of involvement in their cases generally, and defendants' involvement in making key decisions. Concerns about the reliability of the data gathered from only the attorneys are allayed by the findings of Study 4. Although the perceptions of the attorneys and their clients were not in perfect accord, there was substantial agreement on most measures (e.g., degree of client helpfulness, ratings of client involvement), and where differences occurred they do not suggest a systematic bias in the attorneys' reports in order to conform to expected legal norms. Our findings do suggest, however, that attorneys may rate their clients' as somewhat more active than the clients' perceive their own involvement in some cases. Whether this is a result of differing expectations, inflated reports by attorneys or other factors cannot be determined by our study.

We also find in Study 4 that none of the four defendants whose competence was doubted by their attorneys perceived any difficulties themselves. This may be due to lack of insight on the part of the clients, misperceptions on the part of their attorneys, or differing expectations of attorneys and clients in these cases. Finally, a few clients expressed concerns about their own competence, even though their attorneys perceived no problems. Possible explanations include attorney failure to ascertain competence problems, defendant anxiety, or, again, differing expectations.

These discrepancies in perception, which involved a subset of our small sample, suggest avenues for future research into attorney-client interactions. For our more limited purposes, however, this small sample is sufficient to lend confidence to the findings of Studies 1, 2 and 3 that clients whose competence is doubted are disproportionately passive in their overall involvement in their defense, and that the majority of defendants, whether perceived of doubtful competence or not, are actively involved in the key decisions in which legal norms mandate personal involvement.

Frequency of Doubted Competence

Study 1 identified 14.8% of the felony defendants as of doubtful competence. In these three studies, the competence of felony defendants was doubted in approximately 1 of 10 cases: 7.9% in Study 2, 14.7% in Study 3 and 11% in Study 4. The rates of doubted competence were considerably lower in misdemeanor cases (3% in Study 2 and 7.6% in Study 3). Taken together, these studies suggest that attorneys have doubts about their clients' competence in a small but significant proportion of cases. Doubts about competence are more likely to be expressed in felony cases than in misdemeanor cases, and in tried cases than in cases ending with guilty pleas. The relevant differences here would seem to be the increased stakes, the more extensive interactions, and the increased intensity of client involvement expected in tried cases.

Attorneys' Strategies in Doubted Competence Cases

An important finding, replicated in Studies 2-4, is that attorneys often do not obtain formal mental health evaluations when client competence is doubted. Indeed, only in Study 1 did the attorneys refer as many as half of the DC clients for formal assessment of competence. The rates of referral in these three studies were 20% (Study 2), 45% (Study 3) and 25% (Study 4).

It remains for future studies to explore the precise reasons that attorneys spurn the formal evaluation process in many cases of doubted competence. Several factors may be at work here. One, experienced attorneys may know that although they have *some* doubts about a client's competence, the legal threshold is a low one and most defendants referred for evaluation will be found competent. Thus, they may perceive formal evaluation as futile in equivocal cases. Two, the availability and costs-benefits of pursuing a formal adjudication of incompetence may affect attorneys' decisions. Structural features of some service delivery systems may discourage attorneys from looking first to the formal evaluation route (Poythress, Otto, & Heilbrun, 1991); for example, where funding for evaluations resides with local agencies, limited local funds may discourage attorneys' requests for formal evaluation in all but the most disturbed clients. Three, attorneys may perceive that for some clients a formal finding of incompetence would not be in the client's best interest; such a judgment might be related to negative views of the system for treating and restoring clients' competence, or to strategic concerns about the delay that would be involved. The relevance of these and other factors in attorneys' decisions about how to handle cases of doubted competence remains an interesting, but unexamined, issue.

Whatever reason may be operative in a particular case, the findings from these studies are consistent from those of our previous work in suggesting a set of informal norms, similar to the norms applied by physicians in treatment settings, that may shape attorneys' behavior in dealing with cases of doubted competence. Attorneys do not have an inflexible notion of competent participation, and their concerns about client competence are increased where the charges are more serious and the stakes for their client are greater. They were more likely to express doubts about the competence of clients who either were unusually passive or who tended to reject attorneys' advice. Further, doubts about client competence are more frequently expressed if cases are tried, when ongoing client participation in decision-making may be required; a simple or superficial understanding of the legal process may not be enough to allay attorneys' concerns about their clients' competence in these cases.

Finally, attorneys are amenable to alternative interventions for dealing with perceived incompetence. Rather than automatically resorting to the formal mechanism of referral for clinical evaluation of competence, attorneys appear open to other approaches that resemble those used in clinical settings, including the involvement of family members or consultation with a colleague ("second opinion"), as alternative ways of minimizing the impact of client impairment.

The rate of perceived mental impairment in the general defendant populations sampled in Studies 1–4 was too low to permit a thorough examination of the relation between client mental impairment (as perceived by their attorneys) and attorney-client interaction. Because the rate of perceived impairment is likely to be substantially higher in a population of defendants with clinically supported insanity claims, these cases present an opportunity to study the impact of perceived impairment on the decision-making process. This is what was done in the next and final study.

STUDY 5

Decisions concerning the insanity defense provide an interesting context for studying broad questions relating to the allocation of decision-making prerogatives in criminal defense. It is clear, for example, that attorneys are obligated to adhere to the instructions of competent clients who refuse to plead insanity (See, e.g., *Treece v. Maryland*, 1988; see generally American Bar Association, 1986: Standard. 7-6.3 and accompanying commentary). It is not clear, however, that this norm entails the further obligation to facilitate client participation in decisions to pursue, or not to pursue, the defense. Thus, a study of insanity plea decisions presents a unique opportunity to explore the practical meaning of the legal norm of client autonomy in criminal defense.

METHOD

Sample

The Center for Forensic Psychiatry (CFP) in Ann Arbor, Michigan is a state-operated forensic hospital that conducts pretrial evaluations for courts throughout the state. The Center's computerized database was utilized to identify all cases for calendar years 1990 through 1992 in which the Center's forensic examiner had returned a clinical opinion supportive of the insanity defense. We sampled retrospectively to identify recent cases that had reached final disposition, thereby avoiding the ethical difficulties that would arise in investigating "live" cases. One hundred seventy-six such cases were identified. Data were retrieved from CFP case records regarding client characteristics (e.g., demographics, diagnostic and treatment information) and historical variables of interest (e.g., prior criminal record; history of prior psychiatric treatment). Information regarding attorney-client interaction and decision-making was obtained by telephone interviews with the defendants' attorneys conducted by CFP staff members.

Measures

Archival and interview data were entered on an 18-page research protocol designed specifically for this study. Two pages were devoted to data from the CFP case record, while the remainder of the protocol recorded attorneys' responses to inquiries about (i) case outcomes; (ii) strategies; (iii) attorneys' perceptions of clients' attitudes, competence, and level of participation in case decisions; and (iv) interactions with clients about whether to pursue the NGRI defense supported by the CFP examiner's report.

Procedures

The telephone interviews were conducted from July, 1991 through December 1993. Beginning with cases evaluated at the CFP during the 1990 calendar year, successive waves of about 20 cases each were selected for follow-up. A letter was sent on CFP letterhead to the attorney's office; it described the study and advised the attorney that a CFP staff member would be calling in the near future to conduct a telephone interview about the case. Initial phone contacts attempted either to complete the telephone interview or to set a specific date and time for a subsequent call during which the attorney could be debriefed regarding the case. In most cases, multiple phone calls were required to arrange the interview. As protocols were near completion for one wave of mailings, another group of letters was sent out.

Protocols were completed for 139 of the 176 cases (77%). When protocols could not be completed, this was typically due to difficulty reaching an attorney who had changed offices since the CFP evaluation; in a few cases the attorney was contacted but reported little or no memory for specific details and impressions about the case. Based on information recorded in the CFP records (e.g. offense, defendant's diagnosis, demographic characteristics), the completed cases were not significantly different from the uncompleted ones.

Results

Sample Characteristics

The 139 defendants whose attorneys were debriefed were predominately white (69%) males (87%) who were charged with a felony (93%) and were unemployed (77%) at the time of arrest. Most (73%) had been previously convicted of a felony charge and had one or more psychiatric hospitalizations (82%).

As expected with this sample, the overwhelming majority (85%, $n = 118$) received a primary diagnosis of a major psychiatric disorder: schizophrenia ($n = 77$, 55%), mood disorder ($n = 25$, 18%), delusional disorder ($n = 9$, 6%), or other psychosis ($n = 7$, 5%). Other primary diagnoses included: organic disorders ($n = 8$, 6%); mental retardation ($n = 4$, 3%); alcohol/drug abuse or dependence ($n = 3$, 2%); and autistic disorder, anxiety disorder, adjustment disorder, or organic personality disorder (1 each). Primary diagnosis for 1 case was missing.

The Forensic Evaluation

These defendants were referred to the CFP for pretrial evaluation of their criminal responsibility (100%) and their competence to stand trial (89%). Most (87%) of the evaluations were conducted on an outpatient basis. Of those referred for competence evaluation, more than half (64%) were considered by the examiners to be clearly competent, some (6%) were believed to be marginally competent, and the remainder were believed to be incompetent (30%) at the time of evaluation. Most defendants had been hospitalized at some point during the pretrial phase of their cases, either to restore competence (37%) or for other psychiatric treatment (32%). Interestingly, most of the defendants (90%) were on medication, usually anti-psychotic drugs, during the evaluation.

Based on the written CFP Report, it appears that most (85%) of the defendants cooperated during the evaluation. Among the 21 defendants who were uncooperative, 13 refused to answer any questions, 11 were thought to have concealed pathological symptoms, and 4 were thought to have malingered (i.e., fabricated psychiatric symptoms).

Client Participation in Decision to Seek Evaluation

Attorneys were asked to rate the client's participation in the decision to seek the CFP evaluations. In most cases, the client willingly followed the attorney's recommendation to participate in the evaluation, but the

TABLE 1.2. ATTORNEY DOUBTS ABOUT CLIENT COMPETENCE ($n = 139$)

Percent of cases in which attorneys had doubts about client's ability to:	
Understand charges	37%
Understand nature of criminal prosecution	44%
Understand role of defense attorney	32%
Recognize and relate relevant facts	53%
Trust defense attorney	22%
Understand decision s/he was called upon to make	57%
Make rational decisions	63%

attorneys sometimes made the referral without consulting the client (11%) or over the client's objection (8%).

Client Competence as Perceived by their Attorneys

Not surprisingly, attorneys reported that they had "doubts about [their] client's mental capacity to participate in his/her own defense" at some point during the litigation in almost three-fourths (72%) of the cases. Attorneys were not asked to rate the "degree of doubt" or the intensity of their concern about possible client incompetence. These doubts pertained to most competence-related abilities, as shown in Table 1.2. Of particular interest is the fact that the clients' ability to make rational decisions was more often perceived to be impaired (63%) than their ability to understand the charges (37%) or the nature and purpose of a criminal prosecution (44%). Doubts about clients' decision-making ability often led the attorneys to seek consultation or proxy decision-making from third parties: in 45% of the cases, attorneys reported they consulted a parent, or spouse, or other relative when making case decisions.

Case Disposition and Outcome

Table 1.3 reveals case disposition and outcome. Complete information was available for 123 cases. Cases for which complete dispositional information was available did not differ in any significant way from cases in which dispositional information was incomplete. In 14% of the cases, all charges were dismissed. Forty-one percent of cases ($n = 51$) were resolved by plea or stipulation; stipulated findings of not guilty by reason of insanity (NGRI) accounted for about half of the non-tried dispositions ($n = 25$). Where the defendant pled guilty ($n = 21$) or guilty but mentally ill (GBMI) ($n = 5$), the plea was usually (63%) to reduced charges. In cases resolved by plea, 76% involved plea agreements. The insanity defense was raised in

TABLE 1.3. DISPOSITION OF CASES WITH AVAILABLE
NOT GUILTY BY REASON OF INSANITY DEFENSE

	(%) (n = 123)
All Charges Dismissed	13.8
Resolved by Plea	41.5
Guilty	17.1
Guilty But Mentally Ill	4.0
Not Guilty by Reason of Insanity	20.3
Resolved by Trial	44.7
Guilty	1.6
Guilty But Mentally Ill	2.4
Not Guilty by Reason of Insanity	40.6

96% of the cases that went to trial and it was successful in 91% of the cases in which it was raised. The trial cases were almost always (91%) before a judge sitting without a jury. Overall, the insanity defense was successfully pursued in 71% of the non-dismissed cases, representing 61% of the cases in which the CFP had reached an opinion supporting such a defense.

Defendants' Reactions to CFP Evaluation

Curiously, in 4% of cases the attorney did not even advise the client of an available NGRI opinion. In these six cases, two were dismissed, three were resolved by GBMI pleas and one was resolved by a trial finding of NGRI. Most defendants (60%) were receptive to the idea of asserting an insanity defense and an explanatory formulation that attributed their offense to symptoms of their illness. Of particular interest, however, is the finding that 10% of defendants resisted an insanity plea and another 15% were unreceptive to the attribution of mental illness. The remaining defendants were indifferent. To our knowledge, this is the first empirical estimate of the frequency with which defendants who have an available insanity defense are likely to voice opposition to some aspect of the opinion.

Overall Participation in Decision-Making

Attorneys were asked to rate their clients' overall participation in decision-making. The sample was about evenly split between those who were viewed generally as being passively (46%) versus actively (54%) involved in case decision making. About 25% were regarded as uninvolved or "extremely passive" and, on the other extreme, 13% were rated as "extremely active." Most defendants were characterized as generally

THE NATURE OF COMPETENCE

TABLE 1.4. ATTORNEY'S PERCEPTION OF THE RELATION BETWEEN CLIENT PARTICIPATION AND CLIENT COMPETENCE

	General Population of Criminal Defendants (Tampa)[1]		Defendants with Clinically Supported Insanity Claims (Michigan)[2]	
	Competence Doubted $n = 32$ (8%)	Competence Not Doubted $n = 368$ (92%)	Competence Doubted $n = 95$ (72%)	Competence Not Doubted $n = 36$ (28%)
Accepting Advice				
Always	41%	45%	62%	75%
Usually	31%	32%	19%	19%
Sometimes	6%	17%	7%	3%
Rarely	9%	4%	7%	3%
Never	12%	2%	4%	0%
Client Participation				
Active	41%	59%	27%	42%
Passive	25%	32%	43%	46%
Extremely Passive	34%	9%	30%	14%

[1] Combined samples of defendants described in Studies 2 and 3.
[2] Total $N = 131$, rather then 139, due to missing data.

willing to follow counsel's recommendations, but 9% were described as "rarely" or "never" accepting their attorney's advice.

As Table 1.4 shows, however, attorneys' perceptions about client participation were related to whether they expressed doubts about their clients' competence, a finding that also emerged in our studies of a general defendant population. The data in Table 1.4 compare attorneys' perceptions about client participation in our Tampa study of a general population of criminal defendants with the attorney perceptions in the present sample of Michigan defendants with clinically supported insanity claims. In both samples defendants whose competence was doubted were perceived to be markedly more passive in decision-making, and somewhat less "compliant," than clients whose competence was not doubted. The key difference between the two samples is that attorneys expressed doubts about the competence of 72% of the Michigan defendants with clinically supported insanity claims, compared with only 8% of the general population of criminal defendants in Tampa.

The Decision Whether to Pursue an NGRI Defense

Attorneys described the process by which they and their clients decided whether or not to pursue the insanity defense in 134 cases (inadequate

TABLE 1.5. ATTORNEY-CLIENT INTERACTION IN INSANITY DEFENSE DECISIONS (%)

	All Cases ($n = 134$)	Defense Not Raised ($n = 20$)	Defense Raised ($n = 114$)
Disposition Arranged Before Forensic Examiner's Report Received	10%	35%	6%
Client Followed Attorney Recommendation	51%	40%	53%
Client Decided without Attorney Recommendation	5%	15%	3%
Client and Attorney Disagreed	3%	10%	2%
Attorney Made Decision Without Consulting Client	31%	0%	36%

information was available in 5 cases). It was ultimately decided that the NGRI defense would not be pursued in 20 cases, while the decision was made to enter an insanity plea in 114 cases. Table 1.5 summarizes data provided by the attorneys regarding discussions about this important decision with their clients.

In the 20 cases in which the defense was not pursued, the decision-making process usually followed one of two expected patterns. In seven of the cases, the case had already been dismissed or the defendant had already decided to plead guilty before the report was received. In eight of the cases, the attorney discussed the report with the client and recommended that the defense not be raised and the client followed the recommended advice. (In three cases the attorney discussed the report with the client but made no recommendation, leaving it to the client to decide how to proceed). Two of these cases are of special interest because they involved disagreements between the attorney and client—the attorney recommended that the defense be raised and the client rejected this advice; in one of these cases, the attorney unsuccessfully sought the court's permission to advance the defense over the client's objection.

In 85% of the cases, an insanity plea was pursued. In more than half (53%) of these cases, the decision was made with full client participation: in 43% of the cases, the attorney received the report, discussed it with the client, recommended that the defense be pursued, and the client followed the attorney's recommendation without objection; and in another 10% of the cases, the attorney entered an insanity plea based on an implicit delegation of authority from the client—either pursuant to a previous understanding with the client on the course of action to be followed upon receipt of the report or an anticipation of client ratification at a later time.

In only two of these cases did the attorney and client have an overt disagreement. In one case the client decided to raise the insanity defense in the face of the attorney's contrary advice; in this case, the client eventually decided to plead guilty. In a second case, a client who strongly resisted the insanity plea eventually decided to pursue the defense due to pressure by his family; in this case, the defendant was eventually found NGRI at trial.

In more than one-third (36%) of the cases in which the insanity defense was pursued, the attorneys appear to have pre-empted their clients' participation in the decision-making process. That is, the attorneys made the decision to pursue the insanity defense on their own, without meaningful client participation—they did not discuss the matter with the client at all or they presented a negotiated insanity plea to the client as a *fait accompli*.

Explanation for Attorneys' Preemptive Behavior

In the 41 cases in which the client participation was preempted, the attorneys were asked to explain their reasons for not discussing the decision with the client. In response, they usually indicated either that the insanity defense was the only real choice and that there was nothing to discuss (50%), or that they doubted their clients' competence to participate meaningfully in the decision-making process (38%). [In the few remaining cases, the attorneys indicated either that they consciously precluded the defendants' involvement due to anticipated disagreement ($n = 2$) or that they usually make decisions of this nature without client participation ($n = 3$)]. Not surprisingly, preemptive behavior was associated with other indicators of perceived client incompetence, such as whether the client had been hospitalized for treatment before trial, χ^2 (132.3) = 11.88, $p = .008$, and whether the attorney expressed doubts about the client's ability to understand important case decisions, χ^2 (97.1) = 4.07, $p = .04$. Interestingly, however, the attorneys who preempted client participation in the insanity plea decision were no more likely to seek consultation or proxy decisions from relatives than attorneys who elicited client involvement.

DISCUSSION OF STUDY 5

Results from Studies 1–4, which focused on unselected samples of criminal cases, provide a backdrop for the findings of Study 5. The attorneys in those studies described their clients as somewhat passive in general, but reported a high degree of client involvement in the discrete decisions for which well-established legal norms mandate client participation—e.g., whether to testify at trial, waive a jury and request a bench trial, or plead guilty.

Study 5 focused on a single decision—whether or not to pursue an insanity defense in a sample of defendants selected precisely because a supporting clinical opinion had been rendered. Clearly the decision whether to pursue the insanity defense was the pivotal strategic issue in these cases, and the prospect of psychiatric labeling, stigmatization, and indeterminate hospitalization would seem to place this issue squarely within the realm of client autonomy. Not surprisingly, one-fourth of the clients resisted the attributions of mental disorder, insanity, or non-responsibility represented by the forensic findings. Notwithstanding the arguments that can be made against raising the insanity defense, it was pursued in 85% of the cases in this study, including 79% of the cases in which clients had resisted one or more of the clinical findings. Moreover, contrary to our expectations, the rate of reported disagreement between the attorneys and the clients regarding the insanity plea was relatively low.

Surprisingly, the main finding in this study pertains to the *lack* of client involvement: attorneys made the decision without consulting the defendant in about one-third of the cases in which the defense was raised and the degree of client participation was relatively low even when the client was consulted. The key question is what accounts for the observed pattern of attorney dominance. In our view, this pattern is attributable to two related factors—an ambiguous legal and ethical norm relating to the attorney's obligation to facilitate client participation, and a distinct tendency toward paternalistic decision-making in cases involving defendants with documented histories of serious mental illness.

The Ambiguous Legal Norm

It is now well settled that defense attorneys are obligated to adhere to client wishes on basic issues relating to defense or disposition of the case, including the "theory of defense" and the plea. Until recently, however, decisions whether to raise the insanity defense were outside the defendant's sphere of control. In many states, for example, the insanity defense could be interposed by the court and, in some states, by the prosecution, without regard to the defendant's wishes (see, e.g. *Whalem v. United States*, 1968). Moreover, the defendant's preferences on this issue probably were not even binding on the defense attorney. Within the past 20 years, however, the governing legal norm has shifted decisively. A line of cases, beginning with *Frendak v. United States* (1979), has established not only that the defense may not be interposed by the state, but also that the defense attorney must adhere to the wishes of a competent defendant who declines to raise the defense (see *Treece v. State*, 1988). Michigan law is in accord with the prevailing rule. In *People v. Newton* (1989) the court held that a defense attorney who adhered to a competent client's wishes to forego an available insanity defense provided constitutionally adequate representation, strongly implying that an attorney is obligated to follow the client's instruction or withdraw from the case.

Beyond the duty to adhere to the client's known wishes, however, the attorney's legal obligation is ambiguous. Two key questions presented in Study 5 are whether an attorney is obligated to present to the client the possibility of raising a clinically supported insanity defense and, if so, whether the attorney is obligated to facilitate an informed client decision (Bonnie, 1993). Informed client decision-making may be an aspirational ethical ideal but, in Michigan and elsewhere, it is by no means clear that attorneys have a legal obligation to achieve it.

In the absence of any alternative exculpatory claim, the attorney may be justified in assuming, without inviting client participation, that an available insanity plea serves the client's interest in avoiding criminal conviction. If a negotiated insanity plea is entered, or if the defense is raised at trial, the defendant will have the opportunity to object if he wishes to do so.[5] Thus, it can be argued that by deciding to pursue the defense, the attorney does not preclude a client's subsequent veto.

In sum, it is possible that the governing legal norm reflects a "weak" conception of client autonomy. Under a "strong" conception, the attorney would be obligated to present the issue to the client in all cases and to facilitate informed client participation. However, under the weaker conception that appears to prevail in practice, the attorney is expected to adhere to the known wishes of the client but has no affirmative duty to secure the client's involvement.

In light of the high prevalence of attorney preemption for decisions *to pursue* the insanity defense revealed in this study, it is interesting to note that a similar pattern did not emerge in the 20 cases in which the insanity defense was *not* pursued. It appears that clients participated in all of these decisions. In this context, however, the legal norm is not ambiguous: when the attorney decides to forego an available insanity defense, the attorney is

---

[5] In the present *study, for example, the outcomes in the "pre-empted" cases were as follows: dismissal of case (N = 6); NGRI plea (N = 10); guilty or GBMI plea (N = 2); NGRI at trial (N = 18);* and guilty at trial *(N = 2).*

probably obligated to elicit client participation, especially if the attorney advises the defendant to plead guilty.[6]

Attorney Paternalism

It also appears that the attorneys' paternalistic intuitions play a significant role in explaining their behavior. The attorneys explicitly linked their preemptive behavior with perceived client incompetence in 38% of the cases, and responses to other questions about client competence showed that 91% of the attorneys who preempted client participation had doubts about their clients' capacity "to understand the decisions they were called upon to make." In addition, decisions to preempt client involvement were associated with the clients' hospitalization for treatment during the pretrial phase. It is possible that the very fact of client hospitalization impeded client consultation, and the attorneys' preemptive behavior reflected logistical difficulties rather than paternalistic decision-making. For example, we wondered whether the attorneys may have been required by statute to file notice of a possible insanity plea before they had the opportunity to meet with their clients. This explanation seems unlikely, however. The procedural clock would not have been running during the period of pretrial hospitalization for competence restoration. Moreover, even if attorneys decided on their own, due to logistical difficulties, to give notice of a planned insanity plea, they still had plenty of time to discuss the issue with their clients before the scheduled trial.

The tendency of attorneys to take a paternalistic stance in dealing with mentally ill clients has been well-documented in the context of civil commitment, where aggressive advocacy against commitment is often forsaken in favor of a role resembling that of a guardian ad litem (see Poythress, 1978). Even in customary representational contexts, codes of ethics are remarkably ambiguous regarding the allocation of decision-making

---

[6] The usual cases in Michigan, as elsewhere, involve post-conviction claims that the defense attorney should have raised the insanity defense. In these cases, the Sixth Amendment claim usually turns on whether the attorney made an informed professional judgment. Convictions are sometimes set aside. *See*, e.g., *People v. Hunt* (1988); *People v. Snyder* (1981). For our purposes, the key question is whether a conviction will be set aside, even if the attorney made an informed professional judgment, on the ground that he did not present the matter to the client for decision. In cases which went to trial, no rulings setting aside convictions have been identified. However, in *People v. Nyberg* (1984), the court set aside a GBMI verdict (and a life sentence) because the defendant had not been informed "that he had a reasonable likelihood of successfully interposing a valid and a complete defense to the charge." *Nyberg* stands at most for the proposition that an attorney should inform the defendant of any potentially successful defense before advising him to plead guilty.

responsibility. In fact, the codes imply that attorneys are ethically permitted to make decisions on behalf of impaired clients, even in the absence of a legal determination of incompetence.[7] In short, the behavior of the Michigan attorneys in this study appears to reveal an unambiguous instance of "soft" paternalism in legal representation.[8]

CONCLUSION

Four main findings emerged from this series of studies. First, more than half of the defendants are described by their attorneys as passive participants in the overall defense, with about one-in-ten described as uninvolved or "extremely passive". Second, about ten percent of clients are described by their attorneys as being recalcitrant—i.e., as rarely or never accepting the attorneys' advice. Interestingly, passivity and recalcitrance are reported less frequently when attorneys are asked to focus specifically on situations in which the law requires personal client participation, such as the decision to plead guilty or, in tried cases, the decision to waive a jury trial, than when attorneys are asked to characterize clients' overall participation in decision-making. The third main finding emerging from our previous research is that attorneys have some doubt about the mental capacity of their clients in 8–15% of felony cases, although mental health assessments are sought in less than half of these cases. The prevalence of reported client passivity is substantially higher among clients whose competence is doubted than among clients whose competence is unquestioned by their attorneys. Finally, attorneys made the decision to raise an insanity defense without consulting the defendant in about one-third of

---

[7] See, e.g., Model Rules of Professional Conduct, Rule 1.14 (Client Under A Disability) and commentary (1983) ("When the client...suffers from a mental disorder or disability... maintaining an ordinary client-lawyer relationship may not be possible in all respects... If the person has no guardian or legal representative, the lawyer often must act as a de facto guardian.") American Bar Association Ethical Code (EC 7–11) ("If a client under a disability has no legal representative, his lawyer may be compelled in court proceedings to make decisions on behalf of the client.")

[8] An instance of "hard paternalism" is when one overrides the wishes of a competent actor who has made a voluntary choice on the ground that what the person wants to do is not in his or her best interests. Libertarians who object to hard paternalism will usually accept some form of "soft" paternalism under which the intervention is made because the subject is not competent to decide what is in his or her best interests or because of some other defect of voluntariness. The residual controversies relate to the definition of the conditions which justify paternalistic interventions (e.g. impairment of decisional abilities). See generally, Feinberg (1986), pp. 12–16.

the cases in which that defense was raised, and the degree of client participation was relatively low even when the client was consulted.

The findings from these studies illustrate why it is desirable to conceptualize competence in criminal adjudication as two separable constructs—a foundational requirement of "competence to assist counsel" which refers to the minimum conditions required for participation in one's own defense; and a contextualized concept of "decisional competence" which has independent legal significance only in cases in which the defendant is competent to assist counsel (see Chapter 2). If a defendant lacks the abilities required to understand the proceedings and assist counsel, the dignity and reliability of any ensuing adjudication cannot be assured; this is why a defendant's lack of "competence to assist counsel" precludes conviction. However, if the defendant is competent to assist counsel, a discrete defect of decisional competence can potentially be addressed through remedies other than barring adjudication, such as default rules or surrogate decision-making.

Decisional impairments relating to pleas of insanity have arisen with sufficient frequency to lead courts to disaggregate the construct of competence in a manner which tracks the distinction between decisional competence and "competence to assist counsel." The reported cases involve defendants who refuse to plead insanity; in these cases—in which the defendant is regarded as competent to understand the charges and assist counsel but not competent to make a rational decision regarding the insanity plea—courts have sometimes allowed the defense to be raised by a surrogate decision-maker: the defense attorney, a guardian, or the court. As the final study shows, however, "refusing" defendants represent only a fraction of defendants who have clinically supported insanity claims, and the typical case involves an "assenting" defendant whose decision-making ability is questionable. In practice, it appears, attorneys serve as surrogate decision-makers in these cases.

Some would argue that a disposition which deprives the defendant of liberty should not be arranged in the absence of an autonomous decision by the defendant him or herself. From this perspective, the results of the final study are disturbing because they reveal that most defendants who are acquitted by reason of insanity are perceived by their lawyers as having significant impairments of decisional competence, and that one-third of them play no meaningful role in the decision to seek this disposition. Even if surrogate decision-making is regarded as an acceptable response in these cases, as we believe it is, attorneys should take appropriate steps to invite and facilitate the maximum feasible participation of which the defendant is capable. This should be an ethical imperative even if it is not a legal one.

2

Adjudicative Competence in Legal Theory and Practice

At least since the 14th century, common-law courts have declined to proceed against criminal defendants who are "incompetent" to be brought before the court for adjudication. As was true of so much of the common law, the "incompetency plea," as it developed, was rooted in an ancient legal formalism. A criminal prosecution could not proceed against someone who had not entered a plea (guilty or not guilty). A defendant who "stood mute" might be doing so willfully ("mute of malice") or due to deafness or madness ("mute by visitation of God"). Confinement in a small cell, starvation, or the pressure of heavy weights was used to induce a plea from strategically silent defendants, thereby allowing the process to move forward. However, the Crown could not proceed against a "lunatic" or "idiot" whose understanding of the proceedings was so diminished as to prevent a knowing plea. Even after the courts became willing to enter "not guilty" pleas on behalf of defendants who stood mute, the "incompetency plea" survived as an independent bar to adjudication.

The evolution of common-law doctrine is apparent in the court's description of the elements of "fitness to stand trial" in *R. v. Pritchard* in

1836, a famous case involving a defendant who was deaf and mute:

> First, whether the prisoner is mute of malice or not; secondly, whether he can plead to the indictment or not; thirdly, whether he is of sufficient intellect to comprehend the course of proceedings on the trial, so as to make a proper defense—to know that he might challenge [jurors] to whom he may object—and to comprehend the details of the evidence.... It is not enough that he may have a general capacity of communicating in ordinary matters. (p. 135)

Although the medieval interest in whether a defendant remained "mute by malice" no longer has any legal importance, the two other key components of the *Pritchard* formulation (ability to understand the proceedings and to interact with one's attorney in a meaningful way) have continuing significance in applying the "incompetency plea." These two ideas are reflected in the "test" for adjudicative competence enunciated by the U.S. Supreme Court for use by the federal courts in *Dusky v. United States* in 1960: "whether the defendant has sufficient present ability to consult with his lawyer with a reasonable degree of rational understanding—and whether he has rational as well as factual understanding of the proceedings against him."

Fifteen years after *Dusky*, in *Drope v. Missouri* (1975), the Court held that the incompetence doctrine was "so fundamental to an adversary system of justice," that conviction of an incompetent defendant, or failure to adhere to procedures designed to assess a defendant's competence when doubt has been raised, violates the due process clause of the federal Constitution. According to *Drope*: "It has long been accepted that a person whose mental condition is such that he lacks the capacity to understand the nature and object of the proceedings against him, to consult with counsel, and to assist in preparing his defense may not be subjected to a trial." And, it should be added, such a defendant is not competent to enter a plea of guilty in lieu of a trial (*Godinez v. Moran*, 1993). The essential point is that incompetence bars adjudication, whether by plea or trial, and this includes any pretrial proceedings that may be adverse to the defendant's interests. For the sake of brevity, the term "adjudicative competence" will be used to refer to this requirement.

The concept of adjudicative competence thus far described conveys a fairly passive view of the defendant's role in criminal proceedings. A prosecution cannot proceed unless the defendant understands his jeopardy and is able to advise the lawyer who is representing him. In the picture that emerges, the defendant responds, consults and assists, but the active adversaries in the litigation are the prosecutor and the defense attorney. This may be an accurate picture of many, if not most, criminal proceedings, but it is an incomplete picture of the *rights* accorded to the defendant under the Constitution, and of the values embedded in the requirement of adjudicative competence. Under our system of criminal justice, certain decisions must be made by the defendant; they cannot be made by counsel acting on behalf of the defendant. The most important of these is whether to plead guilty. Others are whether to be tried before a jury, or to testify, if the case goes to trial. The defendant also is entitled to make decisions concerning the basic theory of the defense, including whether or not to raise a particular defense, and the attorney is bound to adhere to the defendant's instructions, even if he or she believes that the defendant's interests would not be well-served. The 1998 prosecution of Theodore Kaczinski revealed the tensions and difficulties that can arise when a defendant whose competence is questionable exercises the decision-making prerogatives accorded to him under our criminal justice system.[1]

TOWARD A THEORY-BASED UNDERSTANDING

What does it mean to be "competent" to participate in one's own defense? Forensic clinicians say that the meaning of competence is highly contextualized and that the standard, however formulated, is an "open-textured" one (Roesch & Golding, 1980, pp. 10–13; American Bar Association, 1986, p. 175). Whether a defendant is "competent" under the *Dusky* standard depends on the seriousness and complexity of the charges, on what is expected of the defendant in the given case, on the client's relationship with the attorney, on counsel's skill, and other "interactive" factors (Grisso, 1986, pp. 76–77). The instruments available for structuring forensic interviewing and decision-making in this context typically list the many potentially relevant abilities, even though they may not have particular significance in a given case. These instruments do not prescribe definitive rating criteria, but rely instead upon a clinical judgment based on all the circumstances of the given case (Grisso, 1986, pp. 78–104).

The current practice of competence assessment and adjudication lacks a great deal of normative texture on aspects of the inquiry relating to assistance of counsel and, as a result, is highly discretionary. Appellate courts rarely review and almost never reverse trial court decisions regarding defendants' competence to proceed. In a sequential decision-making

---

[1] Although he eventually pleaded guilty to the many charges against him, the "Unabomber" and his attorneys battled for months over control of the case. The defendant, diagnosed as having paranoid schizophrenia, resisted an insanity plea, and apparently was opposed to the introduction of any evidence tending to show that he was mentally ill, even at the capital sentencing phase of his trial (if the case had been tried).

process of this kind, discretion tends to slide backwards. It should, therefore, come as no surprise that trial judges almost always defer to clinical opinion in pretrial competence determinations (Golding et al., 1984; Hart & Hare, 1992; Reich & Tookey, 1986). Thus, forensic clinicians rather than judges effectively exercise discretion to define competence, which is a source of continuing dissatisfaction to commentators, if not to forensic clinicians and judges.

In short, competence assessment and adjudication tends to be a low-visibility, highly discretionary feature of the criminal process, rarely coming to public attention, and rarely generating appealable error. In fact, most of the reported opinions on competence adjudication involve claims that defendants' attorneys failed to seek competence assessments, or that trial judges failed to order them, rather than claims that the trial judges misapplied the governing substantive criteria. Operationally, the salient truth about the law of adjudicative competence is that asking the question is more important than the getting the "right" answer.

Conceptualizing competence as an "open-textured" construct obscures the critically important distinction between the clinical/descriptive and legal/evaluative dimensions of competence assessment. Adjudication of "competence to stand trial" lacks the normative texture needed to help separate the role of the expert and the role of the judge. Notwithstanding the trend away from "ultimate issue" testimony by mental health professionals in other contexts, forensic clinicians commonly discover that judges practically insist on ultimate issue opinion in reports and testimony on competence to stand trial (American Bar Association, 1986, pp. 118–130).

Perhaps this highly subjective, discretionary approach to competence assessment and adjudication is preferable to any of the available alternatives. It is certainly preferable to a regime in which the defendant's mental and physical disabilities have no legal significance. Moreover, an open-textured inquiry is sometimes superior, notwithstanding its discretionary features, to more structured normative criteria. Typically, this superiority stems from the fact that any effort to limit the factors that may be considered will be underinclusive and any effort to order the factors or to prescribe structured decision rules will not fit all cases. For example, the persistence of "best interests of the child" as the standard for child custody determinations reflects a settled preference for the highly individualized approach. Though the pendulum in criminal sentencing has recently swung in the direction of more determinate normative criteria, the Constitution requires individualized decision-making in capital sentencing adjudication (see, e.g., *Penry v. Lynaugh*, 1989).

In our view, the open-textured approach to competence assessment in criminal adjudication is inferior to the more structured approach developed

LEGAL THEORY AND PRACTICE

by the MacArthur network and explained in Chapters 3 and 5 of this book. It is possible, in this setting, to formulate criteria that facilitate objective decision-making and meaningful judicial supervision while producing normatively sensible outcomes. The proposed approach has several additional advantages. First, it is compatible with the intuitive understanding of clinicians and judges regarding the meaning of competence and with the settled features of existing law. Second, it helps to clarify the issues in areas where the law remains controversial, such as the circumstances under which incompetence bars adjudication and whether the "test" for competence to waive counsel should differ from the usual test for competence. Third, because this approach derives from a theoretical analysis of the purposes served by the pertinent legal rules, it provides a framework for better defining the "psycho-legal abilities" relevant to competence determinations and thereby facilitates research designed to improve the scientific basis of competence assessments in criminal cases.

VALUES SERVED BY THE COMPETENCE REQUIREMENT

When viewed from a contemporary perspective, the requirement of adjudicative competence in criminal proceedings serves three conceptually independent social purposes—preserving the dignity of the criminal process, reducing the risk of erroneous convictions, and protecting the defendant's decision-making autonomy. The *dignity* of the criminal process is undermined if the defendant lacks a basic moral understanding of the nature and purpose of the proceedings against him or her. The *accuracy* or reliability of the adjudication is threatened if the defendant is unable to assist in the development and presentation of a defense. Finally, to the extent that decisions about the course of adjudication must be made by the defendant, he or she must have the abilities needed to exercise decision-making *autonomy*.

DIGNITY

A person who lacks a rudimentary understanding of the nature and purpose of the proceedings against her is a not a "fit" subject for criminal prosecution and punishment. To proceed against such a person offends the moral dignity of the process because it treats the defendant not as an accountable person, but as an object of the state's effort to carry out its promises. Only cases involving defendants who lack a meaningful moral understanding of wrongdoing and punishment or the nature of a criminal prosecution implicate the dignity rationale.

Lists of purposes served by the incompetence doctrine typically include the need to preserve the decorum of the courtroom and the dignity of the trial process (see, e.g., *Harvard Law Review*, 1967, p. 158). However, in our view (Bonnie, 1992), courtroom decorum is not, standing alone, a viable rational for a bar against adjudication. If necessary, a disruptive defendant can be removed from the courtroom and an otherwise competent defendant can waive her right to be present. Moreover, judges should be very tolerant of "disturbing" behavior in the courtroom during plea proceedings and bench trials. In short, the "dignity" rationale for the incompetence doctrine, as used here, refers to the inherent morality of the process carried out in the courtroom, not to its outward appearances.

Accuracy

Beyond the minimal demands of the dignity rationale, the bar against adverse adjudication in cases involving incompetent defendants serves as a prophylactic protection against erroneous convictions. Just as the assistance of competent counsel is regarded as a prerequisite of reliable adjudication, so too is the participation of a competent defendant. As stated by Henry Weihofen (1954), a mentally impaired defendant might be unfairly convicted if he "alone has knowledge" of certain facts but does "not appreciate the value of such facts, or the propriety of communicating them to his counsel" (pp. 429–430). In his Commentaries, William Blackstone (1979, 4:24) described the rationale for the incompetence plea as follows:

> If a man in his sound memory commits a capital offense, and, before arraignment for it, he becomes mad, he ought not to be arraigned for it, because he is not able to plead to it with that advice and caution that he ought. And if, after he had pleaded, the prisoner becomes mad, he shall not be tried; for how can he make his defense? If, after he be tried and found guilty, he loses his senses before judgment, judgment shall not be pronounced; and if, after judgment, he becomes of nonsane memory, execution shall be stayed.

To proceed against a defendant who lacks the capacity to recognize and communicate relevant information to his attorney and to the court would be unfair to the defendant and would undermine society's independent interest in the reliability of its criminal process. This provides the basis for the Supreme Court's statement in *Drope v. Missouri* (1975) that the bar against trying the incompetent defendant "is fundamental to an adversary system of justice" (p. 172).[2]

---

[2] Social scientists should note that courts use "reliability" in constitutional adjudication as a synonym for "validity" or accuracy of outcome.

As critics of the existing legal arrangements have correctly noted, the bar against prosecuting incompetent defendants evolved at a time when the defendant bore responsibility for mounting her own defense (Winick, 1987). Indeed, assistance of counsel was actually precluded in felony and treason cases until the mid-eighteenth century (*Faretta v. California*, 1975). Today, in contrast, assistance of counsel is available as a matter of constitutional right in all serious criminal cases (*Argersinger v. Hamlin*, 1972; *Gideon v. Wainwright*, 1963). Although representation by counsel does not render the traditional rules obsolete, the construct of incompetence itself must be operationalized in the context of the attorney-client relationship. Thus, to the extent that the meaning of incompetence derives from its instrumental function, it refers to the capacity to provide whatever assistance counsel requires in order to explore and present an adequate defense.[3]

AUTONOMY

A third feature of the competence construct, conceptually independent of the two aspects thus far mentioned, derives from legal rules that establish that the defendant must make or have the prerogative to make certain decisions regarding the defense or disposition of the case. A construct of "decisional competence" is an inherent, though derivative, feature of any legal doctrine that prescribes a norm of client autonomy. In theory, one could imagine a system of criminal adjudication that leaves no room for client self determination—one which bars self-representation, does not permit guilty pleas, and commits all decisions regarding defense of the case to counsel rather than the defendant.[4] Under these legal arrangements, a defendant's decisional competence would not be relevant. But this does not describe our system.

As noted above, our law commits some decisions regarding the defense or disposition of the case to the defendant and not to the attorney. According to all authorities, these include decisions regarding the plea, and, if the case is to be tried, whether it should be tried before a jury,

---

[3] "It has long been accepted that a person whose mental condition is such that he lacks the capacity to understand the nature and object of the proceedings against him, to consult with counsel, and to assist in preparing his defense may not be subjected to a trial." *Drope v. Missouri* (1975, p. 171). "The 'test must be whether [the defendant] has sufficient present ability to consult with his lawyer with a reasonable degree of rational understanding—and whether he has a rational as well as factual understanding of the proceedings against him.'" *Dusky v. United States* (1960, p. 402), quoting the Solicitor General).

[4] *Faretta v. California* (1975), holding that a defendant is constitutionally entitled to waive assistance of counsel and to represent himself, makes such a system constitutionally implausible, but it is noteworthy that three Justices dissented.

whether the defendant will be present, and whether the defendant will testify.[5] In more general terms, the defendant is permitted, if not required, to make decisions regarding the objectives of representation, including the basic theory of defense.[6] For some of these decisions (i.e., those involving waivers of constitutional rights), the obligation imposed on courts to assure that the defendant's decision is knowingly, intelligently, and voluntarily made reinforces the principle of self-determination (see, e.g., *Boykin v. Alabama*, 1969, p. 242; *Johnson v. Zerbst*, 1938, pp. 464–465). Not surprisingly, judicial scrutiny is likely to be most intensive when the defendant decides to represent himself (For two recent indications, see *United States v. Mooney*, 2000, and *People v. Welch*, 1999).

COMPONENTS OF ADJUDICATIVE COMPETENCE

Keeping in mind these three rationales for competence adjudication, and drawing on the language of *Dusky v. United States* (1960) and other appellate decisions that interpret and apply *Dusky*, it is possible to specify the competence-related abilities required for adjudicative competence. Adjudicative competence encompasses two related but separable components (Bonnie, 1993).

COMPETENCE TO ASSIST COUNSEL

The first component refers to a foundational "competence to assist counsel." The minimum conditions legally required for participating in one's own defense generally include the capacity to (1) understand the charges and the basic elements of the adversary system (understanding), (2) appreciate one's situation as a defendant in a criminal prosecution (appreciation), and (3) relate pertinent information to counsel concerning the facts

---

[5] See *Rock v. Arkansas* (1987) (whether to testify); *Brookhart v. Janis* (1966) (whether to plead guilty); *Adams v. United States ex rel.McCann* (1942) (waiver of jury trial). See generally American Bar Association (1986), § 4–5.2(a); Model Rules of Professional Conduct (1983), Rule 1.2(a).

[6] See American Bar Association (1986), § 4-5.2(a); Model Rules of Professional Conduct (1983), Rule 1.2(a). In contrast, "decisions on what witnesses to call, whether and how to conduct cross-examination, what jurors to accept or strike, what trial motions should be made, and all other strategic and tactical decisions are the exclusive province of the lawyer after consultation with the client" (American Bar Association, 1986, § 4-5.2(b); see also *Jones v. Barnes* (1983) (regarding lawyer's prerogative to decide what issues to raise on appeal). The distinction between "objectives" and "means" of representation is, of course, indeterminate at the margins.

of the case (reasoning). These three psycho-legal abilities, taken together, operationalize *Dusky*'s requirements that the defendant have a "rational as well as factual understanding of the proceedings" and that he or she be able "to consult with counsel with a reasonable degree of rational understanding." The competence-to-assist-counsel component of adjudicative competence, summarized in this way, serves the dignity and accuracy rationales mentioned above, and the law clearly precludes any adjudication adverse to a defendant who lacks the abilities required to assist in his or her own defense. In this sense, competence to assist counsel is the foundational component of adjudicative competence.

The capacities required to preserve the dignity of the process and to assure reliability are conceptually distinct. Although they probably overlap a great deal empirically, abundant clinical experience demonstrates that they are not congruent, and that the ability to perform one set of tasks does not necessarily predict ability to perform the other.[7] Some mentally disabled defendants who understand the process and their own situations are unable to assist counsel; and, conversely, a delusional defendant may be able to understand counsel's role and to relate relevant information but may believe that the criminal prosecution serves a benevolent divine plan and has no punitive purpose or effect. Despite the conceptual and empirical divergence of these two groups of capacities, however, it is sensible to combine them in a single foundational construct because both of these rationales, dignity and reliability, underlie the traditional bar against prosecution and conviction of incompetent defendants.

Decisional Competence

In most cases, questions about "competence to assist counsel" arise at the outset of the process, before significant interactions with counsel have occurred and before strategic decisions regarding defense of the case have been encountered or considered. The second component of adjudicative competence is "decisional competence," because a defendant who is competent to assist counsel may not be competent to make the specific decisions regarding the defense of his or her case that are encountered as the process of criminal adjudication unfolds. Decision-making involves cognitive tasks in addition to those required for assisting counsel, but the abilities required to establish decisional competence have not yet been definitively established. The Supreme Court's 1993 decision in *Godinez v. Moran* acknowledged the significance of decisional competence, holding that a defendant's trial competence and competence to plead guilty

---

[7] Chapter 4, Study 2, describes our empirical investigation of these issues.

should be addressed under a single standard (the *Dusky* standard) and that the defendant's decision-making abilities are encompassed within that standard. However, the Court did not articulate which abilities are required for decisional competence in criminal adjudication. The most plausible extrapolation of the *Dusky* standard, as applied to decision-making, would require the capacity to: (1) understand information relevant to the specific decision at issue (understanding), (2) appreciate the significance of the decision as applied to one's own situation (appreciation), (3) think rationally (logically) about the alternative courses of action (reasoning), and (4) express a choice among alternatives (choice). Taken together, these four criteria operationalize the "rationality" requirement to which the Supreme Court referred in *Godinez v. Moran* (1993).

Before *Godinez v. Moran*, appellate courts were divided over whether certain decisions—such as pleas of guilty or waiver of counsel—required a "higher" level of decisional capacity than the level embedded in the *Dusky* standard.[8] Although they used different phrases, most state and federal decisions embraced the view that, unlike guilty pleas, waivers of counsel do require a higher level of competence.[9] However, the Supreme Court held in *Godinez* that the *Dusky* standard governs all decision-making contexts, including waiver of counsel. The Court was careful to emphasize, nonetheless, that even though due process does not require a higher standard of competence for waiver of counsel, the states are free to prescribe a higher standard under state law. What such a higher standard might entail is not entirely clear,[10] but these additional requirements, whatever they might be, are extrinsic to the decisional component of the *Dusky* formula, and are therefore not pertinent to the research described in this book.

---

[8] Compare *Sieling v. Eyman* (1973) with *Allard v. Hellgemoe* (1978). The cases are summarized in *Godinez v. Moran* (1993) at p. 396, notes 5 & 6.

[9] Bonnie (1993) has endorsed the view that, while guilty pleas should not ordinarily require a higher level of decisional capacity, waiver of counsel should not be permitted if the defendant's decision is substantially affected by psychopathological factors. Under this approach, the higher standard would also have to be met if the defendant sought to make a decision over counsel's objection (such as refusing to plead insanity or refusing to introduce mitigating evidence in a capital case). This position is grounded in a contextual interpretation of the demands of "soft" paternalism in situations involving objectively high risk-benefit relationships.

[10] According to the views expressed in Bonnie (1993), the higher standard would entail more attention than *Dusky* requires to the defendant's capacity to weigh advantages and disadvantages of the proposed decision in a manner substantially free of pathological influences. This seems to be what the Ninth Circuit had in mind in the line of cases in which it applied the "reasoned choice" standard, including Richard Moran's case (*Moran v. Godinez*, 1992).

LIMITS OF THE UNITARY VIEW

The Supreme Court's decision in *Godinez* indicates that adjudicative competence is a unitary construct including both "foundational" abilities needed for a rational understanding of the proceedings and rational communication with counsel, as well as the abilities needed to make rational decisions as decisions need to be made. This approach promotes efficiency in assessment because it enables the evaluator to address basic decisional capacity in an initial evaluation, without the need to conduct repeated evaluations, and it also promotes consistency in competence assessment and adjudication. However, as one of us has pointed out previously (Bonnie, 1993), this approach has a serious disadvantage because it links the finding of decisional incompetence to the procedural bar against adjudication. Prosecution of a defendant who is not able to understand the proceedings or assist counsel, as defined above, should be categorically barred in order to preserve the moral dignity of the criminal process and avoid an unacceptable risk of erroneous convictions. However, more flexible responses, such as surrogate decision-making or specifically tailored default rules (i.e., no waiver of constitutional rights) could be used to respond to particularized deficiencies in decisional competence. Notwithstanding *Godinez*, for example, some courts have allowed attorneys to enter an insanity defense over the objection of a client who has been found to be competent to stand trial under *Dusky* while being incompetent to make a rational decision regarding the insanity plea (see, e.g., *Hendricks v. Colorado*, 2000; also, Chapter 1, Study 5). This seems like a sensible resolution of the insanity plea cases and other cases involving other particularized decisional deficits (e.g., refusal to introduce mitigating evidence). It is also a sensible way to respond to cases in which the defendant is competent for adjudication with assistance of counsel but not competent to waive counsel. Whether such flexible responses are compatible with the unitary view of competence embraced in *Godinez* remains to be seen.

COMPETENCE ADJUDICATION IN PRACTICE

Participants in the criminal justice system have a variety of motivations for raising questions about the defendant's competence for adjudication other than those directly implicated by the rationales for the doctrine itself. Jail personnel may believe that the defendant needs mental health services that cannot be provided in the jail; in such cases referral for competence assessment serves as a mechanism for obtaining acute psychiatric care for defendants in detention. The prosecution or trial judge may believe that the defendant is mentally disordered and the case should be directed to the mental health system; in such cases a commitment for competence evaluation and a finding of incompetence function as a surrogate for civil commitment. The prosecution may be seeking confinement of a defendant who would otherwise be released on bail; in such cases the incompetence commitment functions as a form of preventive detention. The defense attorney may be seeking consultation and assistance of mental health experts in deciding how to defend the case; in such cases the competence referral serves as a mechanism for obtaining more generalized forensic assistance. Even more far afield from the rationales embedded in *Dusky*, jail administrators may see the incompetence diversion as a mechanism to relieve overcrowding in a jail or, for defendants who require expensive medical (non-psychiatric) treatment, a way to divert those costs from the county to the state.

In systemic terms the requirement of adjudicative competence plays a significant role in the administration of criminal justice. Although "procedural fairness" concerns (dignity, accuracy and autonomy) may not be the main motivation for referral, they are embedded in the everyday practice of competence assessment and adjudication. Steadman and Monahan (1983) estimated, based on 1980 data, that at least 25,000 felony defendants were referred for competence assessments, with perhaps 8,000 of these evaluations being conducted on an inpatient basis. More recently Skeem, Golding, Cohn, and Berge (1998) estimated the number of defendants referred annually for competence evaluations to be 50,000. The studies presented in Chapter 1 found that attorneys express some doubt about their clients' competence in about 10% of felony cases, and that they seek evaluation in about half of these situations. A conservative national estimate, based on referrals in 5% of 1.2 million felony indictments, would be 60,000 pretrial competence assessments per year.[11]

Referral for a competence evaluation infrequently results in a finding of incompetence—perhaps 10–30% of defendants referred for evaluation are regarded as incompetent by evaluators, and found to be so by the courts (Melton et al., 1997, p. 135).[12] In these cases, defendants are committed for restoration of competence, usually to a forensic hospital,

---

[11] The estimate of 1.2 million felony indictments is based on extrapolation from figures from two publications of the Bureau of Justice Statistics on criminal adjudication in state courts in 1994 (Langan & Brown, 1997; Reaves, 1998).

[12] In the remaining cases, however, a pretrial competence evaluation has two important practical effects: it provides an opportunity for mental health consultation for an attorney representing a client with mental disability, and it serves to "cleanse" the case of a possible ground for setting aside a conviction based on a claim that the attorney or the court failed to recognize or explore the possibility of incompetence.

although treatment may also be administered on an outpatient basis (see, e.g., Va. Code Ann. § 19.2–169.2). In the vast majority of such cases, the defendant is returned to the court for trial within 6 months. In a small number of incompetence commitments, typically involving severely and chronically mentally ill defendants or defendants with mental retardation, the defendants are found to be unrestorable. In such cases continued confinement must be predicated on the state's ordinary commitment or guardianship authority if these criteria are met (*Jackson v. Indiana*, 1972).

In many states, the statutory criteria for incompetence do not explicitly require a finding mental illness or mental retardation as a predicate for a finding of incompetence. As a practical matter, of course, deficits in competence-related abilities are usually associated with a mental disorder. However, some physical illnesses, such as those involving great pain or discomfort, can also impair a defendant's ability to consult with counsel and pay attention to the proceedings. Continuances are routinely granted in such cases on the ground that the defendant is not presently "fit" for trial. Although courts do not usually link such rulings to the "competence" requirement, they seem to reflect applications of the same principle.[13]

In the preceding pages, we have tried to summarize the law and practice of competence assessment and adjudication in criminal cases. As a final preliminary note, it is important to emphasize that, because a defendant's "incompetence" bars adjudication, any doubts about the defendant's mental status must be resolved before the case can proceed. In this respect, a claim that the defendant lacks competence to plead or stand trial must be distinguished from a defensive claim of mental disorder or "incapacity" that can be raised at trial: a defendant who was competent to plead and to be brought to trial might nonetheless claim that he was "insane" *at the time of the alleged offense*. Such a claim bears on the defendant's criminal *responsibility* or liability and must be resolved by the jury (or the judge in a bench trial) on the basis of the evidence introduced at the trial. In sum, the doctrines of "incompetence" to proceed and "insanity" or non-responsibility refer to two distinct connections between mental disorder and criminal adjudication—incompetence refers to a defendant's condition at the time of the adjudication and "insanity" or non-responsibility refers to the defendant's condition at the time of the alleged crime.

---

[13] Those cases typically arise in appeal when the defendant claims that the trial court's refusal to grant a continuance was an abuse of discretion. When appellate courts reverse convictions in such cases—which is atypical—the decision is grounded in concerns that the defendant's illness impeded his ability to assist counsel in preparation for trial or in the conduct of trial. See, e.g. *Ward v. State* (1940) (heart condition); *State v. Wilson* (1935) (gunshot wound). Occasionally, a court will invoke the due process clause, e.g. *Miller v. Commonwealth* (1923), and refer to the *Dusky* criteria, e.g. *State v. Kaiser* (1962).

3

Development of an Adjudicative Competence Research Measure

The Network's Adjudicative Competence Research Agenda

THE LIMITATIONS OF FIRST GENERATION MEASURES OF ADJUDICATIVE COMPETENCE

When the MacArthur Adjudicative Competence project began in 1989, several measures were available to the field for evaluating "competence to stand trial." As noted in Chapter 1, the impetus for many of these measures had come from mental health professionals who attempted to operationalize the judicial and statutory standards in order to facilitate assessments. The array of measures ranged from relatively broad checklists or menus of topics (Bukatman, Foy, & Degrazia, 1971; Robey, 1965) that forensic clinicians were encouraged to consider, to highly structured screening measures such as the Competency Screening Test (CST: Lipsitt,

Lelos, & McGarry, 1971) and the Georgia Court Competency Test (GCCT: Wildman et al., 1980), to semi-structured interview guides such as the Competence to Stand Trial Assessment Instrument (CAI: Laboratory of Community Psychiatry, 1973) and the Interdisciplinary Fitness Interview (IFI: Golding, Roesch, & Schreiber, 1984).[1]

These measures emerged during an era in which early empirical studies revealed that some mental health professionals performing competence evaluations were unaware of the relevant legal criteria (Van & Morganroth, 1964), often used techniques and methods that focused on traditional clinical (i.e., symptoms, diagnoses) issues rather than the functional legal abilities implicated by the *Dusky* standard (Hess & Thomas, 1963), and applied an inappropriate "psychosis = incompetence" formula to derive their conclusions about defendants' competence to stand trial (McGarry, 1965). Because courts tended to rubber stamp clinicians' opinions about (in)competence, and because clinicians used the same formula (psychosis = incompetence) to determine when a defendant's competence had been restored, a commitment for competence restoration treatment often proved to be tantamount to a lifetime commitment to a state hospital (Hess & Thomas, 1963; Miller, Dawson, Dix, & Parnas, 1971, p. 1442).

In retrospect, it seems clear that these first generation competence measures made a significant positive contribution to the competence assessment enterprise. Each measure, in its own way, referenced the *Dusky* criteria and thus helped to focus forensic evaluators' attention on functional legal abilities relevant to competence. At the same time, these measures suffered from a variety of conceptual, structural, and psychometric limitations. In terms of the legal conceptualization of competence articulated in Chapter 2, three concerns are readily apparent:

- the legal focus in these early measures is substantially weighted toward assessing defendants' knowledge of the jury trial process; comparatively little guidance is provided for the assessment of issues specific to pleading guilty or entering a plea agreement, the route of disposition for more than 90% of cases;
- in terms the capacities implicated by the *Dusky*, the early measures emphasize "factual understanding" almost exclusively; they offer little or no explicit guidance for distinguishing deficits in "understanding" from deficits in "appreciation," and none operationalizes the assessment of "reasoning" in any significant way;

---

[1] For a review of these and other adjudicative competence measures, see Melton et al. (1997), Chapter 6.

- the early measures primarily assess "understanding" by testing the legal knowledge that the defendant brings to the interview; thus, they tend to test for *actual knowledge* rather than for *capacity*, which the *Dusky* standard mandates.

The structure and purpose of these measures also varied considerably. As noted, the CST and GCCT were intended as screening measures rather than as comprehensive tools for an in-depth assessment of competence-related abilities. The merits of these screening measures included the standardized administration of a fixed set of items and explicit scoring criteria to guide clinicians' judgments of the adequacy of defendants' answers. However, neither of these measures was constructed to yield separate scores that indexed capacity in discrete legal domains (e.g., foundational versus decisional competence) or discrete competence-related abilities (e.g., capacity for "choice" versus "understanding"). Although subsequent research using factor analytic methods sought to identify an inherent structure in these screening measures (Nicholson, Briggs, & Robertson, 1988), the derived structures either did not conform well to the relevant domains suggested by an analysis of *Dusky* (in the case of the GCCT) or the structures did not replicate well across different research samples (CST). Thus, the index of "competence" from these measures was merely a sum of item scores which could be compared to a recommended cutoff score to determine whether some global impairment in competence was likely. Scores below the recommended cutoff served as a signal that a more comprehensive inquiry into competence was warranted.

More comprehensive inquiries into defendants' competence utilized semi-structured interviews which, like the screening measures, had high face validity. Measures such as the CAI and IFI identified discrete areas of inquiry that focused on various elements of legal knowledge (e.g., the roles of principal participants in the adjudicatory process) and/or legal functioning (e.g., capacity to testify relevantly). Although some sample questions for probing these areas were provided, these measures did not facilitate a standardized assessment; rather, these tools employed a flexible, branching interview approach that permitted the clinician to determine both the direction and extent of questioning. The flexibility of the interview approach permitted a potentially wide-ranging and highly individualized assessment; however, it also introduced a degree of subjectivity into competence assessments that some found problematic. In essence, each examiner created his or her own set of questions for each assessment, resulting in a high probability that (a) different examiners would assess competence differently (i.e., use different questions) in the same defendant, and (b) a single examiner would likely employ different questions with different defendants. The lack of standardization in the questions or probes also meant that these measures could not provide objective, criterion-based scoring of defendants' responses. Thus, further subjectivity resulted from the need to rely on individual examiners' own criteria for what constituted a good, adequate, or poor response.

Finally, although some of these measures employed numerical scales for rating perceived impairment, none of them provided an algorithm for combining the ratings into an index, or set of indices, that could be interpreted in light of normative scores developed from research with relevant defendant populations. Indeed, the lack of standardized administration and scoring in these measures militated against the development of norms to guide clinical interpretation.

The state of the field at the beginning of the final decade of the 20th century was aptly summarized by Grisso (1992):

> After two decades of research to improve CST [competence to stand trial] evaluations, CST examiners still are without any instrument offering standardized administration and scoring (as contrasted with CST interview guides and subjective ratings) to assess the domain of CST-related abilities for the general population of defendants who are referred for CST evaluations... Without an objective measure of the legally relevant abilities, development of a research foundation for the field of CST assessment will continue to be limited. (pp. 366–367)

THE RESEARCH AGENDA

The conceptual model described in Chapter 2 provided a much more complex picture of adjudicative competence than had previously existed. Bonnie (1992, 1993) disaggregated the legal competence construct into two domains—a general competence to assist counsel, and decisional competence. Further, borrowing from the legal and clinical literature describing criteria for informed consent in the treatment context, the model suggested that as many as four distinguishable competence-related abilities might be assessed with respect to each domain. This model gave rise to a number of interesting research questions. Among them were:

- What is the normative level of capacity for different groups of criminal defendants—e.g., randomly selected, pretrial, jail inmates versus defendants adjudicated incompetent—across an array of competence-related abilities?
- How does capacity with respect to one legal domain (e.g., general competence to assist counsel) relate to capacity in the other domain (decisional competence)?

- How does capacity with respect to one competence-related ability (e.g., reasoning) relate to another competence-related ability (e.g., appreciation)? If a person is impaired with respect to one capacity, is he or she necessarily impaired with respect to others as well?
- Are defendants' capacities with respect to the two legal domains, or with respect to the four discrete competence-related abilities, differentially affected by clinical condition (i.e., diagnosis) or by symptomatology (e.g., depression versus psychosis versus cognitive impairment)?
- Would expanding the reach of adjudicative competence assessments to include the wider array of facets in Bonnie's model substantially impact the number of defendants judged "incompetent"?

Given the limitations of existing measures for assessing adjudicative competence, the Network selected as its first task the development of a new adjudicative competence research measure that would be sufficiently sophisticated and nuanced to explore such questions. The remainder of this chapter describes the development of a research instrument labeled the MacArthur Structured Assessment of the Competencies of Criminal Defendants (MacSAC-CD).

DESIGN AND DEVELOPMENT OF THE MacSAC-CD

General Design Features of the MacSAC-CD

In developing the MacSAC-CD we aspired to create a set of measures that would satisfy a variety of desirable criteria for psycholegal research tools. First, the measures would be face valid and relate in an obvious way to aspects of adjudicative competence implicated by *Dusky*. Second, separate measures would be constructed to assess various competence-related abilities within each of the legal domains described in Bonnie's reanalysis. Third, all measures would involve standardized administration and criterion-based scoring. Finally, with respect to assessing the "factual understanding" criterion articulated in *Dusky*, the relevant measures would evaluate a defendant's *capacity* to comprehend relevant legal information, not merely his or her current knowledge.

Although face and content validity may be of lesser concern in the development of measures of general psychological constructs, Grisso (1986) noted their extreme importance in the measurement of psycholegal constructs: "There can be no more important criterion for face validity than the opinion of judges and lawyers as prospective consumers of the results of one's ... assessment instrument ... It is possible that no amount of empirical validity will be able to overcome a judicial belief in the face invalidity of an instrument's dimensions in relation to the legal construct" (p. 42). To address this concern we relied on the expertise of Network members and outside consultants with extensive research and practical experience in the area of adjudicative competence in the development, selection, and wording of items for the various measures.

To insure that the various psycholegal abilities were measured independently, separate pools of items were drafted for each psycholegal ability within each domain. Item overlap across measures within the MacSAC-CD was not allowed. Further, careful thought was given to alternative ways of operationalizing different psycholegal abilities. As described in more detail below, different types of tasks were developed to assess "reasoning" capacity across the two domains of legal competence.

The goal of creating a standardized measure that could be used with all defendants posed one of the biggest challenges in instrument development. Clearly, each defendant's case has unique features—specific charges and allegations, different victims, the need to work with a particular attorney, and so forth. Nevertheless, in many respects the expectations of the legal system regarding functional abilities needed for competent participation operate at a more general level. For example, defendants need to be aware of the general roles and responsibilities of prosecutors and jurors, although it is not expected that they will know anything about the particular individuals that fill these roles. Similarly, it is potentially important that a defendant be able to understand that certain offenses include a particular mental element in addition to the prohibited act(s), or that certain rights are surrendered as part of the decision to enter a plea agreement. Again, capacities with respect to these expectations may be assessed using general rather than case specific queries. A defendant who can grasp the general notion of *mens rea* may be instructed in the particular mental element pertinent to his or her case, and the most important fundamental legal rights waived in pleading guilty—such as right to confront accusers, right to a jury trial, and Fifth Amendment protections—are not dependent on the parameters of a particular plea agreement.

A technique that lends itself to standardized inquiries is vignette methodology in which an defendant reveals his or her capacities through discussions of legal issues embedded in a hypothetical case. As described in more detail below, several of the MacSAC-CD measures were created by writing items that require defendants to respond to queries about the plight of a hypothetical defendant rather than to queries about their own case.

Finally, to insure that our measures of factual understanding tested a defendant's capacity rather than merely his or her current knowledge about a legal issue, we designed items that involved specific disclosures of legal information, after which defendants were tested for comprehension using both recall (paraphrase) and recognition (True-False) response formats.

COMPONENT MEASURES OF THE MACSAC-CD

As the discussion above reveals, the MacSAC-CD is not a unitary instrument that was intended to measure in any monolithic way a defendant's "competence to proceed." Rather, it is a research tool comprised of multiple measures, each of which assesses one competence-related ability (understanding, reasoning, appreciation) within one legal domain (competence to assist counsel, decisional competence). The fourth column of Table 3.1 provides the array of measures in the MacSAC-CD and places these measures within the legal and conceptual framework of the *Dusky* criteria described in Chapter 2.[2]

The prefix for each measure indicates the legal domain to which the measure applies: CAC = competence to assist counsel, DC = decisional competence. The suffix indicates the competence-related ability tapped by the measure: U = factual understanding, R = reasoning, A = appreciation (rational understanding). With respect to decisional competence, there are a variety of decisions that a defendant potentially faces depending on the facts and nature of his or her case—e.g., whether or not to plead guilty, whether or not to take the witness stand at trial, whether or not to waive a jury and seek a bench trial. In creating the MacSAC-CD we opted to create two DC:U measures, one of which assessed understanding of issues related to pleading guilty (DC:U-PG), and one which assessed understanding of issues related to waiving a jury (DC:U-WJ).

As noted above, vignette methodology was used to standardize much of the MacSAC-CD. Specifically, the measures that assess understanding (CAC:U, DC:U-PG, DC:U-WJ) and reasoning (CAC:R, DC:R) use items that are constructed around the following vignette:

> Two men, Fred and Reggie, are playing pool in a bar and get into a fight. Fred hits Reggie with a pool stick. Reggie falls and hits his head on the floor so hard that he nearly dies.

---

[2] Within the Decisional Competence domain, the capacity to express a choice was assessed in the MacSAC-CD by a scale (DC:C) comprised of a single item. In the research using the MacSAC-CD (described below) this measure yielded no findings of interest due to lack of variability in responses (fewer than 1% of defendants were unable to express a choice). Thus, we have excluded this item from Table 3.1 for simplicity sake).

TABLE 3.1. LEGAL, CONCEPTUAL & MEASUREMENT LANDSCAPE OF THE MACARTHUR ADJUDICATIVE COMPETENCE MEASURES

Dusky Criteria	Conceptual Domain	Description/Operationalization	MacSAC-CD Measures	MacCAT-CA Items
				Understanding
Factual understanding of the proceedings	Assist Counsel	Know *abstractly* the basic roles of participants, adversary nature of proceedings, possible consequences of conviction.	CAC:U	Items 1–6
	Decisional Competence	Know *abstractly* the parameters of options available (e.g., plea options; whether to testify or request waiver of jury/counsel)	DC:U-PC DC:U-WJ	Items 7–8
				Reasoning
Consult with lawyer	Assist Counsel	Recognize and relate information relevant to constructing a legal defense.	CAC:R	Items 9–13
	Decisional Competence	Capacity to seek relevant information that would inform the decision and; to conduct a risks-and-benefits analysis of options.	DC:R	Items 14–16
				Appreciation
Rational understanding of the proceedings	Assist Counsel	Plausibility of beliefs about how participants and procedures will play out in one's own case	CAC:A	Items 17–21
	Decisional Competence	Plausibility of beliefs that relate to deciding among legal options (e.g., whether to plead guilty, testify, etc.)	DC:A	Item 22

[1] See Chapter 5 of this book, which describes the MacCAT-CA, a clinical measure developed from the MacSAC-CD.

Measures of Competence to Assist Counsel

Understanding (CAC:U)

Within the domain of Competence to Assist Counsel, understanding was conceived as comprehension at a general and abstract level of the personnel and procedures involved in the adjudicatory process. In terms of the *Dusky* criteria, this level of understanding is closest to the requirement of *factual understanding* of the proceedings. The CAC:U measure consists of 7 items that assess comprehension in the following areas: (a) basic characteristics of criminal prosecution and defense, (b) roles of judge and jury at a jury trial, (c) the elements of a criminal charge (*mens rea* and *actus reus*), (d) the nature of a guilty plea, and (e) the consequences of a conviction.

A four-step procedure is used to administer each item on the CAC:U. Step 1 is an open-ended inquiry about a particular issue. This query is called Predisclosure and solicits the defendant's current fund of knowledge. For example, Item 1 begins:

> Let's say that Fred gets arrested and charged with a crime. Fred gets a lawyer. Fred's lawyer is called the attorney for the defense. What is the job of the attorney for the defense? [subject response]
>
> There is another lawyer involved in Fred's case who is called the prosecutor. What is the job of the prosecutor? [subject response]

The defendant's response to predisclosure reflects current knowledge rather than capacity and is not scored.[3] However, this manner of introducing a legal issue permits the evaluation to proceed in a more natural and conversational manner. In order to assess *capacity* to understand relevant legal information, the item proceeds with Step 2, which is called Disclosure. The following information is read aloud to the defendant (who can follow along by reading the disclosure in a booklet provided by the examiner):

> Fred's lawyer tells Fred how the legal system works. There are two sides. On one side is Fred's lawyer, who is called the attorney for the defense. He will try to show that Fred did not commit a crime. Also, as the case goes on, the defense attorney will tell Fred what his choices are. On the other side is a lawyer called the prosecutor. The prosecutor will try to show that Fred did commit a crime and that there is no excuse for what Fred did.

---

[3] In the clinical instrument derived from the MacSAC-CD, described in Chapter 5, the predisclosure response is scored because existing knowledge, *when correct*, may be considered a valid proxy for capacity.

Following the Disclosure the defendant is tested in two ways about his or her comprehension of the disclosed information. At Step 3 a paraphrase response is requested: *"In your own words, tell me what Fred just found out about the legal system"* [subject response]. The examiner utilizes a set of general probes (e.g., *"Tell me more"*) to encourage a full response, and specific probes (e.g., *"What do you mean by __?"*) to encourage the defendant to use his or her own words and synonyms rather than merely parroting words contained in the disclosure. The content of the defendant's narrative is then examined to determine whether it contains specific elements of information determined *a priori* to be scorable for the item. Scoring ranges from 2 (full comprehension) to 1 (partial comprehension) to 0 (no comprehension) depending on the number of scorable elements contained in the defendant's narrative.

Step 4 involves the administration of four True-False items. These items were included in the MacSAC-CD in order to evaluate defendants' relative capacities to display comprehension via recall (paraphrase) versus recognition formats. Major mental disorder and mental retardation are the commonly recognized legal bases for incompetence to proceed to adjudication, and the symptoms of some mental disorders may impair defendants' expressive capacities although, potentially, their receptive comprehension may be relatively good. On this basis some have argued that measures that employ a recognition format may be more appropriate for evaluating understanding (Everington & Luckasson, 1992). Thus, for Item 1 of the CAC:U the defendant is asked to characterize each of the following statements as True or False *based on the information provided in the Disclosure*:

1. On one side is Fred's lawyer who is called the prosecutor.
2. As the case goes on, the defense attorney will tell Fred what his choices are.
3. The job of the defense attorney is to decide whether a person is guilty or not guilty.
4. The defense attorney tries to show that a crime has not been committed.

(The items are read one at a time, and the defendant can read along on a copy provided by the examiner.) A score of 2 is assigned for answering correctly all four items, 1 for answering correctly 3 items, and 0 for answering correctly two (chance) or fewer items. The Paraphrase and True-False item scores are added to yield a score on this item from 0–4.

Reasoning (CAC:R)

Within the domain of competence to assist counsel, we operationalized reasoning in terms of a defendant's capacity to distinguish more legally relevant from less legally relevant case-related facts. To standardize this measure we provide the defendant with additional hypothetical facts about Fred's case and ask him or her to choose, and then to give a rationale for, facts that would be most important for Fred to tell his attorney. The expanded vignette is as follows:

> Fred has been working in the home construction business for 10 years. His main job is to put roofs on houses. One day, after work, Fred decides to go to a baseball game with his friend, Julie. After the game they go to a bar. At the bar Fred has a couple of beers and he starts to play pool with a guy he just met named Reggie. Suddenly, Fred and Reggie begin to argue about the pool game and begin to push each other. Then Fred swings at Reggie with a pool stick and hits him in the chest. Reggie falls down and hits his head on the floor pretty hard. It looks like Reggie is hurt very badly. Fred runs to the phone to call an ambulance. As it turns out, Reggie nearly dies.

The defendant is then given two cards, each of which contains a "fact" that can be assumed to be true. These "facts" are read aloud and the defendant is then asked to choose the fact that would be most important to relate to an attorney and to provide a reason that the chosen fact is more important. For example, one pair of facts is:

> Card 1: After Reggie pushed him, Fred thought that he saw Reggie reaching for a knife.
> Card 2: Fred picked up a paycheck at work before he picked up Julie to go to a baseball game.

Scores on each item range from 0 to 2. One point is given for selecting the more legally relevant fact (here, Card 1), and another for providing a reason consistent with the important legal theme underlying that item (i.e., the possibility of self-defense). The CAC-R consists of 6 such items and a possible range of scores from 0–12. The "correct" facts in these six items reflect the following legally relevant themes: self-defense, absence of intent to harm, provocation, need to protect self, identification of witnesses, and adverse effects of alcohol on behavior.

Appreciation: CAC:A

The competence-related ability of appreciation is conceptually related to the *Dusky* criterion of "rational understanding" of the proceedings. Unlike understanding, which reflects comprehension at a more general and abstract level (i.e., how the legal system is supposed to work), appreciation relates to a defendant's beliefs about how legal actors and processes will play out in his or her own case. Thus, the CAC:A abandons the vignette methodology employed to assess understanding and reasoning and involves the systematic inquiry into the defendant's beliefs about (a) the criminal charges, (b) the likelihood of a conviction, (c) the impartiality of the judicial process, (d) possible helpfulness of the defense attorney, (e) the possible benefits of full disclosure of case information to defense counsel, and (f) severity of punishment one will likely receive if convicted.

Because appreciation is related to "rational understanding," the focus of CAC:A items is on the rationality of a defendant's beliefs in regard to these issues. Items begin with a query of how the defendant thinks a specific issue will play out in his or her own case, compared to how that item might apply to most other people facing the same/similar charges. The item relating to likelihood of conviction begins with the following statement:

> Some people who get in trouble with the law are found guilty of a crime. Now I want you to look at this card. It has five answers on it to indicate how likely you think it is that you will be found guilty. I want you to pick the answer that comes closest to what you think.

For this item the first option printed on the card, which is also read aloud to the defendant, is:

> A. I definitely have a lower chance of being found guilty than most people charged with [the offense that the defendant has been charged with].

Options B–E are worded exactly the same except that they reflect a gradient of increasing probabilities of being found guilty (compared to most people...): B. "probably" have a lower chance..., C. "have about the same chance...", D. "probably have a higher chance...", and E. "definitely have a higher chance...".

The choice selected (A–E) is not scored, but merely provides the basis for the follow up query, which asks the basis for his or her belief (e.g., "*What are the reasons that you think you are definitely (or probably) more (or less), or just as likely to be convicted...?*"). The defendant's reasons are recorded and the examiner then makes a judgment of the facial plausibility of the reasons given: clearly plausible reasons are scored 2, questionably plausible reasons are scored 1, and clearly implausible reasons are scored 0. Clearly plausible reasons for believing one has a "higher chance" might refer to the strength of evidence against the defendant (e.g., "They caught me at the scene," or "My co-defendant ratted me out") or to sociological views of inherent bias in the legal system (e.g., "I am a black man and there is some level of prejudice against blacks in the legal system"). Beliefs that are implausible on their face often reflect disorganized or delusional thinking (e.g., "I am definitely less likely to be found guilty" because "I have special powers to control peoples' thoughts and I'm going to use these powers to influence the jury").

When the plausibility of a defendant's belief is unclear, further probing is used to get an elaborated response. If the belief appears to rest on a dubious assumption, the examiner restates the questions using a premise that negates the defendant's dubious assumption. For example, suppose a defendant asserted that he definitely had a "higher chance" of being found guilty because his attorney was "a public defender." The item might be administered again with the following premise: "*Let's assume that you would be represented by a private, paid attorney rather than by the public defender. Given this situation, pick the answer that comes the closest to what you think about your chance of being found guilty.*" The defendant's reasons for his or her new belief would now be judged on plausibility (0–2) and this would become the item score.

Measures of Decisional Competence

Measures that assess understanding and reasoning within the decisional competence domain also utilize the "Fred and Reggie" vignette in order to allow standardized inquiries regarding these competence-related domains.

Understanding a Plea of Guilty (DC:U-PG)

One understanding measure in the decisional competence domain consists of five items that assess a defendant's understanding of the following issues in participating in a guilty plea/plea agreement: (a) pleading guilty involves an admission of criminal conduct, (b) the constitutional rights waived in pleading guilty, (c) plausible reasons for pleading guilty rather than going to trial, (d) plausible reasons for going to trial rather than pleading guilty, and (e) the prerogative to decide how to plead belongs to the defendant.

The second DC:U measure, DC:U-WJ, assesses capacity to understand issues specific to the decision whether to waive the constitutional right to a trial by jury and request a bench trial. This measure consists of six items that focus on a defendant's understanding of (a) the distinction between a trial by judge and a trial by jury (two items), (b) the fact that a right to a jury trial is guaranteed by the Constitution and that the prerogative to request waiver belongs to the defendant, (c) the right of the defense to participate in jury selection, (d) plausible reasons for requesting a trial by a judge, and (e) plausible reasons for requesting a trial by a jury.

The structure of the items in these DC:U measures is identical to that of the CAC:U items. Each begins with an open-ended query (Predisclosure) that solicits a narrative response that reflects defendant's current fund of knowledge (this response is not scored). This is followed by Step 2 – a Disclosure that forms the basis for testing the defendant's comprehension of legal information to which he or she has been exposed. At Step 3 comprehension is tested by evaluating the completeness of the defendant's paraphrase of the key elements of information embedded in the Disclosure; at Step 4 True-False items are used to assess comprehension based on recognition rather than recall (paraphrase).

Reasoning (DC:R)

The decisional competence reasoning measure contains a variety of items, some of which required the demonstration of reasoning capacity specifically within the legal context of the vignette, others of which assess more general reasoning ability. DC:R items 1–4 assess reasoning within the context of Fred's option whether or not to enter a plea agreement. The defendant is provided with the following description of Fred's legal options:

> One choice is that Fred could plead guilty and have a trial. The chances are high that Fred would be convicted of a crime. If Fred is convicted of attempted murder, it is likely that he would be sentenced to 10 years in prison. Or, if Fred is convicted of simple assault, it is likely that he would be placed on probation.
> The other choice is that Fred could plead guilty. The prosecutor has talked with Fred's lawyer and an offer has been made. If Fred will plead guilty to the less serious charge of simple assault, the charge of attempted murder will be dropped. Fred will get a sentence of six months in jail. There would be no chance for Fred to be found innocent.

The defendant is then told to assume that Fred is his friend and wants some advice about what to do. The defendant is then asked DC:R item 1: "What else would you want to know before you advise Fred?" This query challenges that aspect of reasoning which requires thinking through a decision and deciding what information would be relevant to seek in order to make an informed choice. The request for information not previously disclosed but judged plausibly relevant (e.g., "I'd want to know if there were witnesses at the bar who would testify for Fred") is assigned a score of 2; a request for plausibly relevant information previously disclosed (e.g., "I'd want to know whether Fred was drinking at the bar"— information provided earlier in the CAC:R disclosure) is assigned a score of 1; a request for no information, or a request for information judged irrelevant (e.g., "I want to know what teams were playing at the baseball game Fred and Julie went to") is assigned a score of 0.

DC:R items 2–4 challenge the defendant to (a) describe the primary legal effects of the two options available to Fred, (b) describe the potential personal consequences (to Fred) of the alternative options, and (c) compare the two choices in terms of advantages/disadvantages or risks and benefits. These items are scored using a 2-1-0 format depending on the number of effects/consequences/comparisons that the defendant can produce.

The 9 remaining DC:R items do not refer to the vignette and assess reasoning in a more general way. Some resemble more traditional math or logic problems and require the defendant to draw appropriate conclusions given different major and minor premises or relative probability information. Others test the capacity to think transitively (i.e., if A>B and B>C, then A>C).

Appreciation (DC:A)

As with CAC:A, appreciation in the decisional competence context refers to the plausibility (rationality) of a defendant's beliefs about choices that might occur within the context of his or her own case. The items in the DC:A attempt to discern a defendant's capacity to make relevant decisions in a self-interested manner, or to uncover delusional thoughts or other symptoms of mental disorder that impair the capacity to evaluate rationally the choice that one may face. The CAC:A consists of two items, one keyed to the possible participation in a plea agreement and the other keyed to the possible request to waive a jury trial.

The structure of these items is identical to that of the CAC:A items described above. First the defendant is asked to select a probability statement about the likelihood that he or she would plead guilty or request waiver of a jury (e.g., "Compared to other people facing criminal charges similar to mine, I definitely (probably)/would (would not) [or] would be just as likely to plead guilty (request waiver of a jury)"). Again, the probability option itself is not scored but merely provides a context for a query that solicits the defendant's reasons for the belief. As before, the plausibility of the defendant's reasons are scored 2, 1, or 0. When the initial reason is scored 1, then a follow-up query solicits a second response and reason, and the plausibility score assigned to the second reason becomes the item score.

BASIC FINDINGS FROM THE ADJUDICATIVE COMPETENCE PILOT STUDY

Impetus for the major field study, described in the next section, was provided by a 1991 pilot study that evaluated prototypes of the three understanding measures (Hoge et al., 1996). The pilot study employed an extreme groups design, comparing understanding scores of 42 hospitalized incompetent defendants (group INC) with those of 42 defendants who were, in the judgments of their public defenders, "clearly competent" (group COM). Encouraging results from the pilot study included that:

- high interrater agreement (Pearson r between two research assistants) was obtained for scoring the paraphrase portion of the three prototype measures for both the COM (.85–.90) and INC (.85–.92) groups;
- scores on the prototype understanding measures were significantly lower for the INC group than for the COM group, whether measured by recall (paraphrase) or recognition (True-False) format;
- the prototype understanding measures were sensitive to changes in patients' clinical status; scores for 28 INC patients retested at the time they were recommended for return to court after receiving psychiatric treatment to restore competence were significantly higher than their baseline scores and not statistically different from the scores of the COM group;
- total scores of the three prototype understanding measures were highly correlated (.83–.85).

Further support for proceeding with a major field study came from the studies of the Network's civil competence project (Grisso & Appelbaum, 1995; Grisso et al., 1995), in which measures of all three competence-related abilities—understanding, reasoning, appreciation—similar to those in the MacSAC-CD performed in theoretically expected ways.

THE MACARTHUR ADJUDICATIVE COMPETENCE FIELD STUDIES

Overview and Hypotheses for the Field Studies

In planning this research, a major decision related to the definition of research groups for the study. The one obvious group to be included would be defendants recently hospitalized for competence restoration treatment (designated HI: hospital incompetents) after being adjudicated incompetent to proceed. However, we no longer wanted to continue with an extreme groups design, so questions remained as to the optimal comparison group(s) of defendants to be recruited.

Anticipating that we might ultimately develop a clinical version of the MacSAC-CD for use by forensic mental health professionals, we wanted to include groups that would provide the most relevant norms for the comparison and interpretation of scores. We ultimately decided on two comparison groups. One relevant comparison group would be unscreened (randomly selected) jail inmates (designated JU: Jail Unscreened), whose competence-related abilities would likely vary considerably more than those of the "clearly competent" jail inmates in the pilot study. Members of this group would be "typical" pretrial inmates for whom the presumption of competence to participate in the proceedings was (almost) never challenged, and their scores would represent the competence-related abilities of the "typical defendant." The second comparison group would be comprised of pretrial jail inmates, all of whom were receiving some type of mental health services (e.g., psychotropic medications, counseling, substance abuse treatment). We considered that this JT (jail treated) group would contain the kinds of defendants about whom competence concerns would more likely be raised (even if they were not formally referred for evaluation). Further, this group would likely have significant levels of psychopathology, and thus pose a sterner test for the MacSAC-CD to distinguish these inmates from hospitalized incompetent inmates on the basis of competence-related abilities.

A second consideration in sampling was gender. Overwhelmingly, men are responsible for a greater proportion of crime than are women, particularly more serious felony offenses which are more likely to give rise to attorneys' concerns about defendants' competence (see Chapter 1; see also Steadman & Braff, 1975). Further, a major review of the adjudicative competence literature by Nicholson and Kugler (1991) revealed that the overwhelming majority (89.5%) of participants in previous studies have been men. Thus, to insure that our findings would be (1) applicable to the largest number of defendants whose competence might be questioned, and (2) comparable with research findings to those that have come before, we opted to include only male defendants in the primary field study.

However, we also recognized the importance of breaking ground in the area of adjudicative competence with women. Thus we decided to conduct a second, independent study of the competence-related abilities of women defendants. Although the study with female defendants was substantially smaller in terms of number of research subjects, the two studies were otherwise identical in design and methodology. Here we report first the findings of the primary field study, followed by the main results of the study involving women.

Research Objectives

The primary purpose of the field study was to examine the psychometric properties and construct validity of the MacSAC-CD. Our investigation of the psychometric properties of the instrument included the following:

- Internal consistency. Coefficient alpha and item-scale correlations would be calculated for each measure and compared to conventionally accepted criteria for adequate research measures. Nunnally (1978) suggests α's > .70 and item-total correlations > .30 as satisfactory for research measures (pp. 245, 263, respectively).
- Interscorer agreement. The measures would have satisfactory levels of interscorer agreement as measured by percent agreement and the kappa statistic, which corrects for chance levels of agreement.
- Inter-measure correlations. Because all measures of the MacSAC-CD relate to the competence construct, we predicted positive correlations among them. However, within this array of positive correlations we hypothesized that measures that tapped the same psycholegal ability (e.g., understanding: CAC:U, DC:U-PG, DC:U-WJ) would correlate more highly with one another than they would with measures that tapped a different ability (e.g., appreciation).

We also formulated six hypotheses regarding outcomes that would demonstrate the validity of the MacSAC-CD:

- Relationship to measures of psychopathology and cognitive functioning. The currently accepted legal bases for an incompetence determination generally speak to "mental disease" or "mental defect." While there is no algorithm for translating these legal terms directly into clinical diagnoses or syndromes,[4] the first term is generally considered to refer to the more debilitating mental illnesses, such as bipolar disorder, schizophrenia, and other disorders that may manifest psychotic features, while the latter is generally considered to refer to impaired cognitive/intellectual abilities. Prior studies using other competence measures have found that competence is negatively correlated with psychosis and low intelligence (Grisso, 1992; Nicholson & Kugler, 1991; Roesch & Golding, 1980). Thus, we hypothesized that MacSAC-CD scores would correlate negatively with measures of psychopathology and/or psychosis, and positively with a measure of current cognitive functioning.

---

[4] The DSM-IV notes the "...imperfect fit between the questions of ultimate concern to the law and the information contained in a clinical diagnosis" and that "In most situations, the clinical diagnosis of a DSM-IV mental disorder is not sufficient to establish the existence for legal purposes of a 'mental disorder,' 'mental disability,' 'mental disease,' or 'mental defect.'" American Psychiatric Association (1994, p. xxiii).

- Expected differences among study groups. For the MacSAC-CD to be a valid measure of competence-related abilities, certain relationships among the scores for our three research groups would have to obtain. In order to accurately reflect the current realities of our legal system, scores on the MacSAC-CD measures should be lower for the recently hospitalized incompetent group (HI) than for either the inmates receiving mental health services at the jail for purposes other than competence restoration (JT: jail treated group) or the unscreened jail inmates (group JU) who were selected randomly. Because of the (expected) higher level of psychopathology in the JT group than in the JU group, we expected some decrement in the competence-related abilities of the JT group such that their scores would fall between those of the other two groups.
- Sensitivity to changes in clinical symptoms. Members of the HI group had been judged legally incompetent and hospitalized for competence restoration treatment. To the degree that their impaired competence was related to psychiatric symptoms, then as clinical condition improved so should their competence-related abilities. Thus, compared to their baseline scores upon admission for treatment, we hypothesized that these defendants would obtain higher scores on the MacSAC-CD when retested at the point that the treatment staff judge them to be clinically improved and restored to competence.
- Correlations with clinical judgments of competence. As a measure of competence-related abilities, the MacSAC-CD should correlate positively with other measures of the same construct. Clinical judgment is the most frequently used "measure" of competence and this judgment was obtainable for the defendants in the HI group. We therefore hypothesized that the MacSAC-CD would correlate positively with clinical judgments of defendants' capacity upon hospital admission for competence restoration treatment. However, we hypothesized that this correlation would be of only modest magnitude. Some members of the HI group may have been judged incompetent on the basis of case specific information or other facets of competence not assessed by our research measure (e.g., amnesia). Further, the range of scores on the MacSAC-CD would likely be restricted in the HI group, which might further limit the magnitude of correlations with other measures.
- Cynicism toward the justice system. Some prior competence measures have been criticized because their scoring criteria were influenced by value judgments related to defendants' attitudes toward the justice system. For example, Brakel (1974) criticized the

Competency Screening Test (Lipsitt, Lelos, & McGarry, 1971) because lower scores (i.e., more impaired competence) were assigned to responses which may have been based on defendants' personal or vicarious experience with the legal system that reflected cynicism and distrust of the police, courts, and lawyers. In constructing the MacSAC-CD care was taken in the procedures for administration and probing to minimize the risk that cynical responses would be scored as indicative of impaired competence. Thus, we hypothesized that scores on the MacSAC-CD would not correlate significantly with an index of defendants' skepticism toward the criminal justice system.

METHOD

PARTICIPANTS

Criminal defendants in Virginia and Florida were recruited as participants in this study. Enrollment was limited to English-speaking, male defendants between the ages of 18 and 65. Legally incompetent defendants (group HI) were recruited at state forensic hospitals which provided competence restoration treatment; presumptively competent pretrial defendants (groups JU and JT) were recruited at county jails.[5] At both the hospitals and the jails available mental health records of potential participants were reviewed and inmates were excluded from the study if their chart showed a diagnosis of mental retardation or serious organic disorder. Enrollment screening also included an index of Verbal Cognitive Functioning (see Measures, below), essentially a prorated IQ score based on three subtests of the Wechsler Adult Intelligence Scale – Revised (WAIS-R). However, no potential participant in any group scored below the exclusion cutoff score of 60.

The HI group included 159 forensic patients, 84 from Virginia and 75 from Florida. To minimize the impact of treatment on baseline scores, all participants were recruited and tested within two weeks of admission ($M = 6.1$ days, $SD = 2.8$ days). Twelve percent of the patients approached refused participation in the study (9% in Virginia, 16% in Florida).

---

[5] Participants differed in minor ways between the two states. In Florida, all HI defendants had been committed after a formal judicial hearing. In Virginia, commitment for competence restoration could be accomplished either by formal judicial hearing or, less formally, via a Criminal Temporary Detention Order. In Florida, only jail inmates represented by the Public Defender were eligible for participation; in Virginia, all jail inmates were eligible (although 86% of those actually recruited were represented by public defenders).

JU and JT participants were recruited from two jails in Florida and one in Virginia. Of the 94 JU participants, 41 came from Virginia and 53 from Florida; of the 113 JT participants, 58 came from Virginia and 55 from Florida. The refusal rate for these two groups was almost identical in the two states—Virginia (33%) and Florida (34%).

Measures

In addition to the MacSAC-CD, the research protocol included a brief interview as well as a review of available jail or hospital files to obtain demographic, psychosocial history, criminal history, and clinical history. For the HI group only, a rating of each defendant's level of (in)competence was obtained from a mental health professional involved in the patient's treatment.

The Brief Psychiatric Rating Scale (BPRS: Overall & Gorham, 1962) is a widely used measure of current psychopathology. In this study we used the 18-item, anchored version by Woerner, Mannuzza, and Kane (1988), which employs a Likert scale from 1 (*not present*) to 7 (*severe*) for rating the presence and severity symptoms. Ratings are based on a brief interview (15 minutes) and can be summed to provide a global measure of current mental status; scores on several item clusters can be combined to yield indices of psychoticism, depression, withdrawal, and hostility (Overall & Porterfield, 1963).

An index of current Verbal Cognitive Functioning (VCF) was obtained using the Vocabulary, Similarities, and Digit Span subtests of the Wechsler Adult Intelligence Scale—Revised (WAIS-R). WAIS-R Manual norms were used to convert raw scores to scale scores. The three scale scores were summed and multiplied by two and then converted to a prorated verbal IQ score using the WAIS-R age-normed tables. For people with serious mental illness, cognitive functions are likely to be impaired by their underlying disorder. Thus, for such individuals the prorated IQ score is better conceived as an index of current verbal cognitive functioning than as a true index of baseline intellectual ability.

Clinical judgments regarding the degree of (in)competence of HI participants was obtained from a member of the patient's treatment team at the time that the baseline administration of the MacSAC-CD was administered. The responsible clinician provided a global rating from 1 (*clearly incompetent*) to 6 (*clearly competent*) to reflect his or her judgment of the defendant's competence.

To obtain an index of defendants' skepticism and cynicism about the criminal justices system, we created a 6-item "Perceived Criminal Injustice Scale" (PCIS) by adapting a scale developed by Hagan and Albonetti (1982). The PCIS items use a 5-point Likert scale ranging from +2 (*strongly agree*) to −2 (*strongly disagree*) to solicit defendants' beliefs about the fairness of lawyers, police, juries and judges. For example, a response of "strongly disagree" to the item "Police, lawyers, and judges treat people who commit crimes the same, whether they are rich or poor" would indicate perceived injustice. In this study, the internal consistency of our 6-item scale was $\alpha = .66$.

Procedure

To recruit HI participants, trained research assistants (RAs) coordinated with the admissions offices at the forensic hospitals. As soon as possible after admission, the clinician responsible for the defendant's treatment was contacted and permission was requested to approach the defendant for recruitment into the study. Each patient/defendant was recruited using procedures approved by a university Institutional Review Board. The purpose nature and length of study participation, confidentiality, voluntary participation, and other issues mandated for informed consent were discussed. Each patient was advised that he or she would be paid $10 upon completion of the protocol for the time contributed to the study. The protocols were administered in private offices or interview rooms arranged by hospital staff. After the completion of the protocol, the RA contacted a treating clinician to obtain a global rating of the patient's level of (in)competence.

Recruitment of JT participants was arranged through contacts with mental health staff at the jails, who assisted in identifying inmates receiving any form of mental health treatment at the jail. From these lists of potential JT participants, RAs used a random number table to select individuals to be approached for recruitment. For the recruitment of JU participants, a random number table was used to select names from either a jail census record (Virginia) or from a periodically updated list of inmates currently represented by the public defender (Florida). Otherwise, except that there was no clinician rating of an inmate's level of (in)competence, the procedures were identical to those used with HI participants.

For all groups the order of administration of measures was VCF, Background Interview, PCIS, MacSAC-CD, and BPRS. The order of administration of the MacSAC-CD measures was CAC:U, DC:U-PG, DC:U-WJ, DC:R, DC:C, CAC:R, CAC:A, and DC:A.

RESULTS I—MAIN FIELD STUDY (MALE DEFENDANTS)

Sample Description

As there were relatively few site differences among the samples, data regarding the demographic and criminal justice features of the research

TABLE 3.2. DEMOGRAPHIC AND CRIMINAL JUSTICE FEATURES OF THE RESEARCH SAMPLES

	HI[1]	JT	JU
Demographics			
Age: M	34.2	32.4	29.9
(SD)	(8.8)	(8.8)	(7.9)
Percent non-white	37	32	28
Socioeconomic Status[2] (%)			
Professional/managerial	2	4	1
Administrative/Clerical	8	10	11
Skilled/semi-skilled manual labor	17	30	50
Unskilled/unemployed	73	55	38
Criminal Justice			
Age at first arrest: M	24.1	23.4	21.4
(SD)	(7.0)	(8.2)	(6.2)
Number of prior arrests: M	1.7	1.7	1.8
(SD)	(0.3)	(0.4)	(0.3)
Current felony charges (%)	73	76	48
Prior felony convictions (%)	44	62	67
Ever in prison (%)	33	42	48
Evaluated for competence in past (%)	40	22	3

[1] Socioeconomic status based on last reported employment, using Hollingshead and Redlich (1958) categories.
[2] HI = hospitalized incompetent   JT = jail treatment   JU = jail unscreened.

samples are combined across sites and provided in Table 3.2. HI participants were somewhat older, $F(2, 362) = 7.28, p < .001$, than those in the other groups and were more likely to be unskilled or unemployed, $\chi^2 (52, N = 358) = 72.14, p < .01$. The groups did not differ significantly in terms of racial composition, nor did they differ in self-reported educational attainment (data not reported). The groups did not differ significantly on a variety of criminal history variables, including age at first arrest, number of prior arrests, and proportion previously in jail or prison. The JU group members were less likely to be facing a current felony charge than the HI and JT groups, $\chi^2 (6, N = 232) = 22.12, p < .001$, while the HI group members were less likely to have had a prior felony conviction, $\chi^2 (2, N = 360) = 14.75, p < .001$.

Clinical features of the research samples are presented in Table 3.3. Given the criteria for group selection, many fewer participants in the JU group had a psychiatric diagnosis in their jail record and, predictably, were less likely to be receiving psychotropic medication at the time of enrollment into the study, $F(2, 365) = 215.98, p < .001$.

TABLE 3.3. CLINICAL FEATURES OF THE RESEARCH SAMPLES

	HI	JT	JU
Chart Diagnosis (%)			
Schizophrenia	65	24	2
Affective disorder	28	59	0
Other	7	17	7
Currently Receiving			
Psychotropic Medication (%)	83	87	0
Prior Psychiatric Treatment (%)			
Inpatient	79	64	10
Outpatient	77	64	15
Brief Psychiatric Rating Scale	M		
	(SD)		
Total Score	37.02	38.95	28.72
	(7.6)	(8.6)	(6.38)
Psychoticism Subscale	6.60	5.71	3.74
	(2.8)	(3.1)	(1.05)
Depression Subscale	7.58	10.84	7.57
	(2.71)	(2.64)	(3.18)
Hostility Subscale	6.58	5.79	4.41
	(2.7)	(2.6)	(1.48)
Withdrawal Subscale	5.89	6.80	5.11
	(2.5)	(3.0)	(2.54)
Verbal Cognitive Functioning M	87.97	92.37	90.39
(SD)	(11.5)	(14.3)	(10.95)

HI = hospitalized incompetent   JT = jail treatment   JU = jail unscreened.

A coherent picture emerged when considering the HI and JT participants' chart diagnoses, BPRS-A scores, and current medications. About two-thirds (65%) of the HI group were diagnosed with schizophrenia and about one-quarter (28%) with a major affective disorder, while these proportions were approximately reversed (24% and 59%, respectively) in the JT group. Patterns of medications prescribed and current mental status symptoms were consistent with these diagnostic patterns. HI participants were more likely to be prescribed antipsychotic medications and JT participants were more likely to be prescribed antidepressants, χ^2 (6, N = 232) = 62.20, $p < .001$. Further, the HI group obtained the highest mean score on the BPRS-A psychoticism subscale, F (2, 358) = 36.87, $p < .001$, while the JT group obtained the highest mean score on the BPRS-A depression subscale, F (2, 358) = 39.96, $p < .001$. The HI group had the lowest mean score on the VCF index, F (2, 363) = 4.32, $p < .01$.

Psychometric Properties of the MacSAC-CD

Internal Consistency

Nunnally (1978, p. 245) suggests that a value of .70 or higher for coefficient alpha indicates satisfactory internal consistency for research measures, and as the data in Table 3.4 indicate, alphas for the component measures of the MacSAC-CD were at or above this value, with the highest values being obtained for the understanding measures. Because the DC:A measure consists of only two items, a correlation coefficient rather than an alpha value was calculated ($r = .40$, $p < .001$). Item-total correlations $> .30$ are usually considered good (Nunnally, 1978, p. 263) and the mean item-scale correlation for each of the component measures was at or above this value (although the value for some individual items on the DC:U-WJ and DC:R measures fell below .30). These results indicate that the component measures of the MacSAC-CD meet conventional standards of internal consistency for research measures.

Interrater Agreement

To examine interrater reliability, the nine RAs employed at four data collection sites each scored 30 protocols randomly selected from among protocols completed at sites other than their own. Criterion scores for all protocols were established by a senior research staff member at the

TABLE 3.4. INTERNAL CONSISTENCY AND INTERSCORER RELIABILITY OF THE MacSAC-CD

MacSAC-CD Measure	Internal Consistency		Interscorer Reliability	
	Cronbach's α	Mean Item-scale Correlation	κ	% Agreement
Understanding				
CAC:U	.87	.53	.60	75
DC:U-PG	.88	.54	.74	83
DC:U-WJ	.88	.50	.75	83
Reasoning				
CAC:R	.68	.41	.60	82
DC:R	.71	.32	.60	76
Appreciation				
CAC:A	.74	.48	.48	88
DC:A	.40*	—	.36	75

*Because there are only 2 items on the DC:A, this is a Pearson r rather than α value.

University of Virginia who had worked closely with the research group in the development of the instrument and who was most experienced in administering the protocol. The right-hand portion of Table 3.4 provides κ coefficients and percent agreement data between scores assigned by the RAs and this "master scorer."

The κ values for the understanding and reasoning measures are respectable, and percent agreement values for these measures range from 75% to 83%. Kappa values for the appreciation measures are less impressive, however, although we noted that scores on these measures were quite negatively skewed, and κ values may be depressed due to skewness and reduced variance. In this light, the percent agreement for the CAC:A (88%) and DC:A (75%) are encouraging.

Inter-measure Correlations

As noted above, we anticipated that the MacSAC-CD measures would correlate positively with one another because all relate to the general competency construct. We also expected that measures related to the same psycholegal ability (e.g., reasoning) would correlate more highly with one another than with measures that relate to other abilities. The observed pattern of correlations among the MacSAC-CD measures was partially consistent with these expectations. The correlations between pairs of measures ranged from .36 (CAC:U with CAC:A) to .85 (DC:U-PG with DC:U-WJ) and all correlations were significant at $p < .01$. The correlations among the three understanding measures ranged from .84 to .85 and were higher than with any other measure. In the appreciation domain, CAC:A correlated more highly (.45) with DC:A than with any other measure; however, DC:A correlated more highly with several other measures than with CAC:A. Similarly, in the reasoning domain CAC:R correlated most highly (.63) with DC:R; however, DC:R correlated more highly with the three understanding measures (.72–.78) than with CAC:R.

CONSTRUCT VALIDITY OF THE MACSAC-CD

Relationship of MacSAC-CD to Measures of Psychopathology and Cognitive Functioning

Our first examination of the construct validity of the MacSAC-CD measures concerned their correlations with measures of psychopathology, particularly psychotic features, and verbal cognitive functioning. Ideally the competence measures should correlate negatively with the former but positively with the latter measures of mental functioning. Correlations of

TABLE 3.5. CORRELATIONS BETWEEN MacSAC-CD AND MEASURES OF PSYCHOPATHOLOGY

Measure/Group	BPRS Psychoticism Subscale				BPRS Total Score			
	HI	JT	JU	TOT	HI	JT	JU	TOT
Understanding								
CAC:U	−.44**	−.42**	−.26*	−.48**	−.28**	−.28**	−.20	−.32**
DC:U-PG	−.46**	−.40**	−.30**	−.50**	−.33**	−.25**	−.23**	−.32**
DC:U-WJ	−.47**	−.43**	−.40**	−.51**	−.31**	−.30**	−.24*	−.31**
Reasoning								
CAC:R	−.39**	−.34**	−.38**	−.43**	−.14	−.20*	−.09	−.19**
DC:R	−.43**	−.40**	−.31**	−.47**	−.31**	−.19*	−.16	−.27**
Appreciation								
CAC:A	−.41**	−.41**	−.44**	−.46**	−.22**	−.26**	−.44**	−.29**
DC:A	−.40*	−.26**	−.28**	−.40**	−.20*	−.15	−.18	−.23**

HI = hospitalized incompetent ($n = 159$) JT = jail treatment ($n = 113$) JU = jail unscreened ($n = 94$). (actual n's for some correlations may vary to missing data). *$p < .05$ **$p < .01$.

the individual MacSAC-CD measures with the BPRS Total and Psychoticism subscale scores are shown in Table 3.5.

These data confirm that the MacSAC-CD scores correlated as predicted with measures of psychopathology. Significant negative correlations with the BPRS Psychoticism subscale were obtained across the board in each research group and for the samples combined; negative correlations (22 of 28 significant) were also obtained with the BPRS Total score.

Also as predicted, for the full research sample significant ($p < .01$) positive correlations with the VCF index were obtained for each MacSAC-CD measure. These correlations were somewhat higher for measures of understanding (.51 to .54) and reasoning (.34 to .49) than for measures of appreciation (.12 to .26).

Group Differences in MacSAC-CD Performance

Mean scores for the three groups on all MacSAC-CD measures,[6] shown in Table 3.6, were compared using a multivariate analysis of covariance (MANCOVA) that controlled for age, socioeconomic status, prior contact with the criminal justice system, and prior contact with the

---

[6] The DC:C (choice) measure (not shown in Table 3.6) consists of a single item that asks the participant to choose between two legal options (going to trial versus accepting a plea offer) proffered to "Fred." Only 2.7% of participants were unable to voice a preferred choice. Of these, 9 were HI group members (5.6%) and 1 was a JT group member (.9%).

TABLE 3.6. MEAN SCORES (BY GROUP) ON THE MACSAC-CD MEASURES

Measure		Group			Compare Means HI v. JT+JU
		HI	JT	JU	
Understanding	M (SD)				
CAC:U		18.92	21.20	22.60	$t(313) = -3.92$
		(5.54)	(4.30)	(3.30)	$p < .001$
DC:U-PG		13.30	16.64	17.26	$t(313) = -6.66$
		(4.73)	(3.47)	(2.63)	$p < .001$
DC:U-WJ		16.77	20.04	20.49	$t(313) = -5.80$
		(5.06)	(3.95)	(2.81)	$p < .001$
Reasoning	M (SD)				
CAC:R		8.61	10.05	10.33	$t(313) = -4.70$
		(2.93)	(1.98)	(1.68)	$p < .001$
DC:R		11.74	13.96	14.05	$t(313) = -5.51$
		(3.17)	(2.38)	(2.19)	$p < .001$
Appreciation	M (SD)				
CAC:A		10.45	11.10	11.55	$t(313) = -2.98$
		(2.10)	(1.80)	(1.06)	$p < .005$
DC:A		3.31	3.80	3.92	$t(313) = -5.24$
		(1.09)	(.60)	(.31)	$p < .001$

HI = hospitalized incompetent   JT = jail treatment   JU = jail unscreened.

attorney.[7] Significant differences among the groups were found in this analysis, $F(3, 313) = 4.46$, $p < .001$. Planned contrasts were then performed to test our specific hypotheses about group differences.

For each MacSAC-CD measure the mean score of the HI group was compared to the mean score of the JT and JU groups combined. The results of these comparisons are shown in the right hand column of Table 3.6 and support the construct validity of the MacSAC-CD. For each measure of competence-related abilities (understanding, reasoning, appreciation), the mean score of the HI group was significantly lower than the mean of the combined JT and JU groups. As Table 3.6 reveals, on each measure the JT group mean scores were intermediate between those of the HI and JU groups.

MacSAC-CD Sensitivity to Changes in Clinical Status

We sought additional evidence of the construct validity of the MacSAC-CD by examining the degree to which changes in scores pre- and

---

[7] These were the only background or demographic variables that correlated with MacSAC-CD performance.

TABLE 3.7. MEAN PRE- AND POST-TREATMENT MACSAC-CD SCORES FOR A SUBGROUP (N = 97) OF HOSPITALIZED INCOMPETENT DEFENDANTS

Measure		Administration		Compare Means Pre- v. Post-
		Pre-Treatment	Post-Treatment	
Understanding	M (SD)			
CAC:U		16.19 (6.35)	19.47 (5.45)	$t(96) = -3.87$ $p < .001$
DC:U-PG		12.47 (5.19)	15.19 (3.98)	$t(96) = -4.08$ $p < .001$
DC:U-WJ		15.59 (5.97)	18.96 (4.20)	$t(96) = -4.55$ $p < .001$
Reasoning	M (SD)			
CAC:R		8.10 (3.21)	9.04 (2.84)	$t(96) = -2.16$, $p < .03$
DC:R		11.20 (3.72)	12.57 (3.04)	$t(96) = -2.78$, $p < .001$
Appreciation	M (SD)			
CAC:A		9.90 (2.77)	10.83 (1.87)	$t(96) = -2.70$, $p < .01$
DC:A		3.19 (1.19)	3.58 (.99)	$t(96) = -2.41$, $p < .02$

post-competence restoration reflected improved capacity. To minimize the impact of treatment on baseline scores, all participants were recruited and tested within two weeks of admission ($M = 6.1$ days, $SD = 2.8$ days). From the full HI sample of 159 defendants, the MacSAC-CD was readministered to 97 defendants who received treatment in the forensic psychiatric hospital for at least one week following the initial research interview (actual M interval 38.1 days, $SD = 21.9$).[8] The mean pre- and post-treatment MacSAC-CD scores for these 97 defendants are shown in Table 3.7.

[8] Attrition from the original 159 sample was primarily due to discharges that took place within 1 week of the initial research interview. Such discharges occurred primarily when the hospital staff viewed the defendant as competent upon admission, although some patients may have responded to treatment very rapidly (within 1 week). Others may have been missed because they were transported back to jail/court before the RAs could approach them for follow-up evaluation. There were few statistically significant differences between the defendants available for follow-up and those that were not. Among MacSAC-CD measures, they differed only on CAC:U scores; among background and demographic variables, they differed only on likelihood of pre-arrest employment.

The data in Table 3.7 show that changes in MacSAC-CD scores did parallel the treatment staffs' judgments of improvement in clinical condition and legal competence. As the right hand column of the table indicates, for each measure the post-treatment mean score is significantly higher than the pre-treatment mean score. Relatedly, the mean post-treatment BPRS Total score ($M = 29.6$, $SD = 5.5$) was significantly lower than the BPRS Total score at first research protocol administration ($M = 37.0$, $SD = 8.3$), $t(159) = 7.10$, $p < .001$.

Correspondence with Clinical Judgments of Competence

Another index of validity was the degree to which the initial MacSAC-CD scores of the HI group correlated with the treatment staffs' clinical judgments of capacity. The correlations obtained between initial MacSAC-CD scores and clinicians' global competence judgments (six point scale) were as follows: CAC:U, .39; DC;U-PG, .46; DC:U-WJ, .40; CAC:R, .41; DC:R, .39; CAC:A, .34; and DC:A, .29. These correlations were all statistically significant ($p < .01$). We noted earlier that these correlations might be suppressed somewhat due to, among other things, restricted range of MacSAC-CD scores because clinician judgments about competence were available only for the HI group. Indices of MacSAC-CD performance for the HI group with a somewhat expanded range of scores were created by combining all measures of a particular competence-related ability into a single score (e.g., reasoning = DC:R + CAC:R). For these indices based on combined measures, correlations with clinicians' ratings were as follows: understanding, .60, reasoning, .60, and appreciation, .47 (all p's $< .01$).

MacSAC-CD Scores' Relationship to Attitudes toward the Criminal Justice System

Our final inquiry regarding the validity of our research measure concerned the correlations between MacSAC-CD scores and the Perceived Criminal Injustice Scale (PCIS), a measure of cynicism toward the criminal justice system. For the HI group the correlations ranged from −.03 to .12 and none was statistically significant. For the JT group correlations ranged from −.21 to −.08, and only the correlation with DC:U-WJ was statistically significant, $r = -.21$, $p < .05$. Finally, for the JU group the correlations ranged from −.20 to .05 and only the correlation with CAC:U was statistically significant, $r = -.20$, $p < .05$. These correlations indicate that, within each research sample, MacSAC-CD scores are unrelated to defendants' attitudes toward the criminal justice system.

RESULTS II—FEMALE DEFENDANTS

The second, and smaller study of the MacSAC-CD involved 107 women recruited at the same research sites and using the same inclusion/exclusion criteria as the main field study. An attempt was made to recruit HI participants during the first week of hospitalization. The actual mean time to protocol administration was 6.3 days (SD = 3.3 days). Sample sizes for the three research groups were 38 (HI), 18 (JT) and 50 (JU). The women's competence study involved the same procedures and utilized the same protocol as the main field study.

SAMPLE DESCRIPTION

The mean ages (S.D.) of the HI, JT, and JU women – 34.1 (11.10), 32.9 (7.39), and 31.6 (7.84) years respectively, were not statistically different and, the mean age across groups (M = 32.73, SD = 9.07) did not differ from that of the men in the main field study (M = 32.53, SD = 8.72). The women's groups did differ in terms of racial composition, however. Nearly three-quarters (70%) of the JU group were African-American, as were more than half (58%) of the HI group, while the group of JT women contained about one-third African-Americans (28%), χ^2 (2, 104) = 9.73, $p < .01$. Across all three groups, compared with the racial distribution in the main field study (Table 3.3), proportionately more subjects in the women's study were from a racial minority, χ^2 (1, N = 471) = 8.33, $p < .005$. Compared to men in the main field study, there was no difference in the percentage of women who were unmarried (includes divorced) at the time of recruitment (78% versus 81% men) or in the mean years of education (11.55 versus 11.47 men).

Primary clinical and treatment history data for the three groups are provided in Table 3.8. Defendants with schizophrenia were disproportionately represented in the HI group, χ^2 (2, 21) = 22.25, $p < .001$, while affective disorder was more prevalent in both the HI and JT groups than in the JU group, χ^2 (2, N = 30) = 9.80, $p < .007$. Predictably, a significantly greater proportion of participants in the HI and JT groups than the JU group reported histories of both inpatient and outpatient treatment (ps $< .001$). Expected differences among the three groups' mean scores on the BPRS (total score) and VCF index, however, were not found. Unlike the main field study, in which the two clinical groups (HI and JT) of men had significantly higher BPRS-A scores and the HI group had a lower mean VCF score, the women's groups did not differ significantly on these measures.

TABLE 3.8. CLINICAL FEATURES OF THREE SAMPLES OF FEMALE DEFENDANTS

		HI	JT	JU
Chart Diagnosis (%)				
Schizophrenia		45%	22%	0%
Affective disorder		45%	56%	6%
No diagnosis		0%	22%	84%
Other		10%	0%	10%
Prior Psychiatric Treatment (%)				
Inpatient		79%	72%	14%
Outpatient		76%	67%	34%
Brief Psychiatric Rating Scale				
Total score	M	36.63	32.72	33.48
	(SD)	(7.43)	(8.29)	(7.45)
Verbal Cognitive Functioning	M	88.74	83.61	87.16
	(SD)	(11.08)	(10.99)	(10.86)

HI = hospitalized incompetent   JT = jail treatment   JU = jail unscreened.

TABLE 3.9. RELIABILITY INDICATORS OF THE MACSAC-CD WITH FEMALE DEFENDANTS

MacSAC-CD Measure	Cronbach's α	Item-Scale Correlation
Understanding		
CAC:U	.84	.35–.54
DC:U-PG	.82	.38–.60
DC:U-WJ	.84	.42–.62
Reasoning		
CAC:R	.61	.24–.40
DC:R	.65	.09–.53
Appreciation		
CAC:A	.32	.04–.27
DC:A	.44*	

*Because there are only 2 items on the DC:A, this is a Pearson r rather than α value.

PSYCHOMETRIC PROPERTIES

Reliability indicators for the MacSAC-CD with these women defendants are presented in Table 3.9. In comparison to the findings with male defendants (see Table 3.4), internal consistency as measured by Cronbach's alpha was not quite as good in the female sample. Alpha remained quite good for the understanding measures, but for the reasoning measures the alphas were slightly lower than the recommended minimum ($\alpha > .70$) for research measures and alpha for CAC:A was quite low (.32). Item-scale correlations were in the acceptable range ($r > .30$) for most items on the understanding and reasoning measures; again, however, the results for CAC:A on this indicator of internal consistency were poor.

Inter-measure Correlations

As in the main field study, we expected that the MacSAC-CD measures would correlate positively with one another. Pairwise correlations between measures were all positive (range .08 to .79) and 19 of 21 correlations were significant at $p < .05$ or better (15 of 19 at $p < .001$). We also expected that measures related to a particular competence-related ability would correlate more highly with each other than with measures of a different ability. However, this relationship was found only among the understanding measures (CAC:U, DC:U-PG, DC:U-WJ), whose pairwise correlations with each other ranged from .74 to .79, and none of these measures correlated higher than .64 (CAC:U with DC:R) with any other measure. However, DC:R correlated more highly with each of the understanding measures (rs range = .64 to .71) than with CAC:R ($r = .49$), while CAC:A and DC:A were not correlated with one another ($r = .08$, ns).

CONSTRUCT VALIDITY[9]

Relationship of MacSAC-CD to Measures of Psychopathology and Cognitive Functioning

Table 3.10 displays, for each group and the total women's sample, the correlations between MacSAC-CD scores and measures of psychopathology. Consistent with the results from the main field study, these data reveal that MacSAC-CD scores are negatively correlated, particularly in the HI group, with an index of current psychotic symptoms (BPRS Psychoticism), although here the correlations were not statistically significant for the appreciation measures. Generally negative, if not significant, correlations were obtained with the BPRS Total score, suggesting that psychotic symptoms in particular, rather than global psychopathology, adversely affect competence-related abilities.

---

[9] HI subjects in the women's study were not retested when deemed by the hospital staff to be restored to competence and ready for return to court. Thus, we did not evaluate the sensitivity of the MacCAT to changes in clinical status as was reported in the main field study (see Table 3.7).

TABLE 3.10. CORRELATIONS BETWEEN MacSAC-CD AND
MEASURES OF PSYCHOPATHOLOGY

Measure/Group	BPRS Psychoticism Subscale				BPRS Total Score			
	HI	JT	JU	TOT	HI	JT	JU	TOT
Understanding								
CAC:U	−.51**	−.52*	−.14	−.48**	.17	−.25	−.04	−.18
DC:U-PG	−.44**	−.25	−.33**	−.47**	.02	−.16	−.11	−.12
DC:U-WJ	−.45**	−.18	−.14	−.46**	.07	.19	−.01	−.02
Reasoning								
CAC:R	−.15	.03	−.23	−.22*	.12	.21	−.40**	−.13
DC:R	−.45**	−.60**	−.26	−.54**	.04	−.29	−.11	−.16
Appreciation								
CAC:A	−.12	−.06	−.02	−.08	−.30	.23	−.24	−.21*
DC:A	−.29	.15	−.07	−.23*	.16*	−.06	−.02	−.00

HI = hospitalized incompetent ($n=38$) JT = jail treatment ($n=18$) JU = jail unscreened ($n=106$); actual n's for some correlations may vary to missing data). *$p < .05$ **$p < .01$.

For the full research sample significant positive correlations with the VCF index were obtained for 5 of 7 MacSAC-CD measures. These correlations were somewhat higher for measures of understanding (.40 to .46) than for reasoning (.15 to .31) and appreciation (.01 to .23) measures.

Group Differences in MacSAC-CD Performance

Mean scores for each group on all MacSAC-CD measures are shown in Table 3.11. MANCOVA analysis (controlling for VCF, scores on an index of socioeconomic status, and education level variables whose bivariate correlations exceeded .30 with one or more MacSAC-CD measures) revealed a significant overall effect, $F(14, 162) = 2.39, p < .01$.

An inspection of the table reveals that, as expected, the HI group obtained the lowest mean score on each measure. In planned comparisons, for each MacSAC-CD measure the mean score of the HI group was compared to the mean score of the JT and JU groups combined. The results of these comparisons are shown in the right hand column of Table 3.11. In 4 of 7 comparisons, the HI mean score was statistically different from the mean of the JT and JU groups combined. There were no significant differences between the JT and JU groups on any MacSAC-CD measures.

Correspondence with Clinical Judgments of Competence

For the 38 subjects in the HI group a global rating of current competence was obtained from a forensic hospital clinician on the defendant's

TABLE 3.11. Mean Scores (by group) on the MacSAC-CD Measures for Female Defendants

Measure		Group			Compare Means HI v. JT+JU
		HI	JT	JU	
Understanding	M (SD)				
CAC:U		17.95 (5.08)	19.47 (3.12)	19.95 (4.05)	$t(89) = -2.61$ $p < .01$
DC:U-PG		13.15 (4.24)	15.35 (3.48)	16.02 (3.00)	$t(89) = -3.46$ $p < .001$
DC:U-WJ		17.00 (4.75)	20.41 (2.18)	20.17 (3.15)	$t(89) = -4.73$ $p < .001$
Reasoning	M (SD)				
CAC:R		9.06 (2.69)	9.88 (1.93)	10.02 (1.96)	ns
DC:R		10.64 (2.93)	13.53 (2.24)	13.44 (2.38)	$t(89) = -5.25$ $p < .001$
Appreciation	M (SD)				
CAC:A		11.21 (.89)	11.88 (.48)	11.56 (1.25)	ns
DC:A		3.61 (.83)	3.71 (.98)	3.80 (.51)	ns

HI = hospitalized incompetent   JT = jail treatment   JU = jail unscreened.

treatment team. Correlations between the MacSAC-CD scores and these clinician ratings were as follows: CAC:U, .25; DC;U-PG, .23; DC:U-WJ, .11; CAC:R, .31; DC:R, .16; CAC:A, .09; and DC:A, .32. As was obtained in the main field study with male defendants, the correlations are all positive—suggesting a positive association between global clinical judgments and capacity as indexed by these measures. However, these correlations did not reach statistical significance, perhaps due in part to the substantially smaller n of subjects.

DISCUSSION

General Findings and Conclusions

The main field study (with male defendants) yielded consistently positive results regarding the psychometric properties and the construct validity of the MacSAC-CD. The component measures met or exceeded conventional criteria for adequate internal consistency ($\alpha > .70$, item-total correlations > 30); interscorer reliability for the understanding and reasoning measures as measured by κ (.60–.75) reflected good improvement over chance (.4 $< \kappa <$ .75, Landis & Koch, 1977), although for the appreciation measures the κ values obtained (.36, .48) are conventionally considered to reflect only marginal improvement over chance ($0 < \kappa < .4$) (although distribution skewness and small variances may have depressed correlations on these measures).

The construct validity of the MacSAC-CD was explored through several research questions: (1) Do scores on the instrument correlate in theoretically expected ways with measures of psychopathology—negatively with psychosis but positively with intellectual functioning (theoretical validity)? (2) Do scores on the instrument differentiate relevant legal groups in expected ways given the groups' actual legal competence status (criterion validity)? (3) Do scores on the instrument improve for initially incompetent defendants when they are retested after clinical status has improved such that their competence (by clinical judgment) has been restored? (4) Do scores on the instrument correlate positively with clinical judgments of competence (concurrent validity)? and (5) Are scores on the instrument affected by cynical attitudes about the criminal justice system (divergent validity)? As the data in Tables 3.5 through 3.7 and the text reveal, each of these questions was answered in the affirmative.

The second, smaller study that involved women defendants also provided support for the MacSAC-CD as a reliable and valid adjudicative competence research measure, particularly for the understanding and reasoning components. Coefficient α for the understanding measures ranged from .82 to .84, and for the reasoning measures from .61 to .65. Item-to-scale correlations for these measures were also generally within acceptable range ($r > .39$). Consistently, negative correlations with the BPRS psychoticism subscale (Table 3.10) and positive correlations with an index of verbal cognitive functioning (prorated verbal IQ estimate) were obtained for these measures. Finally, among women defendant samples mean group differences were in the expected direction for all understanding and reasoning measures and mean differences were statistically significant for 4 of 5 measures. The appreciation measures performed more poorly than other MacSAC-CD measures in the women's study, however, and more poorly than in the main field study with male defendants. For example, coefficient α was unacceptably low, as were item-to-total correlations (Table 3.9), and differences among groups were trivial and not statistically significant.

Taken together, these studies provided substantial support for the MacSAC-CD, both as a valid research instrument on adjudicative competence issues and as a prototype for the development (through further investigation) of a clinical measure of competence-related abilities. Grounded in both sound legal theory (Bonnie, 1992, 1993) and in psycholegal assessment theory (Grisso & Appelbaum, 1995), the MacSAC-CD incorporates additional features such as standardized administration and criterion-based scoring while yielding a more differentiated picture of a defendant's competence-related abilities than has been obtainable with earlier, first-generation measures. In Chapters 4 and 5 of this book we explore, respectively, research issues in adjudicative competence and the development of the MacArthur Competence Assessment Tool—Criminal Adjudication (MacCAT-CA), a clinical tool for use in adjudicative competence assessments.

LIMITATIONS

In closing this chapter, we note limitations of this new research measure. First, although the MacSAC-CD provides quantitative indices of three important competence-related abilities that are amenable to standardization and objective measurement, no claim is made that it assesses systematically all of the dimensions or issues potentially relevant to adjudicative competence. It is primarily a cognitive assessment tool that does not evaluate such factors as anticipated comportment of a defendant's behavior with courtroom standards or interpersonal factors that may affect his or her ability to work with a particular attorney.

In some jurisdictions a relevant concern is the defendant's capacity to withstand the anticipated stresses the may come with participation in a criminal trial (e.g., *State v. Valentino*, 1974), another factor not assessed by this instrument. Similarly, although amnesia for the time of the alleged offense is generally not an automatic bar to competence (*Wilson v. United States*, 1968), it is a factor that is relevant to a competence determination and the MacSAC-CD does not explore the adequacy of a defendant's memory for the time of the alleged offense. Finally, it is noted that this instrument does not take into consideration contextual variables, such as relative strength of the evidence or case complexity, that may be relevant in a given case. These considerations reinforce the notion of the MacSAC-CD as a tool that, if revised for used in a clinical context (see Chapter 5), would be only one component of a competence evaluation.

4

Research Issues in Adjudicative Competence

Having established that the MacSAC-CD is a psychometrically sound and valid research instrument, we conducted additional analyses of the data from the main field study to explore three important research issues regarding the competence of criminal defendants. These issues are: (a) the relationships of diagnosis and psychiatric symptomatology to legal capacity, (b) the extent to which defendants' capacities are consistent across different competence-related abilities and different legal domains (assisting counsel versus decisional competence), and (c) the degree to which impaired abilities in the adjudicative competence area are mirrored by impaired competence in the area of competence to make treatment decisions (i.e., to accept or refuse psychotropic medication). In this chapter we report the results of these additional analyses.

STUDY 1: DIAGNOSIS, MENTAL STATUS, AND LEGAL CAPACITY

In their meta-analysis of research related to competence to stand trial, Nicholson and Kugler (1991) noted prior studies have indicated that findings of incompetence are generally associated with a diagnosis of schizophrenia and the presence of psychotic symptoms. However, limitations in the design and instrumentation employed in many prior studies leave unanswered many questions about the relationships among diagnosis, mental status, and legal competence status. Because many researchers examined only one group of defendants (i.e., those adjudicated incompetent), the relationships among these variables in other defendant groups remains unexplored. Further, many investigators employed instruments that did not permit either standardized administration or criterion-related scoring to assess defendants' competence. In light of Bonnie's reformulation of the conceptual landscape of legal competence (Chapter 2) and the availability of a psychometrically sound research measure for assessing multiple competence-related abilities (Chapter 3), it seemed appropriate to revisit these issues.

DEMOGRAPHIC AND CRIMINAL JUSTICE FEATURES OF DIAGNOSTIC GROUPS

In contrast to Table 3.2, which arrays demographic and criminal justice features by groups based on competence status (HI, JT, JU), Table 4.1 presents the demographic and criminal justice features of groups defined by clinical chart diagnosis[1]—schizophrenia, affective disorders, other diagnoses, and no diagnoses—regardless of competence status. As is clear from Table 3.2, however, most of the participants in the schizophrenia group came from the HI sample ($n = 104$, 77%), with the JT sample contributing most of the remainder ($n = 29$, 21%) of this group. Two JU participants, one diagnosed with psychotic disorder not otherwise specified (NOS) rounded out this diagnostic group. The affective disorders group was comprised primarily of individuals from the JT sample ($n = 67$, 60%), with the remainder ($n = 45$, 40%) coming from the HI sample. DSM-III-R disorders represented in the affective disorders group included mood disorders (e.g., major depression, bipolar disorder: $n = 93$, 83%), depressive disorder NOS ($n = 6$, 5%), adjustment disorder with depressed mood ($n = 8$, 7%), and mixed anxiety/depression diagnoses ($n = 8$, 7%). All defendants in the no diagnosis group came from the JU sample.

The diagnostic groups differed by race, χ^2 (18, $n = 358$) = 47.52, $p < .001$, with the schizophrenia group including proportionately more

---

[1] Defendants from the HI group were diagnosed by psychiatrists upon admission to forensic hospitals for competence restoration, while defendants in the JT group were diagnosed by mental health professionals upon admission to the jail. Diagnoses of JU defendants were obtained from jail records and represent diagnoses offered prior to the present incarceration.

TABLE 4.1. DEMOGRAPHIC AND CRIMINAL JUSTICE FEATURES OF
SUBJECTS BY DIAGNOSTIC GROUP

Variable	Schizophrenia	Affective Disorders	Other Disorders	No Diagnosis
Demographics				
Mean age (SD)	33.8 (7.5)	32.6 (9.9)	29.5 (7.7)	31.0 (8.6)
% Non-white	49.5%	26.9%	29.2%	38.6%
% lower SES categories	71%	60%	67%	37%
Criminal Justice				
Mean age at first arrest (SD)	23.6 (6.7)	22.5 (8.7)	20.7 (7.3)	22.6 (6.8)
Mean prior arrests (SD)	1.3 (0.3)	1.3 (0.3)	1.3 (0.4)	1.2 (0.30)
% facing felony charges	62%	66%	62%	71%
% previously in prison	37%	38%	21%	51%
% with a previous competency examination	43%	23%	5%	8%

non-white participants. The groups also differed in terms of SES, χ^2 (21, $n = 351$) $= 84.54, p < .001$, with the no diagnostic group having proportionately fewer members in the unskilled/unemployed categories of the Hollingshead and Redlich (1958) socioeconomic scale. In terms of criminal justice history, individuals in the no diagnosis group were more likely to have served a prior prison sentence, χ^2 (3, $n = 357$) $= 8.50, p < .04$, and to be facing felony charges, χ^2 (3, $n = 356$) $= 15.74, p < .001$, but less likely to have undergone previous competence evaluations, χ^2 (3, $n = 355$) $= 46.24, p < .001$. There were no differences among the groups in terms of number of prior arrests or age at first arrest.

MacSAC-CD PERFORMANCE BY DIAGNOSIS

A comparison of primary interest was the performance of the schizophrenia group versus the other diagnostic groups on the MacSAC-CD. An inspection of the mean scores (and standard deviations) for all groups, shown in Table 4.2, reveals that the schizophrenia group obtained the lowest mean score on each MacSAC-CD measure. A MANCOVA that controlled for other variables statistically related to MacSAC-CD performance (SES, age, criminal justice history, contact with attorney, and research sample [HI, JT, JU] membership) confirmed significant differences between the schizophrenia group and other diagnostic groups, F (3, 908) $= -3.23, p < .001$.

The results of univariate comparisons, shown in the right hand column of Table 4.2, reveal that except for CAC:A, the mean score differences

TABLE 4.2. MEAN SCORES ON THE MacSAC-CD MEASURES BY DIAGNOSTIC GROUP

Measure	Schizophrenia	Affective Disorders	Other Disorders	No Diagnosis	Schiz. v. Other Groups (pooled) Comparison
Understanding					
CAC:U M	17.03	21.11	21.00	21.17	$t = -3.54, p < .001$
(SD)	(5.76)	(3.63)	(3.87)	(3.25)	
DC:U-PG	12.82	16.86	16.76	17.00	$t = -3.03, p < .002$
	(4.77)	(3.31)	(3.65)	(2.68)	
DC:U-WJ	16.30	20.21	20.52	20.15	$t = -2.72, p < .001$
	(5.21)	(3.52)	(3.97)	(3.03)	
Reasoning					
CAC:R	8.18	10.21	10.62	10.28	$t = -4.05, p < .001$
	(2.95)	(1.75)	(1.94)	(1.68)	
DC:R	11.52	13.87	13.89	14.09	$t = -2.32, p < .02$
Appreciation					
CAC:A	10.36	11.00	11.24	11.58	not significant
	(2.21)	(1.80)	(1.37)	(1.02)	
DC:A	3.20	3.90	3.91	3.57	$t = -2.50, p < .01$
	(1.16)	(0.39)	(0.32)	(0.81)	

between the schizophrenia group and the other diagnostic groups pooled were statistically significant for each measure. Comparisons among the other three diagnostic groups (affective disorders, other disorders, no diagnosis) yielded no significant differences in performance on MacSAC-CD measures.

Although poorer MacSAC-CD performance is clearly associated with schizophrenia, an inspection of the means and standard deviations in Table 4.2 clearly indicates overlap in the score distributions of the diagnostic groups. Some defendants with schizophrenia obtained high scores on the measures, while some members of the other groups obtained scores that were quite low. In the legal system, the ambiguities in complex data related to level of functioning in various competence-related abilities ultimately get translated into decisions that are categorical—defendants are pronounced "competent" or "incompetent." In order to examine our data in an analogous fashion, we created research definitions of "impaired psycholegal functioning" for each MacSAC-CD measure and examined the distribution of diagnostic groups across these "impaired" and "unimpaired" categories.[2]

---

[2] In deciding to conduct this analysis, we were acutely aware of the limits of the "fit" of this analogy, and we make no assertions that experimentally defined "impairment" on one or more MacSAC-CD measures, as defined in further text, should in any way be dispositive of either clinical judgment or legal competence decisions in actual cases.

To minimize the proportion of presumably normal and competent defendants who would be designated "impaired" on our instruments, we created a Jail Screened (JS) group by "sanitizing" the JU group; this involved removing six participants with unusually high BPRS scores (BPRS > 40) and one defendant with a previous diagnosis of schizophrenia. We then experimentally defined "impaired" functioning on each understanding or reasoning measure of the MacSAC-CD as any score two or more standard deviations below the mean score of this new JS group; for the appreciation measures (CAC:A, DC:A) we defined as "impaired" any subject who received a score of "0" on any item. The experimentally defined cutoff scores and proportions of schizophrenia, affective disorders, and no diagnosis group members scoring in the "impaired" range for each measure are shown in Table 4.3.

The data in Table 4.3 reaffirm the significant relationship of schizophrenia to impaired psycholegal functioning when capacity is translated into categorical outcomes using our research criteria. Almost 60% of defendants with schizophrenia displayed impaired functioning in each psycholegal domain, and nearly three-quarters (72%) scored in the impaired range on at least one MacSAC-CD measure. Using diagnosis alone as an indicator, the risk for impaired functioning in the abilities measured by the MacSAC-CD for defendants with schizophrenia was about three times that of defendants with affective disorders and more than five times that of undiagnosed defendants.

TABLE 4.3. PERCENT OF PARTICIPANTS SCORING IN THE IMPAIRED RANGE BY DIAGNOSTIC GROUP

Legal Domain & Measure	Schizophrenia	Affective Disorders	No Diagnosis
Competence to Assist Counsel			
CAC:U	44%	13%	5%
CAC:R	23%	5%	0%
CAC:A	29%	11%	4%
Any CAC measure	59%	20%	7%
Decisional Competence			
DC:U-PG	42%	13%	3%
DC:U-WJ	32%	8%	5%
DC:A	32%	3%	2%
DC:R	27%	5%	2%
Any DC measure	58%	16%	9%
Any MacSAC-CD measure	72%	25%	14%

Mental Status and MacSAC-CD Performance within Diagnostic Groups

To understand better the possible sources of impaired legal functioning in our participants, we examined the relationship between mental status variables (VCF; BPRS Total and subscale scores) and the various diagnostic groups. Significant differences were found among the diagnostic groups, multivariate F (3,349) = 35.78, $p < .001$, and univariate analyses revealed significant differences on each mental status variable. Planned comparisons revealed that compared to the affective disorders group, the schizophrenia group had a significantly lower mean VCF score ($M = 86.44$, $SD = 11.18$, versus $M = 93.45$, $SD = 13.85$), less BPRS depression symptomatology (depression subscale $M = 7.86$, $SD = 3.13$, versus $M = 10.03$, $SD = 3.84$), but more psychotic symptomatology (psychoticism subscale $M = 7.58$, $SD = 3.01$, versus $M = 4.99$, $SD = 2.23$). The mean scores for these two diagnostic groups did not differ on BPRS Total score or subscale scores for hostility or emotional withdrawal. These findings suggest that the greater impairment in legal functioning for the schizophrenia group (Tables 4.2 and 4.3) is associated with more active psychotic symptoms and cognitive impairment (the latter, perhaps, adversely affected by the former).

Table 4.4 presents the correlations among the mental status variables and MacSAC-CD measures for the schizophrenia and affective disorders groups.[3] The first column of the table reveals that for both diagnostic groups, performance on MacSAC-CD measures is positively related to current VCF. An inspection of the magnitudes of the correlation coefficients, however, suggests that the competence-related abilities of understanding and reasoning are more influenced by VCF than is appreciation. The next two columns indicate the relationship between the BPRS Total and psychoticism subscale scores and competence-related abilities. Although the correlations are negative and (in most instances) significant for both mental status indices, the relative magnitude of the correlation coefficients indicates that psychotic symptoms specifically, rather than global psychopathology,[4] exert the greater influence on performance scores. Fairly consistently, the psychoticism subscale correlated more strongly with performance in the affective disorders group, suggesting

---

[3] Due to the small number of participants with other diagnoses, that group was excluded from this analysis.
[4] Correlations between BPRS subscales for hostility and withdrawal were generally non-significant and displayed no consistent relationship to MacSAC-CD performance. Scores on the BPRS depression subscale generally correlated *positively* with performance (range = .05 to .29), with about half of the correlations reaching statistical significance.

TABLE 4.4. CORRELATIONS (RANGE) BETWEEN COMPETENCE-RELATED ABILITIES AND KEY MENTAL STATUS VARIABLES FOR THE SCHIZOPHRENIA AND AFFECTIVE DISORDERS GROUPS

	VCF	BPRS Index			BPRS Psychoticism Subscale Symptom		
		BPRS Total	Psychoticism Subscale	Conceptual Disorganization	Hallucinations	Unusual Thoughts
Understanding[1]							
Schizophrenia	.54 to .60	−.19 to −.21	−.24 to −.28	−.39 to −.47	−.02 to −.08	−.05 to −.10
Affective Disorders	.44 to .48	−.24 to −.32	−.48 to −.58	−.39 to −.51	−.32 to −.37	−.23 to −.35
Reasoning[2]							
Schizophrenia	.35 to .52	−.05 to −.18	−.21 to −.25	−.25 to −.48	−.06 to .02	−.08 to −.12
Affective Disorders	.19 to .41	−.10 to −.18	−.40 to −.48	−.44 to −.49	−.08 to −.17	−.26 to −.27
Appreciation[3]							
Schizophrenia	.11 to .28	−.15 to −.23	−.26 to −.36	−.26 to −.33	−.08 to −.09	−.21 to −.33
Affective Disorders	.05 to .18	−.08 to −.09	−.35 to −.37	−.40 to −.42	−.15 to .01	−.15 to −.31

[1] Table entries show range of correlations of mental status variables with CAC:U, DC:U-PG, and DC:U-WJ.
[2] Table entries show correlations of mental status variable with CAC:R and DC:R.
[3] Table entries show correlations of mental status variable with CAC:A and DC:A. VCF = verbal cognitive functioning.
Significance values for different correlations vary somewhat due to different n's for analysis. Generally $r \geq .17$ is significant at .05, $r \geq .25$ is significant at .01, and $r \geq .33$ is significant at .001. For specific values, see Tables 4 & 5 from Hoge et al. (1997).

that psychotic symptoms may play a relatively greater role in that group's competence-related abilities.

Finally, the right-hand portion of Table 4.4 presents correlations between MacSAC-CD measure scores and specific item scores for the BPRS psychoticism subscale. Reading horizontally for the schizophrenia group, conceptual disorganization appears to have the greatest impact on competence-related abilities. Although unusual thoughts were also associated with poor performance on the appreciation measure, hallucinations appears unrelated to competence-related abilities in this group. For the affective disorders group, both conceptual disorganization and unusual thoughts appear to adversely impact all competence related abilities, although for this group the presence of hallucinations was also related to poorer performance on the understanding measures. Comparing the item-to-performance correlations vertically within each competence-related ability, the higher coefficients for the affective disorders group suggest that psychotic symptoms play a somewhat stronger role in determining that group's performance level.

DISCUSSION

The primary findings from these analyses confirm what investigators have found in earlier studies that used somewhat more global and undifferentiated measures of capacity (psychotic symptoms regardless of diagnosis, and a diagnosis of schizophrenia more so than other diagnoses) are significantly associated with impaired competence. Significantly poorer performance on all MacSAC-CD measures was found for the schizophrenia group, even when controlling for formal legal status (competent versus incompetent). In addition to significant mean differences in capacity measured dimensionally (Table 4.2), schizophrenia is associated with a much higher rate of "impairment" when competence-related abilities are defined categorically (Table 4.3).

While these findings suggest that attorneys, judges, and mental health professionals should be particularly alert to the risk for impaired competence in defendants with a current or past diagnosis of schizophrenia, the magnitude of the standard deviations in Table 4.3 indicates that the diagnostic groups' score distributions overlap for all measures. Similarly, Table 4.4 reveals that fully a quarter of the defendants diagnosed with schizophrenia did not score in the experimentally defined "impaired" range on any of the MacSAC-CD measures, while 14% of those with no diagnosis had one or more scores in the impaired range. Thus, our findings also stop well short of equating "incompetence," or even "impaired abilities" with either schizophrenia or psychosis.

That 14% of the no diagnosis group scored in the "impaired" range on one or more of the MacSAC-CD measures points to possible limitations in the study design. Rather than using structured diagnostic assessments, we relied upon the clinical diagnoses found in participants' medical records. Some defendants with minimal symptoms or primarily negative symptoms, or those who minimized their symptoms, may not have been identified and treated in jails. These "no diagnosis" defendants may have experienced undetected symptoms that adversely affected their competence-related abilities.

The second finding from these analyses relates to the role of specific symptom patterns and capacity. Data from Table 4.4 indicate that current cognitive functioning is perhaps related more strongly to MacSAC-CD performance among defendants with schizophrenia than in those with affective disorders. Not surprisingly, psychotic symptoms adversely affected capacity in both diagnostic groups, thought somewhat more strongly in the affective disorders group. Of additional interest was the finding that other symptom clusters captured by BPRS subscales (e.g., depression, hostility, emotional withdrawal) generally related in no systematic or significant way to competence-related abilities (see footnote 5). Recall from Chapter 1 that doubts about clients' competence, particularly with respect to the decision making ability, often arose when the attorneys perceived the defendants to be more passive and uninvolved. Although more research is needed to explore these issues and replicate these findings, the apparent irrelevance of withdrawal symptoms (emotional withdrawal, motor retardation, blunted affect) to MacSAC-CD performance suggests that, absent other factors (e.g., psychotic symptoms or low VCF), attorneys' reliance on withdrawal-like symptoms as an indicator of impaired capacity may be misplaced not if it affects their involvement in their case in terms of motivation or ability to make decisions or supply information.

STUDY 2: A COMPARISON OF CRITERIA FOR ADJUDICATIVE COMPETENCE

A second analysis used data from the field study to explore three conceptual and legal assumptions relevant to the theoretical model of adjudicative competence presented in Chapter 2.

Assumption 1

The first domain in Bonnie's model, *competence to assist counsel*, encompasses three distinguishable abilities—the ability to *understand* information that relates to the charges and the criminal process, the ability to *appreciate* one's own situation as a defendant, and the ability to *reason* sufficiently about one's case so as to consult reasonably with counsel. Readers will recall that these three abilities are measured in the MacSAC-CD by the CAC:U, CAC:A, and CAC:R, respectively. One key assumption in the model is that impairment of one of these abilities does not necessarily mean that the other abilities are also impaired. Thus, our hypothesis was that, given a rational criterion for impairment on each measure for these three abilities, defendants who scored in the impaired range on any one of them would not necessarily score in the impaired range on the others.

Assumption 2

The second assumption tested was that the use of different tests for decisional competence would yield different outcomes with respect to impaired capacity. Decisional competence includes the capacity to understand the nature and consequences of alternative choices, the ability to appreciate the significance of a decision in one's own case (as opposed to understanding decision outcomes in the abstract), and being able to reason about information pertinent to the decision. Thus, parallel to the hypothesis for the first assumption, we anticipated that defendants would show differential impairment, as experimentally defined, on measures of decisional competence—DC:U, DC:A, and DC:R-PG and DC:R-WJ.

Assumption 3

Another key assumption is that the second legal domain in Bonnie's model, *decisional competence*, encompasses abilities not required for competence to assist counsel. This assumption underlies the normative claim that adjudicative competence criteria must be more demanding in a legal system that demands a degree of autonomous participation by the defendant in making important decisions—such as whether to plead guilty, or whether to testify—than in a system that allocates all decisions to the attorney. Under this assumption, we hypothesized that some incompetent defendants might score in the unimpaired range on all measures of capacity to assist counsel (CAC:U, CAC:A, CAC:R), yet display impairment on measures in the decisional competence domain (DC:U, DC:A, DC:R-PG, DC:R-WJ).

Refining Experimental Groups: Groups HI(C) and JS

We redefined two of our research groups for purposes of this analysis. First, we established a relatively pure group of incompetent defendants from the original HI sample using the global rating of adjudicative competence obtained from a treatment team member when the MacSAC-CD was administered at recruitment (see Chapter 3). The 70 patients rated as either "moderately incompetent" or "grossly incompetent" (language that anchored the two lowest rating points) were designated as a Hospitalized Incompetent-Clinically Validated (HI-C) group.

Second, as in the first analysis (above), we purified the JU group by excluding subjects with significant psychopathology as evidenced by either a chart diagnosis of schizophrenia ($n = 1$) or a BPRS-A Total score that exceeded 40 ($n = 6$). This group was designated the JS, or "Jail Screened" group. As before, we experimentally defined "impaired" functioning on each understanding or reasoning measure of the MacSAC-CD as any score two or more standard deviations below the mean score of this new JS group; for the appreciation measures (CAC:A, DC:A) we defined as "impaired" any subject who received a score of "0" on any item.

RESULTS

Table 4.5 indicates the percentage of HI(C) defendants that scored in the experimentally defined "impaired" range for each MacSAC-CD measure. These data were used to assess the assumptions and hypotheses described above.

TABLE 4.5. HI(C)1 DEFENDANTS SCORING IN THE IMPAIRED RANGE ON EACH MacSAC-CD MEASURE[1]

Legal Competence	HI(C) Group (N = 70)	
Domain & Measure	n	%
Competence to Assist Counsel		
CAC:U	39	55.7
CAC:R	23	32.9
CAC:A	29	41.8
Impaired on *any* CAC Measure	52	74.6
Decisional Competence		
DC:U-PG	35	50.0
DC:U-WJ	30	42.9
DC:R	28	40.6
DC:A	27	38.1
Impaired on *any* DC Measure	47	67.0
Impaired on *any* CAC or DC Measure	61	87.3

[1] HI(C) = clinically affirmed incompetent defendants.

Hypothesis 1

Our first hypothesis was that defendants who were impaired with respect to any one of the psycholegal abilities (understanding, reasoning, appreciation) within the legal domain of competence to assist counsel (CAC) would not necessarily be impaired with respect to the others. The upper panel of Table 4.5 presents findings relevant to this hypothesis.

The first line in the upper panel reveals that more than half of the subjects ($n = 39$) scored in the impaired range on CAC:U. A smaller percentage of subjects were impaired on the reasoning (CAC:R) or appreciation (CAC:A) measures. However, not all of the subjects impaired on CAC:R or CAC:A were among those impaired on CAC:U. Rather, 13 subjects—almost 20% of the entire sample and 25% of those who were impaired on any CAC measure—were impaired in terms of reasoning and/or appreciation, but not in terms of understanding. These results support the assertion that, within the domain of competence to assist counsel, impairment on one psycholegal ability is not necessarily associated with impairment on others.

Hypothesis 2

We similarly hypothesized that within the legal domain of decisional competence (DC), defendants who were impaired with respect to any one of the psycholegal abilities (understanding, reasoning, appreciation) would not necessarily be impaired with respect to the others. The data relevant to this hypothesis are presented in the second panel of Table 4.5. The greatest percentage of subjects (50%, $n = 35$) showed impairment on the understanding measure that related to issues around weighing a guilty plea. Again, fewer subjects scored in the impaired range on the second understanding measure (5 fewer), the reasoning measure (7 fewer), and the appreciation measure (8 fewer). Overall 12 subjects—17% of the entire sample and 25% of the subjects who were impaired on any DC measure—were impaired in the areas of reasoning and/or appreciation but not with respect to understanding issues related to considering a guilty plea.

Hypothesis 3

The third hypothesis asserted a degree of independence between the two domains of decisional competence. We surmised that some incompetent defendants might score in the unimpaired on all measures of capacity to assist counsel, yet they would display impairment on one or more measures in the decisional competence domain.

The first panel in Table 4.5 reveals that approximately 75% of the sample was impaired on at least one CAC measure, leaving a quarter of the sample ($n = 18$) unimpaired with respect to competence to assist counsel. The last line in the table, however, reveals that 87.3% of the sample was impaired on at least one MacSAC-CD measure. By subtraction, 9 subjects—50% of those unimpaired in the CAC domain, 13% of the entire HI(C) sample, and 15% of those who scored in the impaired range on any MacSAC-CD measure—showed impairment in the decisional competence domain only. These results suggest that capacities related to decisional competence are important determinants of adjudicative competence independent of the role played by abilities associated with the more fundamental capacities related to assisting counsel.

DISCUSSION

These results provide support for the empirical assumptions underlying Bonnie's conceptualization of adjudicative competence. Within each domain of adjudicative competence (competence to assist counsel; decisional competence) the data indicate that understanding, reasoning, and appreciation are separable and somewhat independent aspects of functional legal ability—defendants judged legally (and clinically) impaired may reveal deficits in one of these areas without necessarily displaying impairment in others. These findings have implications for the development of clinical measures of adjudicative competence because, as noted earlier (Chapter 3), many prior measures have had an explicit, if not exclusive, focus on defendants' abstract understanding of the law or the adjudicatory process. The inclusion of explicit reasoning tasks, such as those required by the CAC:R or DC:R measures, and measures of appreciation as to how legal actors and the legal process will play out in one's own case may be necessary in order to assess a broader array of capacities relevant to adjudicative competence determinations. Such measures may permit a more differentiated analysis of a defendant's capacities vis-à-vis the separable *Dusky* criteria (see Table 3.2). That is, rather than pursuing categorical clinical judgments of "competent" or "incompetent," clinicians armed with an appropriate clinical measure can provide a more nuanced analysis of a defendant's particular capacities and limitations for the court to consider in reaching its ultimate judgment about competence.

Second, these data reveal the importance of decisional competence as a discrete domain within adjudicative competence. About one quarter of defendants judged legally and clinically incompetent scored in the impaired range on at least one decisional competence measure despite scoring in the unimpaired range on measures of competence to assist counsel. Data such as these can inform policy judgments regarding adjudicative competence criteria. As Chapter 2 indicated, the meaning of a defendant's decisional capacities within the well-established *Dusky* formula is not clear at present. Future elaborations on the functional capacities required for adjudicative competence may be informed by research that reveals important distinctions between merely assisting counsel (in a comparatively passive sense) and the capacity to actively engage in decision making relevant to constructing a criminal defense or to weighing options that are presented in the course of the adjudicatory process.

STUDY 3: COMPARISON OF ADJUDICATIVE COMPETENCE AND CIVIL COMPETENCE

ABILITIES FOR CRIMINAL DEFENDANTS WITH SCHIZOPHRENIA

The modern trend in the law is to treat various legal competencies as independent and discrete from one another (Melton et al., 1997). Generally, people involved in the legal system are presumed to be competent although that presumption can be challenged in a variety of contexts and they may be judged legally incompetent upon review of appropriate evidence. However, an adjudication of incompetence for one legal purpose usually does not render a person legally incompetent in another context. This principle of separate competencies is particularly evident in civil law. In the area of guardianship, for example, statutes draw explicit distinctions between *plenary* and *limited* guardianship, often stating a clear preference for the latter in an effort to preserve individual autonomy and self-determination wherever possible.[5] Similarly, statutes governing involuntary hospitalization (civil commitment) often require separate determinations of competence to admit oneself for voluntary treatment and competence to make treatment decisions (e.g., to accept or refuse psychotropic medications) once in the hospital (whether admitted on a voluntary or involuntary basis).[6]

In the adjudicative competence context, a second capacity that is often relevant for many incompetent defendants is their competence to consent to treatment. Our third research question used data from the main field study to examine the treatment competence of criminal defendants

---

[5] See, e.g., Florida Statutes Annotated Chapter 744 (West Supplement 2000).
[6] See, e.g., Florida Statutes Annotated Chapter 394.467 (West Supplement 2000).

and the relationship between adjudicative competence and competence to consent to treatment with psychotropic medications.

Research Participants

Participants in this study were a small sample ($N = 28$) of defendants who had been adjudicated incompetent to proceed and admitted to forensic hospitals (i.e., from the HI group) for psychiatric treatment to restore competence and a comparison group of 30 defendants from the JU group.[7] Although these 28 HI subjects represent only a small portion of the HI group ($n = 159$), they were indistinguishable from the remaining members of the HI group in most relevant respects. They did not differ significantly from the remaining HI participants in terms of age, race, marital status, prorated VIQ, number of times previously in jail or prison, or performance on 5 of 7 MacSAC-CD measures. This smaller sample of HI participants did report a slightly higher level of educational attainment ($M = 11.64$ years versus 10.62 years) and did display more psychopathology on the BPRS-A ($M = 40.78$) than the remainder of the HI group ($M = 38.00$).

Measures

In addition to the MacSAC-CD field study protocol described in Chapter 3, the participants in this study completed research measures developed in the Network's civil competence project. The civil competence measures assess the same abilities that are reflected in the MacSAC-CD—understanding, reasoning, and appreciation, but with a substantive focus on information relevant to consenting to (or refusing) mental health treatment (mainly, psychotropic medications). In the civil competence project parallel measures were created reflecting information relevant to the treatment of schizophrenia, depression, or angina. Because the participants in this study were all diagnosed with schizophrenia, we used the civil measures tailored to that disorder. We provide here a brief description of these measures of competence to consent to treatment. For a more extended presentation, readers are referred to Grisso, Appelbaum, Mulvey, and Fletcher (1995) and Grisso and Appelbaum (1995).

Capacity for understanding information was assessed using the Understanding Treatment Disclosures (UTD) measure. This measure

---

[7] Additional HI defendants with other diagnoses ($n = 7$) and JT defendants with varying diagnoses ($n = 15$) were recruited for this study; however, these group sizes are too small for statistical analyses and we have elected to report findings only for the HI schizophrenia subjects.

involves the standardized presentation of five paragraphs of information. Embedded in each paragraph is a key element that corresponds to information required for informed consent to treatment (e.g., nature of the proposed treatment, potential risks and benefits, alternative treatments, etc.). After each paragraph is presented, comprehension is assessed using a paraphrase (recall) task. The person's response is scored 2, 1, or 0, depending on the extent of information recalled. This process is repeated until all five paragraphs have been presented and comprehension for each has been tested.[8] Total scores for the UTD range from 0 to 10.

Appreciation in the treatment competence context was assessed using the Perceptions of Disorder (POD) measure, which consists of two components. Items on the Non-acknowledgment of Disorder (NOD) scale challenge patients to (a) acknowledge their own symptoms as described in the medical record, (b) recognize the severity of their symptoms, and (c) acknowledge their diagnosis provided to them from the hospital chart. Items on the Nonacknowledgment of Treatment (NOT) scale challenge patients to acknowledge (a) the potential value of obtaining any treatment (generally) for their condition, (b) the potential benefit of a specific proposed treatment (medication), and (c) the reduced likelihood of improvement without treatment. Scores for each of these subtests (NOD and NOT) range from 0 to 6 depending on the extent of a person's acknowledgment of his symptoms, illness, and potential utility of treatment.

Finally, the Thinking Rationally about Treatment (TRAT) measure was constructed to assess reasoning capacity. The main portion of the TRAT employs a vignette in which the person is presented a hypothetical story about a patient who must make some decisions about treatment for schizophrenia. Three treatment alternatives, including a description of risks and benefits associated with each, are provided. The person is then instructed to assume that he or she is assisting the hypothetical patient to make a decision about which treatment to select. A series of five questions is posed to the person, each of which assesses a cognitive function related to thinking rationally about the choice. These functions are (a) the capacity to identify information outside the scope of the vignette that would potentially inform the decision, (b) the ability to identify consequences of a selection (e.g., explaining the choice on the basis of anticipated outcomes), (c) comparative thinking—the simultaneous consideration of similar aspects of two treatment alternatives such that they are considered in relation to one another, (d) complex thinking—explicit reference to all three potential treatment options (versus avoiding or neglecting one or

---

[8]See Grisso et al. (1995) for other variations for presenting treatment disclosures. We describe here the procedure used in our study.

more of them), and (e) generating consequences—the ability to envision potential real-life consequences that could result from, for example, the side effects associated with a treatment.

Three additional cognitive tasks of a more general nature (i.e., not related to the vignette or to the patient's specific illness) complete the TRAT procedure. These tasks assess (a) the consistency of expression of one's views or values, (b) the capacity to make logical inferences of a transitive nature, and (c) probabilistic thinking—the capacity to correctly state the relative values of numerical probabilities presented as frequencies of occurrence. Potential scores on the TRAT range from 0 to 19 and serve as an index of reasoning ability.

RESULTS

CRIMINAL DEFENDANTS' PERFORMANCE ON CIVIL COMPETENCE MEASURES

The first column of Table 4.6 displays the mean score on each of the civil competence measures for the 28 HI defendants admitted for competence

TABLE 4.6. MEAN SCORES ON TREATMENT COMPETENCE MEASURES: DEFENDANTS WITH SCHIZOPHRENIA AND CONTROLS FROM THE MAIN FIELD STUDY AND THE TREATMENT COMPETENCE STUDY

	MacSAC-CD Field Study		Treatment Competence Study[1]	
Ability/Measure	Schizophrenia ($n = 28$)	Controls[2] ($n = 30$)	Schizophrenia ($n = 75$)	Controls[3] ($n = 75$)
Understanding/UTD M	6.33	8.31	6.18	8.40
(SD)	(2.09)	(1.23)	(3.00)	(1.70)
Reasoning/TRAT	10.00	13.52	10.12	13.68
	(3.93)	(2.28)	(4.10)	(3.40)
Appreciation/NOD	3.91	—	3.96	—
	(1.70)		*	
NOT	4.41	—	4.89	—
	(2.34)		*	

[1] Data from Grisso & Appelbaum (1995), Tables 4, 7, and 8.
[2] Data for 30 jail unscreened (JU) defendants who also completed the treatment competence measures. Control subjects in both studies did not receive the NOD and NOT measures.
[3] Non-mentally ill adults from the community.
*Not reported.
UTD = Understanding Treatment Disclosures.
TRAT = Thinking Rationally about Treatment.
NOD = Nonacknowledgement of Disorder.
NOT = Nonacknowledgement of Treatment.

restoration treatment; for comparison, column 2 displays the mean scores for 30 JU defendants who also completed the treatment competence measures. For further comparison, the right hand portion of the table presents data from the MacArthur treatment competence study, including mean scores for 75 people admitted to both public and university-affiliated psychiatric hospitals with a diagnosis of schizophrenia (column 3) and 75 matched community controls (column 4) who had never been hospitalized for the treatment of mental disorder. These data reveal that across the two studies very similar mean scores were obtained for both schizophrenia groups and both control groups. As was found in the treatment competence study, the mean scores for the MacSAC-CD field study HI schizophrenia group were significantly lower than the mean scores of the control group on the UDT and TRAT measures.

COMPARISONS OF PERFORMANCE ACROSS CRIMINAL AND CIVIL STANDARDS

We used the experimental criteria for impaired performance described in Study 1 (above) to classify each defendant as either "impaired" or "unimpaired" on adjudicative competence; a defendant was classified as "impaired" if he scored in the impaired range on any one of the MacSAC-CD measures. We used the criteria established by Grisso and Appelbaum (1995, p. 167) to determine defendants' impairment on treatment competence. A UTD score between 0 and 4 reflected impairment in understanding and a TRAT score between 0 and 5 reflected impairment in reasoning. Scores of 0 on NOD or 0–2 on NOT reflected impairment in appreciation.[9] Table 4.7 displays the percentage of study participants in terms of impairment across adjudicative and treatment competence capacities.

The data in Table 4.7 indicate rather clearly that impairment with respect to one legal issue is likely to be a poor proxy for impairment in another. Of the 20 HI defendants (71%) who scored in the impaired range on at least one adjudicative competence measure, only 8 of them (40%) were also impaired with respect to decision making about treatment for schizophrenia. Of the 8 HI defendants (28%) who had been adjudicated incompetent but did not score in the impaired range on any MacSAC-CD measure (and thus may have been incompetent on the basis of factors not

---

[9] These cutoffs represent scores of 2 or more standard deviations below the mean scores for the total treatment competence sample and ascribe "impairment" to less than 5% of the control subjects in that study.

TABLE 4.7. FIELD STUDY DEFENDANTS' IMPAIRED PERFORMANCE ON ADJUDICATIVE COMPETENCE AND TREATMENT COMPETENCE MEASURES

	Schizophrenia		Controls[3]
	HI	HI(C)[2]	JU
% Impaired[1]	n = 28	n = 20	n = 30
Adjudicative Competence only	43%	40%	7%
Treatment Competence only	11%	10%	0%
Both Adjudicative and Treatment Competence	29%	40%	0%
Neither Adjudicative nor Treatment Competence	17%	10%	93%

[1] A defendant was classified as "impaired" if he scored in the impaired range on any measure of competence related ability for the relevant legal context (adjudicative or treatment competence).
[2] This "clinically validated" incompetent group is a subset of the larger HI group, established using the criteria described in Study 2.
[3] Thirty jail unscreened (JU) defendants who also completed the treatment competence measures.

assessed by that instrument), only 3 of them (37.5%) scored in the impaired range on at least one treatment competence measure.

DISCUSSION

The findings from Study 3 support current legal thinking that distinguishes among legal competencies and treats them, for evidentiary purposes, as separate issues. In particular, these findings suggest that there may be a significant subset of adjudicated incompetent defendants who may nevertheless have the requisite capacities to decide competently about the array of treatment modalities that may be offered to remediate their symptoms. Although social policy may dictate that defendants' treatment decisions (e.g., to refuse psychotropic medication) be overridden on other grounds (e.g., society's interest in serving justice, through adjudication, to victims allegedly harmed by the accused; see *Weston v. US*, 2001), it should not be assumed that defendants who are "incompetent to stand trial" or "incompetent to proceed" are necessarily lacking in the capacities needed to make treatment decisions.

The data here are based on a small research sample limited to defendants with schizophrenia, and these results need to be replicated.

However, the findings are consistent with those of the larger MacArthur treatment competence study (Grisso & Appelbaum, 1995), a study whose findings suggest that capacity for treatment decision making may be even better preserved in patients diagnosed with depression. More generally, the finding of relative independence between capacities relevant to separable legal issues is consistent with the finding of Cascardi and Poythress (1996) in which treatment competence was found to be a poor proxy for capacity for voluntary admission to psychiatric treatment.

5

Development of the MacArthur Competence Assessment Tool-Criminal Adjudication (The MacCAT-CA)

The research described in Chapter 3 established that the MacSAC-CD was a reliably-scored, valid measure of criminal defendants' ability to participate in the legal process, that was also grounded in a legal theory of competence. The MacSAC-CD, however, was judged not appropriate for clinical-forensic use for a number of reasons. Some of the items lacked face validity for the legal setting, preliminary findings indicated that some of the MacSAC-CD measures yielded redundant information (e.g., paraphrase and recognition measures of understanding), and administration time for the MacSAC-CD ranged from 1.5 to 2.0 hours (which was significantly longer than the time required to administer any of the existing competence assessment instruments). This argued for development of a briefer competence assessment instrument.

In light of the above, the MacSAC-CD was streamlined from an instrument comprising 7 measures and 47 items to one containing 3 measures and 22 items. Decisions about item deletion and retention were based on a number of concerns including their psychometric properties (e.g., item-to-total correlations in the original scales; impact of item deletion on coefficient alpha) and face validity in the legal context.

The resulting measure, the MacArthur Competence Assessment Tool-Criminal Adjudication (MacCAT-CA), assesses three psycho-legal abilities relevant to criminal defendants' participation in legal proceedings: understanding, reasoning, and appreciation. Items that assess both foundational competence and decisional competence were retained in each of these measures.

THE MacCAT-CA

Table 5.1 provides a description of the MacCAT-CA items. Items 1 through 8 assess understanding, items 9 though 16 assess reasoning, and the final 6 items assess appreciation. As should be evident from the item content (see also Table 3.1), understanding is conceptually most akin to the *Dusky* (1960) criterion of "factual understanding" of the proceedings, reasoning is conceptually closest to the *Dusky* criterion of capacity to assist counsel, and appreciation is conceptually most akin to the "rational understanding" criterion.

For the psycho-legal abilities of understanding and reasoning, the MacCAT-CA retains the vignette methodology of the MacSAC-CD and assesses these capacities in an abstract and general sense (e.g., the defendant is not asked about the prosecutor or judge that will participate in his or her own case; see Chapter 3 for a more detailed discussion of this methodology). The understanding and reasoning measures provide a consistent and rigorously administered set of questions about the legal system and options that are available to "Fred" as his case proceeds to adjudication. A defendant's understanding of and reasoning about Fred's case and circumstances allows the examiner to make inferences about his or her capacities (relevant to a normative group of criminal defendants) for purposes of his or her own case.

In contrast, the appreciation measure evaluates the rationality of a defendant's beliefs about how the legal process will apply in his or her case. Appreciation items explore a defendant's beliefs concerning whether he or she will be treated differently from other defendants in similar circumstances (e.g., facing similar charges) and the reasons for such beliefs. These items investigate whether peculiar, idiosyncratic, or outright

TABLE 5.1. MacCAT-CA ITEMS AND MEASURES

Measure	Item Content
Understanding	
	1. Roles of defense attorney and prosecutor
	2. Elements of an offense
	3. Elements of a lesser included offense
	4. Role of the jury
	5. Role of the judge at trial
	6. Consequences of conviction
	7. Pleading guilty
	8. Rights waived in making a guilty plea
Reasoning	
	9. Self-defense
	10. Mitigating the prosecution's evidence of intent
	11. Possible provocation
	12. Fear as a motivator for one's behavior
	13. Possible mitigating effects of intoxication
	14. Seeking information that informs a choice
	15. Weighing consequences: Identifying advantages and disadvantages of a legal option
	16. Making comparisons: Weighing the risks and benefits of alternative legal options
Appreciation	
	17. Likelihood of being treated fairly
	18. Likelihood of being assisted by defense counsel
	19. Likelihood of fully disclosing case information to the defense attorney
	20. Likelihood of being found guilty
	21. Likelihood of punishment if found guilty
	22. Likelihood of pleading guilty

delusional thinking influence a defendant's perceptions of, and participation in, the legal process.

Each item on each measure is scored 0–1–2, yielding scores ranging from 0–16 on understanding, 0–16 on reasoning, and 0–12 on appreciation. *Consistent with our conceptualization of competence as a context-dependent legal issue, scores from these measures are not combined, and there is no single, overall, global index of "competence" derived from the MacCAT-CA.*

THE NIMH NORMING STUDY

Although preliminary research examining the performance of the MacSAC-CD indicated that it was a reliable and valid measure of a criminal defendant's competence to participate in the legal process, the MacCAT-CA was not yet suitable for use in legal settings. First, the psychometric properties of the MacCAT-CA were not established. Although it was reasonable to assume that the MacCAT-CA's reliability and validity would be acceptable given its heritage, the MacCAT-CA constituted a significant departure from the MacSAC-CD in some important ways. As such, basic research examining the instrument, its psychometric properties, and validity was necessary.

Second, one of the potential values of the MacCAT-CA was that it could allow the forensic examiner to consider and describe the defendant's abilities and capacities *normatively*—that is, in comparison to the typical performance of relevant defendant groups (e.g., defendants adjudicated incompetent to proceed, "typical" pretrial defendants whose competence was not questioned, etc.). To allow for such comparisons, norms for the newly developed MacCAT-CA still had to be developed. Research to examine the psychometric properties of the MacCAT-CA and to develop norms for clinical interpretation was funded by a grant from the National Institute of Mental Health.

METHOD

SELECTION OF STUDY SITES

In order to develop national norms for the MacCAT-CA, data were gathered from subjects in eight states, the selection of which was influenced by three factors: (a) type of forensic service system employed, (b) presence of state sponsored forensic evaluator training, and (c) geographic dispersion.

State systems for providing forensic evaluations vary considerably in organizational structure. Grisso, Cocozza, Steadman, Fisher, and Greer (1994) developed a typology of forensic service delivery systems that included five system types (Traditional Inpatient, Modified Traditional, Community Based, Private Practitioner, Mixed [i.e., a combination of two or more of the preceding models] and a "Not Classified" category). Because the system under which forensic evaluations are conducted might affect clinical and legal decision making about defendants' competence, states which employed the various systems were selected for inclusion in the study.

States also vary with respect to the presence or absence of training requirements for forensic examiners (Everett, 1996; Farkas, DeLeon, & Newman, 1997; Otto & Heilbrun, 2002). For example, in Massachusetts, the courts can appoint as forensic evaluators in criminal cases only those professionals who have successfully attended a week-long forensic training

TABLE 5.2. MacCAT-CA Data Collection Sites

State	System Type	Forensic Evaluator Training Provided
Washington	Traditional	No
South Carolina	Modified Traditional	No
Oklahoma	Community Based	No
Louisiana	Private Practitioner	No
Wisconsin	Mixed	No
Utah	Not Classified	No
Michigan	Modified Traditional	Yes
Alabama	Community Based	Yes

program and completed forensic evaluations under the supervision of a senior forensic examiner. Other states do not require any kind of training for appointment. Because training requirements might affect decision-making with respect to defendants' competence, states with varying training requirements were selected for inclusion in the study. Finally, the research team wanted a sample of defendants from around the United States in order to best approximate a "national" sample for the development of norms.

The six states selected to represent the different "types" of pretrial forensic service system delivery identified by Grisso et al. (1994) were Washington, South Carolina, Oklahoma, Louisiana, Wisconsin, and Utah. Two additional states, Michigan and Alabama, were selected because they provided comprehensive forensic evaluator training programs to clinicians who conduct court-appointed forensic evaluations (see Table 5.2).

The selection of states within each of the four discrete system types (Traditional, Modified Traditional, Community Based, Private Practitioner) was driven by a preference for those that were relatively pure in terms of service delivery mechanisms (Joseph Cocozza, personal communication). Otherwise, selection decisions were made based on concerns of cost-efficiency in implementing the study (e.g., proximity to the investigators, estimated volume of available cases) and geographic representativeness.

Selection of Participants

Comparison Groups

The same three populations of defendants sampled in the MacSAC-CD field study were considered important to sample for purposes of evaluating the psychometric properties of the MacCAT-CA and for the development of interpretive clinical norms.[1] The group of hospitalized incompetent

---

[1] See Chapter 3 for further description of these populations.

(HI) defendants was necessary in order to provide the distributions of scores typical of legally incompetent individuals. Inclusion of both JU (jail unscreened) and JT (jail treated) comparison groups was important for different reasons. JU inmates were included in the study to provide data on how the "normal," presumed competent defendant population performs on the MacCAT-CA measures. In contrast, the JT defendants comprised the most relevant comparison group in terms of establishing the clinical validity of the MacCAT-CA, since the most rigorous test of the clinical utility of the instrument would be its ability to distinguish mentally disordered, incompetent (HI) defendants from those who were mentally disordered, but competent.

Participant Inclusion Criteria

In order to be eligible for participation in the study, potential participants had to be English-speaking defendants, charged with a felony offense, and between 18 and 65 years of age. Defendants were excluded if they had a jail or hospital chart diagnosis indicating an organic disorder or if they obtained a score <60 on a screening measure of IQ (see Measures, below). Potential HI subjects were excluded if they could not complete the research protocol within 10 days of admission to the hospital for competence restoration treatment.

Defendants of all races and both genders were eligible for the study, as neither variable was expected to be associated with significant differences in MacCAT-CA performance (see Chapter 3). Given the typical composition of forensic populations, a predominately male sample was anticipated.

Sample Size

The target numbers of participants per group in each state were 52 HI, 52 JT, and 26 JU. The target number of participants for the study was therefore 1040, a number sufficient to insure stable covariate matrices for the multivariate analyses of the data and to insure stable interpretive norms. With this number of participants, effect sizes comparable to those obtained in the MacArthur field study could be detected with 81% probability, comparing groups at the individual state level.

Identification of HI Subjects

In each state, HI subjects were recruited from inpatient forensic facilities with whom the research team established cooperative agreements.

Although, prior to hospitalization and enrollment in the study, each HI participant was evaluated clinically and subsequently adjudicated incompetent to proceed, there remained the potential problem of false positives in this group as a result of treatment effects. For example, defendants might have received psychotropic medication or other treatment in jail while awaiting their competence hearing and/or admission to the forensic hospital, or may have responded very rapidly within the window of time for recruitment into the study (within 10 days of entry into the hospital), resulting in improvement in competence-related abilities prior to administration of the research protocol. To the degree that such persons did appear in the HI group, results might be biased against the clinical utility of the MacCAT-CA measures, since these "prematurely restored" participants' scores would likely inflate the HI group means on the MacCAT-CA measures.

This problem was addressed by having a hospital treatment team member provide a global rating of incapacity (on a scale from 1 = *clearly incompetent*, to 6 = *clearly competent*) at the time the HI participants were recruited into the study. This rating was used in data analyses to identify a clinically affirmed subgroup of incompetent defendants [HI(C)]. Although the research team does not believe that, in clinical practice, clinicians' judgments or ratings should "trump" court decisions, for research purposes this assessment permitted identification of a relatively "pure" group of incompetent defendants and, thus, allowed for more fair comparisons in testing the classification utility of the MacCAT-CA.

Identification of JU and JT Inmates

In each state the research team established cooperative agreements with public defender offices and/or courts, thus gaining permission to approach jail inmates who were awaiting trial for possible participation in the study. A contact person in the public defender office or jail provided a list of potential participants from their inmate rosters. At all sites except Oklahoma we were able to enlist the assistance of mental health staff at the jail in identifying those inmates who were receiving mental health services. From the lists of those receiving services (JT) and those not receiving services (JU), research assistants (RAs) randomly selected inmates to approach for the study.

To insure that all JU and JT inmates recruited into the study were presumptively competent at the time of completion of the research protocol, RAs in each state followed up with the admissions clerk at the forensic hospital for a period of two months after protocol administration. Any JT or JU participant who had been admitted to the forensic hospital for competence restoration treatment during that period was dropped from the study due to concerns that he or she may have been incompetent when recruited. JT or JU participants who were not adjudicated incompetent within two months of protocol administration were presumed to have been competent at that time. In this way the research team hoped to avoid the problem of false negatives, which would bias the results against the clinical utility of the MacCAT-CA measures, since the scores of these "competent" participants would likely diminish the JT and JU group means on the MacCAT-CA measures.

SELECTION OF MEASURES

Predictor Variables

Data were collected in several domains as potential predictors of competence-related abilities. These domains included psychosocial history variables, present level of intellectual functioning (estimated IQ), and level of psychopathology. Self-report and review of jail or hospital records were used to obtain demographic information, including diagnosis, current medications, mental health treatment history, socioeconomic status (SES), and criminal justice history.

For each participant, current level of intellectual functioning was estimated using the Information and Picture Completion subtests of the Wechsler Adult Intelligence Scale-Revised (WAIS-R). Prorated IQs based on these subtests are highly correlated with full scale IQ (mean corrected validity coefficient across 9 age groups = .86) and are highly reliable (mean reliability coefficient = .90) (Kaufman, Ishikuma, & Kaufman-Packer, 1991).

Two measures of psychopathology were employed in this study. As in the MacSAC-CD field study, we used the 18-item anchored version (Woerner, Mannuzza, & Kane, 1988) of the Brief Psychiatric Rating Scale (BPRS), which yields a single index for total psychopathology based on a sum of interviewer ratings on 18 symptom scales (e.g., anxiety, hostility, suspiciousness, etc.) and subscale scores that index psychoticism, depression, hostility and withdrawal (see Chapter 3).

To provide an index of psychotic symptomatology that was independent of the RAs' BPRS ratings, a second measure of psychopathology was administered. The 25-item PSY-5 psychoticism scale (Harkness, McNulty, & Ben-Porath, 1995) was derived from the MMPI-2 item pool and measures the gross degree of correspondence between an individual's inner models of reality and the external social and physical world (Harkness, McNulty, & Ben-Porath, 1995). In studies with various clinical and non-clinical samples, estimates of internal consistency have ranged from .70 to .84. The scale also yields appropriate mean differences across samples as well as expected patterns of correlations with measures of theoretically-driven and divergent constructs.[2]

As noted above, for the HI group only, a hospital treatment team member provided a global rating of each defendant's competence to proceed (on a scale from 1 = *clearly incompetent*, to 6 = *clearly competent*) at the time the patient was recruited into the study. This rating was used to identify a relatively pure group of incompetent defendants in data analyses (HI(C)). It also served as an independent, albeit gross, measure of competence for evaluating the concurrent validity of the MacCAT-CA.

Criterion Variables

The primary outcome variables were scores on the three measures of psycholegal ability—understanding, reasoning, and appreciation—that comprise the MacCAT-CA (see above).

PROCEDURES

Site Preparation

In each state, agency agreements with forensic hospitals, public defender offices, courts, and jails were negotiated by a local site coordinator who also assisted in the recruitment of RAs. All RAs were brought together for four days of training on the administration of the research protocol prior to beginning data collection.

Participant Recruitment

At each site within each state, RAs worked through agency contacts established by the site coordinators to access potential subjects. Upon completion of the informed consent process, the Information and Picture Completion subtests of the WAIS-R were administered to obtain an estimated IQ. Those defendants whose prorated IQ was below 60 were dropped from the study as not meeting inclusion criteria. The remaining subjects then completed the full research protocol. The order of administration of measures was Psychosocial History, BPRS, PSY-5 Psychoticism scale, and MacCAT-CA. Upon completion of the protocol, $10 was

---

[2] The PSY-5 Psychoticism scale was added to the protocol shortly after data collection began. Thus, scores were available for only 647 subjects (89%).

deposited in the institutional (jail or hospital) account of each subject and RAs retrieved information from the participant's institutional file.

MacCAT-CA Protocol Scoring

RAs scored all protocols that they collected. Scored protocols were mailed to the research team at the University of South Florida for data entry. Prior to data entry, the scoring of the MacCAT-CA was reviewed by a second RA trained in the scoring of this instrument. When questionable scoring was noted, it was reviewed by one of the primary investigators, who considered the disputed scoring and determined the correct score. Periodic feedback was provided to RAs regarding problems detected in their scoring of the protocols.

RESULTS

SAMPLE CHARACTERISTICS

Recruitment of Participants by State

A total of 729 subjects were recruited into the study, which is 71% of the targeted number (1040). Table 5.3 displays the numbers of subjects

TABLE 5.3. RESEARCH SAMPLE: GROUPS BY STATES

	JU (26) N (%)	JT (52) N (%)	HI (52) N (%)	Total (130) N (%)	% of Total N
State					
Washington	9 (35)	6 (12)	53 (102)	68 (52)	9.3
South Carolina	30 (115)	25 (48)	15 (29)	70 (54)	9.6
Oklahoma	34 (131)	2 (4)	64 (123)	100 (77)	13.7
Louisiana	15 (58)	24 (46)	29 (56)	68 (52)	9.3
Wisconsin	31 (119)	49 (94)	18 (35)	98 (75)	13.4
Utah	28 (108)	49 (94)	36 (69)	113 (87)	15.5
Michigan	24 (92)	50 (96)	38 (73)	112 (86)	15.4
Alabama	26 (100)	44 (85)	30 (58)	100 (77)	13.7
Group Totals & (%) of Target N	197 (95)	249 (60)	283 (68)	729 (71)	
Group % of Actual N	27%	34%	39%	100%	

JU = unscreened jail inmates; JT = jail inmates receiving mental health services; HI = hospitalized incompetent defendants.

recruited into each group, by state. Lower than expected recruitment in the JT group was affected primarily by problems in Oklahoma and Washington; in Oklahoma we were unable to establish procedures with jail personnel by which JT subjects could be identified, and in Washington problems were encountered due to working with multiple defender agencies.

Lower than expected recruitment in the HI group was affected by a number of factors. In some states the number of potential HI participants was lower than expected based on our projections from prior years' data on hospital admissions. Also, some of the potential HI participants were too disordered or aggressive to be approached for research participation during the early days of hospitalization. By the time these patients were stable enough to be approached, the elapsed time placed them outside the window of time (within 10 days of admission) for recruitment into the study. We also had a higher rate of refusal from potential HI participants (22%) than from JT (9%) or JU (9%) subjects. While the HI refusal rate is higher than is desirable, it is actually lower than is sometimes reported in studies of acutely mentally ill persons. For example, in studies of competence to consent to voluntary hospitalization (Appelbaum, Mirkin, & Bateman, 1981) and consent to treatment (Grisso, Appelbaum, & Hill-Fotouhi, 1997) refusal rates of 33% and 43%, respectively, have been reported.

TABLE 5.4. DEMOGRAPHICS BY GROUP

Variable	JU	JT	HI
Mean Age	31.33	32.46	36.01
(SD)	(9.18)	(9.35)	(10.66)
Male	93.9%	88.8%	89.4%
Female	6.1%	11.2%	10.6%
White	35.0%	50.2%	49.8%
Non-White	65.0%	49.8%	50.2%
Mean Years of Education	11.26	11.35	11.44
(SD)	(1.98)	(2.51)	(2.68)
Socioeconomic Status[1]	56.10	56.25	57.94
(SD)	(10.96)	(12.45)	(13.13)

JU = Unscreened jail inmates; JT = Jail inmates receiving mental health services; HI = Hospitalized incompetent defendants.
[1] Calculated using Hollingshead and Redlich's (1958) two factor index of social position.

Demographic Data

Table 5.4 provides descriptive information about the hospitalized and jailed defendant samples (HI n = 283, JT n = 249, JU n = 197).[3] As expected, participants were predominantly male (90%), and gender was distributed similarly across the HI, JT, and JU samples, χ^2 (2, N = 729) = 3.90, p = .14. While there was a balance of white and non-white participants in the study, they were somewhat disproportionately distributed across the three samples, χ^2 (2, N = 729) = 12.99, p < .002. HI participants as a group were significantly older than participants in the JU, t (724) = 25.01, p < .001, and JT samples, t (724) = 16.40, p < .001.

The mean years of education reported by participants was 11.36 (SD = 2.45), and level of education did not vary significantly across groups. Using Hollingshead and Redlich's (1958) two factor index of social position, participants identified the highest level of employment ever held. The mean scores, shown in Table 5.4, equate with social class IV (e.g., clerical and sales workers, technicians). The group means did not differ significantly in terms of highest SES attained by participants.

The participants in the various samples reported similar amounts and types of prior involvement with the criminal justice system. The mean number of self-reported misdemeanor[4] and felony arrests for the total sample was 5.24 (SD = 9.52) and 1.91 (SD = 2.79), respectively. The differences between the groups in terms of their estimated number of felony or misdemeanor arrests were not statistically significant.

Mental Status Data

Group means on measures of psychopathology and cognitive functioning are presented in Table 5.5. The groups did not differ in terms of their estimated current cognitive/intellectual functioning. As expected, participants in the HI group, overall, showed greater levels of psychopathology than did their counterparts in the JT and JU samples. There was a significant group effect as measured by the MMPI-2 Psychoticism scale, with the HI sample demonstrating greater levels of psychopathology than either the JT sample, $t(646)$= 2.55, p = .011, or the JU sample, $t(646)$ = 6.46, p < .001. Participants in the HI sample also obtained higher scores on the BPRS total score than the JT and JU samples, ts (726) = 3.65 and 11.58, respectively, as well as higher scores on the BPRS psychoticism,

---

[3] Different degrees of freedom for the analyses that follow reflect missing data on these variables for a small number of participants.
[4] One participant who reported an improbable 1,000 misdemeanor arrests was deleted from this analysis.

TABLE 5.5. MENTAL STATUS CHARACTERISTICS BY GROUP

	JU M (SD)	JT M (SD)	HI M (SD)	Univariate F
Estimated WAIS-R IQ	85.23 (11.99)	85.49 (14.61)	83.21 (14.05)	2.17
MMPI-2 Psychoticism Scale	63.32 (14.13)	70.48 (18.40)	74.68 (19.64)	20.93*
BPRS Total Score	29.16 (6.99)	35.95 (9.07)	38.80 (10.04)	68.26*
BPRS Psychoticism Subscale	3.41 (1.16)	4.96 (2.61)	7.55 (3.72)	131.96*
BPRS Depression Subscale	8.70 (3.96)	10.76 (4.55)	8.20 (3.99)	24.48*
BPRS Hostility Subscale	5.00 (2.26)	6.15 (2.69)	6.74 (3.09)	23.53*
BPRS Emotional Withdrawal Subscale	3.91 (1.50)	4.62 (2.33)	5.40 (2.95)	22.27*

JU = Unscreened jail inmates; JT = Jail inmates receiving mental health services; HI = Hospitalized incompetent defendants; BPRS = Brief Psychiatric Rating Scale-Anchored.
*$p < .001$.

ts (722) = 10.49 and 15.74), hostility, ts (722) = 2.61 and 6.85, and emotional withdrawal, ts (722) = 3.69 and 6.61, subscales (all $ps < .01$). Similar to findings in the MacSAC-CD field study (Chapter III), HI participants were less depressed than JT participants, $t(722) = 6.75, p < .001$, but did not differ from JU participants, $t(722) = 1.30, p = .19$.

PSYCHOMETRIC PROPERTIES OF THE MACCAT-CA

One primary objective of this research was to examine the psychometric properties of the instrument. In the following sections we report findings related to the internal consistency, interrater reliability, criterion-related validity (comparisons of group means), concurrent validity, convergent validity, and classification utility of the MacCAT-CA.

Internal Consistency

Cronbach's alpha and the mean and range of interim correlations were calculated for each of the MacCAT-CA measures. These values serve as indices of scale reliability and item homogeneity, respectively (Fiske, 1971). The alphas ranged from .81 (reasoning) to .85 (understanding) to

.88 (appreciation), indicating good internal consistency for these measures. Similar findings were reported by Rogers, Grandjeon, Tillbrook, Vitacco, and Sewell (2001), who examined the performance of the MacCAT-CA in three samples of criminal defendants (total $N = 149$).

The mean inter-item correlations were .36 (range = .21–.53), .42 (range = .31–.53), and .54 (.48–.62) for the reasoning, understanding, and appreciation measures, respectively, indicating appropriate homogeneity of item content for all three measures.

Interrater Reliability

To evaluate interrater reliability, a sample of 48 completed protocols was drawn from the data base (2 HI, 2 JT, and 2 JU from each state). Scoring assigned by the original RA who completed the protocol was removed, and 42 protocols were mailed to each RA for re-scoring.[5] One RA failed to return one of the protocols; hence, the interrater reliability analysis was based on 47 total cases scored by each of the eight RAs. In order to compute an intraclass correlation for each measure, three analyses of variance (ANOVAs) were conducted on the total scores from the understanding, reasoning, and appreciation measures, respectively. In each of the ANOVAs, rater was treated as a random variable (Shrout & Fleiss, 1979). Interscorer reliability for the three measures as estimated by this procedure ranged from very good to excellent, with intraclass $R = .75$ for appreciation, .85 for reasoning, and .90 for understanding. Although explicit scoring guidelines are provided for each item, the scoring criteria are more rigorous for the understanding items, and less so for the appreciation measure (where a clinical judgment about the plausibility of a defendant's "reasons" is required). The pattern of ICCs for the three measures is consistent with the degree of rigor in the scoring guidelines. More recently, Rogers et al. (2001) reported "superb" interrater reliability ($r > .90$) using their sample of 149 criminal defendants.

Criterion-Related Validity

Criterion-related validity was examined by comparing the mean MacCAT-CA scores of our groups known to differ in terms of legal competence status. Criterion-related validity would be affirmed by a finding that legally incompetent defendants (group HI) did in fact show impaired performance (lower scores) on the MacCAT-CA measures relative to the legally competent defendants (groups JU and JT).

---

[5] RAs did not receive the six protocols that they had originally scored. Therefore, only 42 "new" protocols were mailed to each RA.

TABLE 5.6. MEAN MacCAT-CA SCORES BY GROUP AND MANCOVA RESULTS

	JU $n=197$	JT $n=249$	HI $n=283$	HI(R) $n=90$	HI(C) $n=170$	Univariate F* (2, 720)	Univariate F** (3, 696)
Understanding							
Mean	12.50	12.56	9.11	10.78	8.14	79.12	73.35
SD	3.08	3.25	4.19	3.41	4.17		
Reasoning							
Mean	13.27	12.90	9.33	11.14	8.23	95.92	88.27
SD	2.64	2.90	4.31	3.75	4.23		
Appreciation							
Mean	11.44	11.02	7.89	9.87	6.58	121.07	129.08
SD	1.01	1.63	4.01	3.00	4.08		

Clinician ratings of competence were unavailable for 23 HI defendants, who were not included in the second MANCOVA.
JU = Unscreened jail inmates; JT = Jail inmates receiving mental health services; HI = Hospitalized incompetent defendants; HI(C) = Clinically affirmed incompetent HI defendants; HI(R) = Residual HI defendants.
*Univariate F for MANCOVA comparing JU, JT, and HI samples. **Univariate F for MANCOVA comparing JU, JT, HI(R) and HI(C) samples.
All F values significant at $p < .001$.

Table 5.6 provides the means and the standard deviations of each sample for each of the three MacCAT-CA psycholegal ability measures. These means differed significantly in a MANCOVA in which type of pretrial forensic evaluation service delivery system and mandated training requirements were entered as covariates, multivariate $F(18, 2160) = 9.79$, $p < .001$. For each measure, planned orthogonal comparisons revealed that the HI sample scored significantly lower (i.e., their competence-related abilities were more impaired) than the JU sample (understanding, $t(720) = 11.37$; reasoning, $t(720) = 12.72$; appreciation, $t(720) = 13.74$, all ps $< .001$). The planned comparisons contrasting the means from the HI and JT samples provides a more stringent test of group discrimination. Similarly, the HI group mean was significantly lower than the JT group mean for each MacCAT-CA measure (understanding, $t(720) = 10.04$; reasoning, $t(720) = 10.66$; appreciation, $t(720) = 12.84$, all ps $< .001$).[6]

---

[6] Similar between-groups analyses were conducted on groups within each state. Multivariate analyses of variance revealed significant group differences in each state, and within each state univariate analyses were significant for each of the MacCAT-CA measures. The HI group mean was significantly lower than that of the JU or JT group in every comparison. These findings support the criterion-related validity of the MacCAT-CA and indicate that the measures performed in similar ways in all eight study states. See Edens, Poythress, Nicholson, and Otto (1999).

As noted previously, we obtained a hospital treatment team member's global rating of competence for each patient recruited into the HI group, in part as a precaution against "false positives" in the HI group (e.g., defendants who, although adjudicated incompetent, had become restored through treatment at jail while awaiting hospital admission). These clinician ratings were used to disaggregate the HI group into two distinct groups for further comparison. The HI(C) group was composed of 170 subjects confirmed as at least "marginally incompetent" by the treating clinician, and the HI(R) sample was the *residual* group of 90 HI defendants, each of whom received a clinician rating indicating at least "marginal competence" at the time of protocol administration. Means and standard deviations for the MacCAT-CA measures for these two groups appear in the right side of Table 5.6.

The MANCOVA was repeated after separating the HI sample into HI(C) and HI(R) groups. A significant multivariate effect was obtained, $F (18, 2088) = 9.82, p < .001$, for this analysis. Planned comparisons indicated that the HI(C) sample obtained lower mean scores on each of the MacCAT-CA measures when compared to the HI(R) group, $ts (696) = 6.05$, 6.98, and 9.93 for understanding, reasoning and appreciation, respectively; all $ps < .001$. Furthermore, despite obtaining higher scores than the HI(C) sample, the HI(R) sample obtained lower mean scores on each of the MacCAT-CA measures when compared to both the JU sample, $ts (696) =$ 5.19, 5.53, and 4.70 for understanding, reasoning and appreciation, respectively; all $ps < .001$, and the JT sample, $ts (696) = 3.88, 3.66$, and 3.62 for understanding, reasoning and appreciation, respectively; all $ps < .001$, suggesting greater impairment in competence-related abilities (see Table 5.6).

The preceding analyses documented the statistical significance of the differences between groups of participants on the MacCAT-CA measures. Table 5.7 provides information regarding the magnitude of those between-group differences. The measure of effect size used to estimate group differences was Cohen's d, which is defined as $d = (X_1 - X_2)/s$, where X_1 and X_2 are the means of the two groups being compared and s is the pooled within-group standard deviation (Cohen, 1988). Thus, Cohen's d expresses the difference between means relative to within-group variation. Conventionally, effect sizes $> .50$ are considered medium effects, and effect sizes $> .80$ are considered large effects (Cohen, 1988, p. 82).

As the first two columns of Table 5.7 show, large effect sizes (approximately one standard deviation) were obtained in comparisons involving all hospitalized incompetent defendants across the three MacCAT-CA measures. Further, as can be seen in the third and fourth columns of the table, substantially larger effect sizes were obtained from comparisons involving the clinically-affirmed incompetent defendants. In every case, the between-group differences exceeded one standard deviation, ranging from almost 1.25 to more than 1.5 standard deviations. Even moderate effects were observed in comparisons involving incompetent defendants who were not clinically-affirmed as such.

Convergent Validity

Support for the construct validity of the MacCAT-CA is found in the pattern of correlations between MacCAT-CA measures and select clinical variables. Ideally, measures of competence-related abilities should correlate positively with estimated IQ, but they should correlate negatively with measures of psychopathology, particularly with measures of psychoticism. As revealed in Table 5.8, this is the pattern of relationships

TABLE 5.7. EFFECT SIZES (COHEN'S D) FOR COMPARISONS BETWEEN SAMPLES OF JAILED DEFENDANTS AND HOSPITALIZED INCOMPETENT DEFENDANTS

Measure	Comparison					
	JU-HI	JT-HI	JU-HI(C)	JT-HI(C)	JU-HI(R)	JT-HI(R)
Understanding	.90	.91	1.20	1.21	.54	.54
Reasoning	1.06	.96	1.45	1.33	.70	.56
Appreciation	1.13	1.00	1.69	1.54	.84	.55

JU = Unscreened jail inmates; JT = Jail inmates receiving mental health services; HI = Hospitalized incompetent defendants; HI(C) = Clinically affirmed incompetent HI defendants; HI(R) = Residual HI defendants.

TABLE 5.8. CORRELATIONS BETWEEN MacCAT-CA AND CLINICAL MEASURES

Variables	Understanding	Reasoning	Appreciation
Estimated WAIS-R IQ	.41	.34	.14
BPRS Total Score	−.23	−.29	−.36
BPRS Psychoticism Subscale	−.40	−.48	−.52
BPRS Depression Subscale	.18	.18	.18
BPRS Hostility Subscale	−.01	−.10	−.28
BPRS Emotional Withdrawal Subscale	−.34	−.27	−.19
MMPI-2 Psychoticism Scale	−.33	−.31	−.21

BPRS = Brief Psychiatric Rating Scale-Anchored. MMPI-2 = Minnesota Multiphasic Personality Inventory-2.
$p < .001$ for all correlations except Hostility/Understanding ($p = .71$) and Hostility/Reasoning ($p = .007$).

obtained in the present study, providing evidence of convergent validity for the MacCAT-CA.

Consistent with the findings from the MacArthur field study using the MacSAC-CD research prototype (Chapter 3, Table 3.5) the MacCAT-CA measures correlated negatively with disturbed thinking as measured by the BPRS psychoticism subscale and MMPI-2 Psychoticism scale, and with global psychopathology as measured by the BPRS total score. Present cognitive ability, as measured by performance on select subtests of the WAIS-R, correlated positively with performance on the MacCAT-CA. Also consistent with findings from the field study, presumed competent jail defendants showed higher levels of depression as measured by the BPRS than hospitalized incompetent defendants.

Concurrent Validity

The global ratings of competence for HI group subjects, obtained from a member of the participant's treatment team at the time of recruitment into the study, provided a gross, independent index of competence that was used to evaluate concurrent validity of the MacCAT-CA. Concurrent validity of the MacCAT-CA measures would be indicated by significant, positive correlations with clinicians' ratings.

Clinicians' ratings of competence were moderately and positively correlated with performance on the MacCAT-CA (understanding: $r = .36$; reasoning: $r = .42$; appreciation: $r = .49$; for all correlations, $p < .001$). The magnitude of the correlations between MacCAT-CA scores and clinicians' ratings may be deflated in part due to restriction in range (i.e., only hospitalized incompetent defendants received such clinician ratings).

Classification Utility

Sequential logistic regression analyses were conducted to evaluate whether the MacCAT-CA measures contributed to the accurate classification of defendants' competence status beyond that achieved using demographic/historical variables and clinical status characteristics. Five demographic/historical variables—age, gender, race, education, and history of prior felony offenses—were included in the analyses, as were five clinical status characteristics—estimated WAIS-R IQ and the four BPRS-A subscale scores. In each of the analyses described below, the set of demographic/historical predictors was entered first into the regression equation as a block, followed by the five clinical status characteristics, also entered as a block. Finally, the three MacCAT-CA measures were entered into the regression equation.

TABLE 5.9. LOGISTIC REGRESSION ANALYSIS: CLASSIFICATION OF PRESUMED COMPETENT DEFENDANTS AND HOSPITALIZED INCOMPETENT DEFENDANTS

	Classification Accuracy		
Analysis 1: JU/JT versus HI Step/Predictors	Competent JU/JT	Incompetent HI	Total
Step 1 – Demographic/Historical Variables	90.4%	23.7%	64.5%
Step 2 – Clinical Characteristics	86.6%	59.5%	76.0%
Step 3 – MacCAT-CA Measures	89.1%	63.8%	79.3%
Analysis 2: JT versus HI Step/Predictors	Competent JT	Incompetent HI	Total
Step 1 – Demographic/Historical Variables	47.3%	66.3%	57.5%
Step 2 – Clinical Characteristics	66.7%	71.7%	69.4%
Step 3 – MacCAT-CA Measures	77.0%	69.9%	73.2%

JU = Unscreened jail inmates; JT = Jail inmates receiving mental health services; HI = Hospitalized incompetent defendants; HI(C) = Clinically affirmed incompetent HI defendants.
Demographic/historical predictors included age, gender, race, education, and prior felony convictions. Clinical status predictors included BPRS-A factor subscales (psychoticism, depression, hostility, emotional withdrawal) and estimated WAIS-R IQ.
For the JU/JT versus HI analyses, $n = 718$. For the JT versus HI analyses, $n = 522$.

The classification task for the first set of analyses was that of differentiating HI defendants from the combined (JU/JT) sample of defendants presumed to be competent. The upper half of Table 5.9 presents classification rates for each of the steps in the sequential logistic regression. As the table shows, overall classification accuracy using demographic/historical characteristics alone (64.5%) was only slightly more accurate than classification using the base rate for competence in the sample (61.2%). The demographic/historical variables were particularly poor for purposes of identifying incompetent defendants. Adding the clinical characteristics increased the overall classification accuracy to 76.0%, including 59.5% of the incompetent defendants. Finally, adding the MacCAT-CA measures made a significant contribution to prediction of competence status after demographic and clinical characteristics had been entered into the equation, χ^2 (3, $N = 718$) = 82.4, $p < .05$. After addition of the MacCAT-CA measures, overall accuracy increased (79.3%), as did the percentage incompetent defendants (63.8%) who were classified correctly.

As noted previously, discrimination of defendants adjudicated as incompetent from (presumably) competent defendants who are receiving mental health treatment in the jails is a more difficult validity hurdle for a measure of adjudicative competence than is discrimination of incompetent defendants from randomly selected jail inmates, the majority of whom presumably do not suffer from a major mental disorder. Therefore, the set of logistic regression analyses described above was repeated after excluding JU defendants from the analyses. The base rate of incompetence in this new subsample of defendants was 53.2%. Classification rates from the second set of sequential logistic regression analyses are presented in the lower half of Table 5.9. In these analyses, demographic/historical predictors yielded accurate classifications in 57.5% of the cases, again close to the base rate for the sample. The addition of clinical status characteristics substantially improved classification accuracy (69.4%) of the cases (71.7% and 66.7% of the incompetent and competent groups, respectively). Finally, addition of the MacCAT-CA scales further increased accurate classifications to 73.2%, primarily through a sizable increase in the correct identification of competent defendants. The incremental contribution of the MacCAT-CA measures was again statistically significant, χ^2 (3, $N = 522$) = 69.5, $p < .05$.

For a variety of reasons, the HI defendants in our study constituted a potentially heterogeneous group with respect to the criterion in question. As discussed earlier (Chapter 2) it is clear that in some instances defendants are adjudicated incompetent and admitted to forensic psychiatric facilities for competence restoration because of political and economic considerations. For example, competency referral and adjudication may be used to secure inpatient services for individuals who fail to meet statutory standards for civil commitment. Further, individual differences in response to treatment and variability in the duration and quality of the treatment provided in jail prior to admission to a state forensic unit also serve to increase heterogeneity among HI defendants.

Given these concerns about heterogeneity in the HI group, the two sets of analyses described above were repeated using the HI(C) participants (i.e., the subsample of HI defendants whose incompetence was affirmed by a member of the hospital staff familiar with the case). Findings from these analyses are provided in Table 5.10.

Logistic regression analysis using the demographic/historical variables correctly classified 73.9% of the cases overall, which is close to the base rate for competence in the entire sample (72%). This set of predictors was particularly poor at identifying the clinically affirmed incompetent defendants. The addition of the clinical predictors improved the overall classification to 83.6%, although the highest accuracy rate (89.1%) was obtained after the addition of the MacCAT-CA measures to the regression equation. The incremental increase in classification accuracy with the addition of MacCAT-CA scores as predictors was statistically significant, χ^2 (3, $N = 605$) = 107.9, $p < .05$.

The lower half of Table 5.10 presents the results from logistic regression analyses after the JU^T defendants were excluded. Prediction based on

TABLE 5.10. LOGISTIC REGRESSION ANALYSIS: CLASSIFICATION OF DEFENDANTS PRESUMED COMPETENT AND CLINICALLY-AFFIRMED HOSPITALIZED INCOMPETENT DEFENDANTS

	Classification Accuracy		
Analysis 1: JU/JT versus HI(C) Step/Predictors	Competent JU/JT	Incompetent HI(C)	Total
Step 1 – Demographic/Historical Variables	97.5%	11.5%	73.9%
Step 2 – Clinical Characteristics	92.3%	60.8%	83.6%
Step 3 – MacCAT-CA Measures	94.8%	74.1%	89.1%
Analysis 2: JT versus HI(C) Step/Predictors	Competent JT	Incompetent HI(C)	Total
Step 1 – Demographic/Historical Variables	85.6%	35.5%	65.3%
Step 2 – Clinical Characteristics	84.0%	67.5%	77.3%
Step 3 – MacCAT-CA Measures	88.9%	76.5%	83.9%

JU = Unscreened jail inmates; JT = Jail inmates receiving mental health services; HI = Hospitalized incompetent defendants; HI(C) = Clinically affirmed incompetent HI defendants.
Demographic/historical predictors included age, gender, race, education, and prior felony convictions. Clinical status predictors included BPRS-A factor subscales (psychoticism, depression, hostility, emotional withdrawal) and estimated WAIS-R IQ.
For the JU/JT vs. HI(C) analyses, $n = 605$. For the JT vs. HI(C) analyses, $n = 409$.

demographic/historical variables yielded correct classification in 65.3% of the cases; the great majority of JT defendants, but only about one-third of HI(C) defendants, were classified correctly. Adding clinical characteristics as predictors increased overall classification accuracy to 77.3%. A comparable percentage of JT defendants and about two-thirds of HI(C) defendants were classified correctly. Notably, addition of the MacCAT-CA further increased correct classifications to 83.9% overall, including almost 90% of criterion-competent and three-fourths of criterion-incompetent defendants. As in the preceding analyses, the incremental contribution of the MacCAT-CA measures to prediction using demographic and clinical characteristics was statistically significant, $\chi^2 (3, N = 409) = 92.8, p < .05$.

INTERPRETIVE NORMS FOR THE MACCAT-CA

The primary data for clinical interpretation of the MacCAT-CA are contained in Tables 5.11 through 5.13. These tables present the cumulative probability distributions and standardized distributions for different legally relevant groups with respect to the three psycholegal abilities measured by the MacCAT-CA. As depicted in the tables, for each measure, two cutting scores are recommended to guide clinical interpretation. These cut scores do not translate into a categorical "finding" of

TABLE 5.11. INTERPRETIVE NORMS FOR THE MacCAT-CA UNDERSTANDING MEASURE

	Presumed Competent (JU/JT groups)			Presumed Incompetent (HI) Group		
	Cumulative frequency	Percentile rank	Linear z	Cumulative frequency	Percentile rank	Linear z
Raw Score						
			Clinically-Significant Impairment			
0	0	0.0	−3.96	5	0.9	−2.17
1	2	0.2	−3.64	10	2.7	−1.94
2	3	0.6	−3.32	26	6.4	−1.70
3	6	1.0	−3.01	34	10.6	−1.46
4	11	1.9	−2.69	49	14.7	−1.22
5	24	3.9	−2.38	60	19.3	−0.98
6	31	6.2	−2.06	81	24.9	−0.74
7	41	8.1	−1.75	94	30.9	−0.50
			Mild Impairment			
8	57	11.0	−1.43	117	37.3	−0.26
9	71	14.3	−1.12	139	45.2	−0.03
			Minimal or No Impairment			
10	91	18.2	−0.80	166	53.9	0.21
11	120	23.7	−0.49	194	63.6	0.45
12	171	32.6	−0.17	214	72.1	0.69
13	227	44.6	0.15	238	79.9	0.93
14	311	60.3	0.46	253	86.7	1.17
15	379	77.4	0.78	269	92.2	1.41
16	446	92.5	1.09	283	97.5	1.64

For defendants presumed competent, $M = 12.54$; $SD = 3.17$; $SEM = 0.15$. For hospitalized incompetent defendants, $M = 9.11$; $SD = 4.19$; $SEM = 0.25$.

legal competence or incompetence. Rather, they are used to guide clinicians' judgments about the degree of impairment on the specific psycholegal ability represented in the table.

In each table, the normative interpretation for an individual whose score is equal to or greater than the higher cutting score is that he or she is unimpaired with respect to the psycholegal ability measured; for an individual whose score is equal to or less than the lower cutting score, the normative interpretation is that he or she is significantly impaired with respect to the psycholegal ability measured. Scores that fall between the two cutting scores in any given table represent a mild degree of impairment; the impact of performance in the mildly impaired range on judgments about competence will vary depending upon the legal context, specifics of the case, and other considerations. Such "gray area" scores should serve as a signal to the clinician for further exploration of the

TABLE 5.12. INTERPRETIVE NORMS FOR THE MACCAT-CA REASONING MEASURE

	Presumed Competent (JU/JT groups)			Presumed Incompetent (HI) Group		
	Cumulative frequency	Percentile rank	Linear z	Cumulative frequency	Percentile rank	Linear z
Raw Score						
		Clinically-Significant Impairment				
0	0	0.0	−4.68	7	1.2	−2.16
1	1	0.1	−4.33	11	3.2	−1.93
2	1	0.2	−3.97	19	5.3	−1.70
3	3	0.4	−3.61	29	8.5	−1.47
4	4	0.8	−3.25	46	13.3	−1.24
5	8	1.3	−2.89	65	19.6	−1.00
6	12	2.2	−2.53	84	26.3	−0.77
7	24	4.0	−2.18	97	32.0	−0.54
8	37	6.8	−1.82	117	37.8	−0.31
		Mild Impairment				
9	53	10.1	−1.46	134	44.3	−0.08
10	80	14.9	−1.10	156	51.2	0.16
		Minimal or No Impairment				
11	103	20.5	−0.74	179	59.2	0.39
12	152	28.6	−0.38	204	67.7	0.62
13	194	38.8	−0.03	225	75.8	0.85
14	276	52.7	0.33	244	82.9	1.08
15	360	71.3	0.69	271	91.0	1.32
16	446	90.4	1.05	283	97.9	1.55

For defendants presumed competent, Mean = 13.07; SD = 2.79; SEM = 0.13. For hospitalized incompetent defendants, Mean = 9.33; SD = 4.31; SEM = 0.26.

defendant's capacities during the remaining portions of the competence evaluation. As is described in more detail below, on the understanding and reasoning measures identical criteria were used to establish cutoffs. However, for theoretical and statistical reasons, a different rationale was used to establish cutoffs on the appreciation measure. Hence, the findings for the understanding and reasoning measures are discussed separately from the findings for the appreciation measure.

Interpretation of Scores on the Understanding and Reasoning Measures

Tables 5.11 and 5.12 present cumulative frequency distributions, percentile ranks, and linear z scores for the understanding and reasoning measures for various legally relevant defendant groups. To determine recommended cutoffs for describing normatively "impaired" and "unimpaired" performance on these measures, we adopted the conventional

TABLE 5.13. INTERPRETIVE NORMS FOR THE MACCAT-CA APPRECIATION MEASURE

	Presumed Competent (JU/JT groups)			Presumed Incompetent (HI) Group		
	Cumulative frequency	Percentile rank	Linear z	Cumulative frequency	Percentile rank	Linear z
Raw Score						
			Clinically-Significant Impairment			
0	1	0.1	−8.01	20	3.5	−1.97
1	1	0.2	−7.29	28	8.5	−1.72
2	2	0.3	−6.58	42	12.4	−1.47
3	2	0.4	−5.86	50	16.3	−1.22
4	2	0.4	−5.15	71	21.4	−0.97
5	4	0.7	−4.44	87	27.9	−0.72
6	6	1.1	−3.72	99	32.9	−0.47
7	13	2.1	−3.01	111	37.1	−0.22
8	21	3.8	−2.29	126	41.9	0.03
			Mild Impairment			
9	38	6.6	−1.58	146	48.1	0.28
10	88	14.1	−0.86	172	56.2	0.53
			Minimal or No Impairment			
11	176	29.6	−0.15	211	67.7	0.78
12	446	69.7	0.56	283	87.3	1.02

For defendants presumed competent, Mean = 11.21; SD = 1.40; SEM = 0.07. For hospitalized incompetent defendants, Mean = 7.89; SD = 4.01; SEM = 0.24.

strategy of examining the degree of departure (in standard deviation units – SDs) from the mean of presumptively competent defendants associated with each possible score for the measure.

The lower cutoff was set at −1.5 SDs from the mean of the presumed competent group. Scores that are at least 1.5 SDs below the mean of the presumed competent group on these measures are considered to reflect normatively impaired functioning (identified as "Clinically-Significant Impairment" in the tables). Our rationale for adopting this cutoff (rather than the more stringent 2 SDs below the mean) is based in part on research findings described in Chapter I, which indicate that although defense attorneys question their clients' competence between 8% and 15% of cases, referrals for competence evaluations are made in only about one-half of those cases. These findings suggest that research samples of incarcerated pretrial defendants will contain some inmates whose functional abilities are genuinely impaired and who may be incompetent, even though they are recruited into presumptively competent groups (such as our JU and JT groups).

The higher cutoff score on the MacCAT-CA measures was set at -1.0 SDs from the mean of the presumed competent group. Scores that are at or above this cutoff are considered to reflect normatively unimpaired functioning (identified as "Minimal or No Impairment" in the tables). Scores that fall between the two cutoffs ($-1.5\ SD < x < -1.0\ SD$) are considered to reflect "Mild Impairment" in the individual's functional capacities.

An inspection of Table 5.11 reveals that scores of 10 through 16 on the *Understanding* measure are at 1.0 or less *SDs* from the mean of the presumed competent group. The normative interpretation in this range is that a defendant exhibits minimal or no impairment with respect to understanding. This cutoff identified 84.1% of the presumed competent group and 50.9% of the HI group as unimpaired in understanding. The table also shows that scores of 0 through 7 are below the lower cutoff of -1.5 SD from the mean of the competent group. This cutoff identified 9.2% of the presumed competent group and 33.2% of the HI group as impaired in understanding. The remaining defendants, 6.7% and 15.9% of the JU/JT and HI groups, respectively, achieved scores of 8 or 9, which constitutes the mild range of impairment in understanding.

Similarly, Table 5.12 reveals that scores of 11 through 16 on the reasoning measure are 1.0 or more *SDs* below the mean of the competent group. For a score in this range, the normative interpretation is that a defendant exhibits minimal or no impairment in his or her capacity to reason about legally-relevant material. This cutoff identified 82.1% of the presumed competent group and 44.9% of the HI group as unimpaired in reasoning ability. Scores of 0 through 8 are more than 1.5 *SDs* below the mean of the presumed competent group; scores in this range are thought to reflect clinically-significant impairment in reasoning capacity. This cutoff identified 8.3% of the presumed competent group and 41.3% of the HI group as impaired in reasoning ability. Based on these cutoffs, scores of 9 or 10 constitute the mild range of impairment on the reasoning measure. This degree of normative impairment was exhibited by 9.6% and 13.8% of the JU/JT and HI groups, respectively.

Interpretation of Scores on the Appreciation Measure

Table 5.13 presents cumulative frequency distributions, percentile ranks, and linear z scores on the appreciation measure for two legally-relevant groups: defendants presumed competent and hospitalized incompetent defendants. Although we contemplated applying the criteria used with the understanding and reasoning measures to the appreciation measure in order to characterize the degree of impairment reflected by different scores, the considerations described below prompted the research team to adopt a different strategy.

First, we considered that the cognitive and mental activities that underlie appreciation are significantly different from those assessed by the understanding and reasoning measures. Performance on understanding items primarily involves prior exposure to, and memory for, specific legally-relevant information. Either a history of personal involvement in the system (e.g., having been previously arrested and prosecuted) or vicarious exposure (e.g., media portrayals of the adjudicatory process, high school civics classes) may provide such exposure. To some extent, performance on the reasoning items draws on these same abilities. In addition, however, reasoning items also involve the ability to apply logic to discern relevant (from less irrelevant) information, and to make correct inferences and deductions.

In contrast, appreciation is most likely to be impaired when a person's fundamental beliefs and assumptions about the legal system and his or her involvement in it are faulty as the result of mental disorder. Indeed, appreciation items are constructed in such a way as to solicit faulty reasoning secondary to irrational (delusional) beliefs. Significant delusional thinking with respect to any single aspect of the adjudicatory process may be sufficient to justify a judicial determination of incompetence (underscoring the importance for clinicians to note and further investigate any responses to appreciation items that earn 0 credit). Further, notwithstanding that some individuals present relatively encapsulated delusional beliefs, marked thought disorder or delusional thinking are logically more likely to impact one's beliefs and one's thinking across multiple legal issues (i.e., to contaminate one's performance on related problems). Thus, the appreciation measure is more likely to function as a dichotomous variable, and the psycholegal ability is more likely to be "impaired" or "not."

Findings from the norming study are consistent with this conceptualization of appreciation. Among defendants presumed competent, the distribution of scores on the appreciation measure was more highly skewed and leptokurtic than were the distributions of scores on the understanding and reasoning measures. Among HI defendants, the distribution of appreciation scores approximated a bimodal distribution, with scores clustering at the extremes of the distribution.

Because of the limited variability in appreciation scores among defendants presumed competent, using the criteria for cutting scores employed with understanding and reasoning measures would have produced only two clusters of scores—those indicating clinically-significant impairment in appreciation and those indicating minimal or no impairment. But given the lower interscorer reliability and greater measurement error of individual items, it was considered desirable to retain a "Mild Impairment" range in order to reduce the risk of erroneously classifying an unimpaired examinee as significantly impaired and vice versa.

In light of these considerations, the statistical criteria used to identify cutoff scores and demarcate regions of impairment in understanding and reasoning were modified for use with the appreciation measure. As shown in Table 5.13, scores of 11 or 12 on the appreciation measure reflect minimal or no impairment in this domain of competence, whereas scores in the 0 to 8 range suggest significant impairment. Scores of 9 or 10 are considered to reflect questionable impairment in this domain. However, because of the potential significance of failure on an appreciation item, whenever a defendant's response to an item earns a score of 0, clinicians should inspect response content closely. When closer inspection of the response makes it clear that the score of 0 resulted from delusional or other disordered thinking (as opposed to inadequate effort or failure to respond), further clinical inquiry may justify concluding that the defendant's capacity to appreciate his or her own legal situation is significantly impaired, even though the total score may fall in the Mildly Impaired range.

Using the recommended cutoffs noted above, 80.3% of the presumed competent group and 39.2% of the HI group were classified as unimpaired in their capacity to appreciate legally-relevant information. In addition, 4.7% of the presumed competent group and 44.5% of the HI group were classified as significantly impaired. Finally, appreciation scores for 15.0% of the JU/JT and 16.3% of the HI defendants fell between these two extremes, suggesting mild impairment in their ability to appreciate their legal situations.

PREDICTION/CLASSIFICATION PERFORMANCE CHARACTERISTICS

Tables 5.14 through 5.16 display the prediction/classification performance characteristics for the understanding, reasoning, and appreciation measures, respectively. At each score level for each measure, the overall classification accuracy (hit rate), sensitivity and specificity, false positive and false negative rates, and positive and negative predictive powers are provided.

The figures in Tables 5.14 through 5.16 probably represent lower end estimates of the predictive and classification utility of the MacCAT-CA. We have noted earlier concerns about the heterogeneity of the HI group and ways that defendants with little or no impairment in competence-related abilities may be recruited into that group. At the same time, agitated defendants whose acute psychiatric symptoms produce significant impairment in competence-related abilities may be excluded from such

TABLE 5.14. PREDICTIVE POWER OF THE MACCAT-CA UNDERSTANDING MEASURE FOR COMPETENT (JU/JT) AND INCOMPETENT (HI) DEFENDANTS USING DIFFERENT CUTOFF SCORES

Scale Score	Hit Rate	SENS	SPEC	FPR	FNR	PPP	NPP
0	.621	.025	1.000	.000	.975	1.000	.618
1	.624	.039	.996	.004	.961	.846	.620
2	.634	.067	.993	.007	.933	.864	.627
3	.643	.102	.987	.013	.898	.829	.634
4	.660	.163	.975	.025	.837	.807	.647
5	.668	.230	.946	.054	.770	.730	.659
6	.684	.297	.930	.070	.703	.730	.676
7	.689	.343	.908	.092	.657	.703	.685
8	.694	.413	.872	.128	.587	.672	.701
9	.698	.473	.841	.159	.527	.654	.716
10	.701	.551	.796	.204	.449	.632	.737
11	.693	.633	.731	.269	.367	.599	.758
12	.657	.721	.617	.383	.279	.544	.777
13	.609	.795	.491	.509	.205	.498	.791
14	.520	.862	.303	.697	.138	.440	.776
15	.464	.958	.150	.850	.042	.417	.848
16	.388	1.000	.000	1.000	.000	.388	—

SENS = Sensitivity. SPEC = Specificity. FPR = False Positive Rate. FNR = False Negative Rate. PPP = Positive Predictive Power. NPP = Negative Predictive Power.

research participation by hospital staff due to concerns for the safety of research assistants. These factors result in a research group of HI subjects that is more like the JU/JT participants than would be a truly representative group of incompetent defendants.

PATTERNS OF IMPAIRMENT ACROSS DOMAINS OF PSYCHOLEGAL ABILITY

Table 5.17 presents information regarding the percentages of competent and incompetent defendants who exhibited clinically-significant impairment on individual MacCAT-CA measures or combinations of those measures. Separate percentages are reported for all HI defendants as well as for the subset of HI defendants whose incompetence was clinically-affirmed by a member of the forensic hospital staff (HI(C)).

The last column of the table provides estimates of the positive predictive power associated with different patterns of impairment. Inspection of the table reveals that only about 15% of defendants presumed competent exhibited clinically-significant impairment in any domain or combination of domains assessed by the MacCAT-CA. Given our definition of clinically-significant impairment and findings from research described in

DEVELOPMENT OF THE MacCAT-CA

TABLE 5.15. PREDICTIVE POWER OF THE MacCAT-CA REASONING MEASURE FOR COMPETENT (JU/JT) AND INCOMPETENT (HI) DEFENDANTS USING DIFFERENT CUTOFF SCORES

Scale Score	Hit Rate	SENS	SPEC	FPR	FNR	PPP	NPP
0	.621	.025	1.000	.000	.975	1.000	.618
1	.626	.039	.998	.002	.961	.917	.621
2	.636	.067	.998	.002	.933	.950	.628
3	.647	.102	.993	.007	.898	.906	.636
4	.669	.163	.991	.009	.837	.920	.651
5	.690	.230	.982	.018	.770	.890	.668
6	.711	.297	.973	.027	.703	.875	.686
7	.712	.343	.946	.054	.657	.802	.694
8	.722	.413	.917	.083	.587	.760	.711
9	.723	.473	.881	.119	.527	.717	.725
10	.716	.551	.821	.179	.449	.661	.742
11	.716	.633	.769	.231	.367	.635	.767
12	.683	.721	.659	.341	.279	.573	.788
13	.654	.795	.565	.435	.205	.537	.813
14	.568	.862	.381	.619	.138	.469	.813
15	.490	.958	.193	.807	.042	.429	.878
16	.388	1.000	.000	1.000	.000	.388	—

SENS = Sensitivity; SPEC = Specificity; FPR = False Positive Rate; FNR = False Negative Rate; PPP = Positive Predictive Power; NPP = Negative Predictive Power.

TABLE 5.16. PREDICTIVE POWER OF THE MacCAT-CA APPRECIATION MEASURE FOR COMPETENT (JU/JT) AND INCOMPETENT (HI) DEFENDANTS USING DIFFERENT CUTOFF SCORES

Scale Score	Hit Rate	SENS	SPEC	FPR	FNR	PPP	NPP
0	.638	.071	.998	.002	.929	.952	.629
1	.649	.099	.998	.002	.901	.966	.636
2	.667	.148	.996	.004	.852	.955	.648
3	.678	.177	.996	.004	.823	.961	.656
4	.706	.251	.996	.004	.749	.973	.677
5	.726	.307	.991	.009	.693	.956	.693
6	.739	.350	.987	.013	.650	.943	.705
7	.746	.392	.971	.029	.608	.895	.716
8	.756	.445	.953	.047	.555	.857	.730
9	.760	.516	.915	.085	.484	.793	.749
10	.727	.608	.803	.197	.392	.662	.763
11	.660	.746	.605	.395	.254	.545	.789
12	.388	1.000	.000	1.000	.000	.388	—

SENS = Sensitivity; SPEC = Specificity; FPR = False Positive Rate; FNR = False Negative Rate; PPP = Positive Predictive Power; NPP = Negative Predictive Power.

TABLE 5.17. PERCENTAGES OF DEFENDANTS SHOWING IMPAIRMENT IN SPECIFIC
ABILITIES AND COMBINATIONS OF ABILITIES ASSESSED BY THE MACCAT-CA MEASURES

Abilities Impaired	Competency status				
	JU/JT n (%)	HI n (%)	HI(C) n (%)	PPP_1	PPP_2
None	380 (85.2%)	106 (37.5%)	40 (23.5%)		
Understanding (only)	18 (4.0%)	13 (4.6%)	6 (3.5%)	.42	.25
Reasoning (only)	16 (3.6%)	19 (6.7%)	9 (5.3%)	.54	.36
Appreciation (only)	8 (1.8%)	45 (15.9%)	34 (20.0%)	.85	.81
Understanding & Reasoning	11 (2.5%)	19 (6.7%)	14 (8.2%)	.63	.56
Understanding & Appreciation	3 (0.7%)	2 (0.7%)	2 (1.2%)	.40	.40
Reasoning & Appreciation	1 (0.2%)	19 (6.7%)	15 (8.8%)	.95	.94
Understanding & Reasoning & Appreciation	9 (2.0%)	60 (21.2%)	50 (29.4%)	.87	.85

See text for definitions of impaired capacity.
JU/JT = combined sample of unscreened jail defendants and defendants receiving mental health treatment in jail; HI = hospitalized incompetent defendants; HI(C) = clinically-affirmed hospitalized incompetent defendants.
PPP_1 = Positive Predictive Power associated with discrimination of HI and JU/JT defendants;
PPP_2 = Positive Predictive Power associated with discrimination of HI(C) and JU/JT defendants.

Chapter 1 regarding defense attorneys' willingness to go forward with defendants whose competence is doubted, this finding is not surprising. Conversely, more than 60% of HI defendants exhibited impairment in one or more of the MacCAT-CA domains, and that percentage increased to more than 75% when only clinically-affirmed HI defendants were considered. Nevertheless, even among HI(C) defendants, almost 25% do not show significant impairment in any of the psycholegal abilities measured by the MacCAT-CA measures.

Another noteworthy observation regarding the data presented in the table is that clinically-significant impairment (as we have defined it) in either understanding or reasoning alone is not predictive of findings of incompetence (i.e., positive predictive power or PPP < .5). In addition, impairment in both understanding and appreciation also yields a PPP of below .5; however, this latter result is perhaps attributable to the rarity of such a combination of impairments. In contrast, every other pattern of impairment involving capacities assessed by the appreciation measure—whether alone, in combination with impairment in reasoning, or in combination with impairment in capacities assessed by both the understanding and reasoning measures—is strongly predictive of findings of incompetence (i.e., PPPs of greater than .85).

DISCUSSION

CLINICAL UTILITY OF THE MACCAT-CA

The MacCAT-CA was conceived and constructed as a clinical tool that offers significant improvements over the previously available measures for use in competence to proceed evaluations. Several important features were incorporated in the MacCAT-CA that, collectively, distinguish it from other available competence assessment instruments. These include: (1) derivation of item content from a comprehensive theory of legal competence; (2) assessment of multiple psycholegal abilities (understanding, reasoning, and appreciation) via scales constructed using a "bottom-up" procedure (Bagby, Nicholson, Rogers, & Nussbaum, 1992); (3) assessment of the capacity to assimilate new information, in addition to present knowledge about the legal system; (4) standardized administration, (5) objective, criterion-referenced scoring, and (6) availability of normative data for purposes of comparison.

The primary purpose of the NIMH-sponsored norming study was to establish the psychometric properties of the MacCAT-CA and develop interpretive norms to guide forensic examiners who might use this instrument in evaluations of adjudicative competence. The findings suggest that the MacCAT-CA measures of understanding, reasoning, and appreciation have good interrater reliability and strong internal consistency, as well as evidence of construct validity (expected patterns of correlation with measures of cognitive ability, psychopathology, and clinical judgments of degree of impaired competence).

The psychometric properties of the MacCAT-CA compare favorably with those reported for other measures of adjudicative competence (Melton et al., 1997, Table 6.4; Nicholson, 1993), such as the 22-item Competency Screening Test (CST; Lipsitt, Lelos, & McGarry, 1971) and the 21-item Georgia Court Competency Test-Mississippi State Hospital revision (GCCT-MSH; Nicholson, Briggs, & Robinson, 1988). Although the individual MacCAT-CA measures contain fewer items, they produced estimates of internal consistency reliability that are similar to those reported for the other competency measures. In addition, the effect sizes associated with differences between competent and incompetent defendants on the MacCAT-CA measures are comparable to those obtained with the CST and GCCT-MSH. A meta-analysis of studies comparing the performance of competent and incompetent defendants on these measures yielded a mean effect size of 1.05 SDs across six studies ($n = 429$) involving the CST and a mean effect size of 1.20 SDs across four studies ($n = 539$) involving the GCCT (Nicholson & Kugler, 1991). In the present study, effect sizes for the MacCAT-CA scales ranged from almost 1 SD for comparisons with all incompetent defendants to more than 1.5 SDS for comparisons with clinically-affirmed incompetent defendants. Interestingly, the understanding measure, which covers information similar to that assessed by other knowledge-based competency measures (e.g., the characteristics of criminal prosecution and defense, the nature of criminal charges, the consequences of conviction), tended to yield smaller effects than the reasoning and appreciation measures, which tap domains of competence-related abilities not assessed by other measures.

In addition to making meaningful distinctions between groups of (presumed) competent and adjudicated incompetent defendants, we conducted a series of logistic regression analyses to evaluate the utility of the MacCAT-CA in classifying individual (competent or incompetent) defendants. Each series involved sequential (hierarchical) entry of predictor classes (demographic variables, clinical status characteristics, and MacCAT-CA measures), permitting examination of the incremental contribution of the MacCAT-CA measures to prediction of competency group membership. Findings from these analyses indicated that the MacCAT-CA measures have some ability to predict competency status. Perhaps the most powerful and fairest test of the utility of the MacCAT-CA measures was provided by the logistic regression analyses involving the defendants receiving mental health treatment in jail (JT) and the clinically-affirmed hospitalized incompetent defendants (HI(C)). Discrimination of JT from incompetent defendants offered a stronger challenge to the predictive power of the MacCAT-CA measures, and exclusion of HI defendants whose psychological improvements were not clinically-affirmed increased the likelihood that adjudicated incompetent defendants constituted a genuinely impaired subsample. As Table 5.10 reveals, almost 90% of the JT defendants and more than 75% of the HI(C) defendants could be classified correctly using the demographic/historical, clinical status, and MacCAT-CA predictors. Moreover, the MacCAT-CA measures made a significant incremental contribution to classification accuracy based on demographic/historical and clinical status characteristics alone, increasing classification accuracy by 5% among competent defendants and 9% among incompetent defendants.

In Tables 5.11 through 5.13 we presented distributions of scores on the MacCAT-CA measures for defendants who are presumed competent and those who have been adjudicated incompetent to proceed, and we suggested cutoffs and ranges of scores for characterizing a defendant's psycholegal abilities as significantly impaired, mildly impaired, or not impaired. This is the first multi-state, large sample study to develop interpretive norms for an adjudicative competence measure. These normative data, along with the additional information in Table 5.20 regarding patterns of significant impairment across these psycholegal abilities for presumed competent and incompetent defendants, should facilitate forensic examiners' interpretation of defendants' performance on the MacCAT-CA and inform clinical judgments regarding defendants' abilities to understand, reason about, and appreciate legally relevant information.

CAUTIONS IN THE USE OF THE MACCAT-CA TO ASSESS "COMPETENCE"

Although the MacCAT-CA will be useful in evaluating criminal defendants whose competence has been questioned, it is not offered as a measure of legal competence *per se*. Indeed, for a variety of reasons we caution potential users of this instrument not to rely on individual cutoffs or combinations of cutoffs as a basis for declaring a defendant to be, categorically, "competent" or "incompetent." Rather, the optimal (and intended) use of the MacCAT-CA results and the norms is to enable clinicians to a) characterize a defendant's degree of impairment in discrete psycholegal abilities, and b) describe the defendant's overall pattern of performance relative to a relevant comparison group.

As data in Table 5.20 indicate, even among clinically-affirmed hospitalized incompetent defendants, almost 25% did not exhibit significant impairment (as we have defined it) in any of the psycholegal abilities measured by the instrument. Even among defendants who scored in the significantly impaired range on all three measures, about 15% might be false positives if declared "incompetent" on that pattern of performance alone.

Although false positive and false negative rates will vary as a function of base rate in research samples, other considerations further militate against using the MacCAT-CA to make dichotomous judgments about competence. For example, there are assumptions embedded in the structure and scoring of the MacCAT-CA (e.g., that each item is weighted equally in evaluating capacity) that may be at odds with the calculus used by judges or juries to determine competence. As noted at the end of Chapter 3, there are psycholegal abilities (e.g., memory for specific events related to one's own case) legal demands (e.g., comportment of one's behavior in court with expected norms), and non-psychological factors (e.g., legal complexity of the case) that a court may consider in making the categorical judgment about "competence." Courts may even take into consideration social and political factors (e.g., the needs of the community for getting closure on a particular case) unrelated to either clinical factors or explicit legal criteria that clinicians might aspire to assess.

In light of these considerations, we believe that a purely objective clinical test of adjudicative competence is neither possible nor desirable. Following Morse (1978) and others, legal categories generally involve judgments about the sufficiency or adequacy of competence-related abilities that must take into account social and moral considerations that stand outside the realm of scientific inquiry. For these reasons we have not attempted to combine the MacCAT-CA's indices of understanding, reasoning, and appreciation into a single index that would indicate a defendant's categorical status regarding adjudicative competence.

As Grisso (1987) noted, political and financial influences on professional practice have driven clinicians to offer such categorical opinions even in the absence of a sound scientific basis for doing so, and the deriving of such "ultimate opinions" has been defended in some academic circles (Rogers & Ewing, 1989). Recognizing that the realities of forensic practice will lead some clinicians to offer such categorical findings, our position guards against this being done on the basis of MacCAT-CA data alone. The MacCAT-CA, is not a "stand alone" instrument that, in and of itself, constitutes a competence evaluation. Rather, when used as part of a comprehensive evaluation that includes information regarding relevant history (e.g., psychiatric history), current mental status, case-specific memories and details of the defendant's current charges, the defendant's understanding of courtroom procedure and protocol, and the defendant's "test-taking set,"[7] the MacCAT-CA should enhance the thoroughness and quality of clinical investigations of adjudicative competence. Grounded in a comprehensive theory of adjudicative competence, the MacCAT-CA offers the additional features of standardized administration and criterion-related scoring that are missing from many contemporary interview-based measures and may lead to better informed judgments of competence whether rendered by forensic practitioners or legal triers-of-fact.

---

[7]As in other forensic assessment contexts, the possibility of impression management or malingering by defendants is a consideration in competence evaluations. The MacCAT-CA does not contain validity scales for assessing degree of effort or validity of responding, and clinicians must rely on collateral testing or other techniques to assess the examinee's approach to the assessment process.

6

New Research on Adjudicative Competence

The program of research on adjudicative competence begun by the MacArthur Network and continued under the sponsorship of NIMH has provided a new conceptual framework and new instrumentation that have been well received in the field. The substantive features (i.e., assesses multiple competence-related abilities across two conceptually distinct competence domains) and the structural features (i.e., standardized administration and scoring; norm referenced interpretation) of the MacCAT-CA have made it an increasingly popular tool for mental health professionals conducting evaluations for attorneys and courts; it is also being used widely as a research tool in an era of rejuvenated interest in adjudicative competence research.

In closing this volume we describe briefly several areas of research currently planned or underway using the MacCAT-CA. These include studies of competence-related abilities in populations other than the adult criminal population on which the MacCAT-CA was normed, and studies that evaluate the performance or utility of the MacCAT-CA with adult criminal defendants in other countries.

THE COMPETENCE-RELATED ABILITIES OF YOUTH IN JUVENILE COURT

The juvenile court system in the United States came into existence around the turn of the last century and evolved around a philosophy of rehabilitation for troubled youth. The court's explicit focus has always been on treatment rather than retribution, and disposition in juvenile court has historically attempted to link youth and their families with psychological or social services that provided the best opportunity to interrupt a trajectory of career delinquency and facilitate prosocial attitudes and behavior in the juvenile. In the past half-century the juvenile court process has gradually become somewhat more formalized as many of the rights and protections enjoyed by adult defendants have been extended to youth (*Kent v. U.S.*, 1966; *In re Gault*, 1967). Nevertheless, juvenile courts have remained primarily rehabilitative in their orientation and, in this environment, adjudicative competence has rarely been a salient issue. Until recently, many states had no explicit statutes that addressed adjudicative competence at the juvenile court level, and on the rare instances in which a youth's capacities to proceed have been raised, it is likely that procedures and criteria in place for adults became the *de facto* parameters for clinical assessments and competence determinations with youth.

The competence-related abilities of youth in juvenile court has become a much more salient issue in the past decade (Sickmund, 1994; see generally, Grisso & Schwartz, 2000). Waiver to adult court, at the discretion of the juvenile court judge following a hearing, has always been an available but infrequently exercised option for those youth deemed not amenable to treatment and needing adult sanctions in order to satisfy public safety concerns. A rising tide of juvenile offending, and particularly violent offending, through the middle of the last decade led policy makers to adopt a "get-tough-on-crime" posture that has resulted in more punishment-oriented juvenile justice system and increased efforts by the state to transfer seriously delinquent youth from juvenile court to criminal court (Fagan & Zimring, 2000; Redding, 1997). Simultaneously, the lower age limit for criminal court jurisdiction has been decreased radically in some instances, with some statutes providing for the transfer of pre-teens to adult court for certain offenses. Because of the requirement that defendants be competent to participate in *all* proceedings associated with the adjudicatory process, adjudicative competence has become a more salient issue both for delinquency proceedings themselves and for participation in transfer hearings for waiver to adult court (McGaha, Otto, McClaven, & Petrila, 2001).

In contemplating the structure of adult adjudicative competence criteria that are extended to youth on a formal (i.e., through legislation) or *de facto* basis, a number of commentators have found them to be flawed. The predicate conditions commonly acknowledged in the law for impaired competence are mental illness and mental retardation and, as the research in Chapters 3 and 5 illustrates, it is usually more severe mental disorder (e.g., psychotic symptomatology) that results in impairment of legally relevant proportions. Some legal theorists and developmental psychologists (e.g., Cauffman & Steinberg, 1996; Cauffman, Woolard, & Reppucci, 1999; Grisso, 1997a,b; Scott & Grisso, 1997; Scott, Reppucci, & Woolard, 1995; Steinberg & Cauffman, 1996) however, have raised the issue of developmental immaturity as a condition of youth and adolescence that may well limit their functional legal abilities required for competent participation in the adjudicatory process. Cognitive and psychosocial deficits, rather than mental illness or mental retardation, may "cause" some youth to be incompetent to proceed.

Existing research provides some support for the developmental immaturity hypothesis (Cooper, 1997; Cowden & McKee, 1995; McGaha et al., 2001; McKee, 1998; Savitsky & Karras, 1984), although the age at which youths' capacities tend to become indistinguishable from adults' remains unclear. Other things being equal (e.g., IQ, absence of psychopathology), the literature suggests that up to about age 14 the competence-related abilities of youth are inferior to those of adults, while youth 15 years of age and older tend to have capacities more comparable to those of adults.

Because of limitations in the measures of competence-related abilities employed and other design limitations in prior studies, there is a dire need for further investigation of these issues. Two recent studies have used the MacCAT-CA as a criterion measure to explore the competence-related abilities of youth. Rutherford (2000) recruited 70 youths awaiting disposition in the juvenile justice system from detention facilities in North Carolina and Mississippi and compared their scores on the MacCAT-CA with those of 40 non-delinquent youth (controls) recruited from the community, and with the scores of the JU group from the NIMH-funded study in which norms for the MacCAT-CA were developed (Chapter 5). Rutherford found that, controlling for group differences in estimated IQ and demographic variables (e.g., SES, family criminal history), scores on the understanding and reasoning measures were significantly lower in the detention center sample than in the control sample (the appreciation measure was not administered to the control youth).

For a second analysis the combined samples were divided into age groups of 10–12 ($n = 18$), 13–14 ($n = 36$), 15–16 ($n = 51$), and age 17 ($n = 5$). Significant differences were found among the groups' mean scores on the reasoning and appreciation measures, and a trend ($p < .10$) was observed for differences among means on the understanding measure. Except for the mean score of the 17 year old group on the appreciation measure (11.23) being slightly lower than that of the 15–16 year old group (11.43), in every instance MacCAT-CA scores increased from one age bracket to the next higher. Generally, similar findings were obtained when the relationship between age group and MacCAT-CA performance was examined separately for the two groups. Finally, comparisons with the adult JU group from the norming sample revealed that mean scores for the combined youth groups were significantly lower on all three MacCAT-CA measures. Analyses comparing the mean scores for youth in different age groups with those of the JU adults revealed significantly lower scores on the understanding and reasoning measures for youth in age brackets 10–12, 13–14, and 15–16; on the appreciation measures significantly lower mean scores were obtained by the 10–12 and 13–14 age groups.

In another study, Warren and Lexcen (2001) employed the MacCAT-CA as a measure of competence-related abilities to examine the capacities of 126 male juveniles in an inpatient psychiatric facility in Virginia. The investigators used age as a proxy for developmental maturity and compared MacCAT-CA scores for youth across three age brackets: 8–13 ($n = 45$), 14–15 ($n = 40$), and 16–17 ($n = 41$). Performance across age groups increased for each of the MacCAT-CA measures. The groups' mean scores ranged from 8.95 to 12.05 on the understanding measure, from 10.84 to 13.41 on the reasoning measure, and from 9.19 to 10.19 on the appreciation measure. In a multivariate analysis of variance that compared these three groups' means and the mean of the adult JU group in the norming sample (Chapter 5), statistically significant differences were obtained for each measure.

Rutherford's findings, as well as those of Warren and Lexcen, provide evidence for a positive relationship between age and functional legal ability, at least through mid adolescence (about age 15) at which point juveniles' performance becomes more comparable to that of adults (although considerable individual differences exist among youth at any given age). Suggestive as these studies are, however, both are limited in terms of their use of age as a proxy for developmental maturity; neither of them employed any measures of specific cognitive or psychosocial constructs (e.g., judgment, risk taking) that might shed light on the specific developmental mechanisms that might adversely impact competence.

In this regard, a somewhat more sophisticated investigation of the developmental immaturity hypothesis is currently underway by the MacArthur Foundation Research Network on Adolescent Development and Juvenile Justice (Laurence Steinberg, Network Director).[1] In this multi-site study,

---

[1] Hereinafter we will refer to this as the Juvenile Justice Network to distinguish it from the original Research Network on Mental Health and the Law. Further information about the Juvenile Justice Network can be found at http://www.mac-adoldev-juvjustice.org/

stratified samples of youth at various ages both from the juvenile justice system (juvenile detention facilities) and local schools in the same communities (non-delinquent controls) are being recruited as research participants. In addition to using age as one potential indicator of developmental maturity, the research protocol employs a battery of measures designed to assess specific cognitive and psychosocial abilities (e.g., judgment; risk taking) that developmental theory suggests should affect the functional legal abilities associated with adjudicative competence. Again, the MacCAT-CA is being employed as the criterion measure for these capacities. At this writing data analysis is just beginning; dissemination of the results of this Network's investigation should begin in 2002.

Research such as that conducted by Warren and Lexcen (2001) and the MacArthur Youth Network will enhance our understanding of the competence-related abilities of youth and, in all likelihood, provide critical empirical data that may guide future policy makers in decisions regarding the most appropriate procedures to use when questions of adjudicative competence arise regarding delinquent youth. In its role as the criterion measure, the MacCAT-CA is contributing to these efforts to explore developmental hypotheses and provide policy-relevant research regarding the competence-related capacities of youth.

At the same time—and this is a point acknowledged both by us and these investigators—the MacCAT-CA is limited in this role because it is a measure of capacities related to prosecution in the criminal court context. In terms of face validity, the content of several MacCAT-CA items (see Table 5.1) pertain to legal actors (e.g., juries), dispositions (i.e., possible finding of "guilt"), and outcomes (e.g., adult sanctions such as jail or prison) that are not directly applicable to delinquency proceedings. Perhaps more problematic is the conceptual framework that underlies scoring of the appreciation measure. This measure was designed to identify irrational beliefs, stemming from psychopathological process, about how one might be treated in the legal system. Impairment on appreciation items should ordinarily reflect delusional or disorganized thinking that can be attributed to a mental disorder (usually psychosis). As these symptoms and disorders occur infrequently in adolescents, this scoring framework should be of limited relevance in most youth samples. Yet, youth do often give responses to appreciation items that seem facially implausible, and this creates potential scoring difficulties that may have contributed to poor internal consistency indices for appreciation (Cronbach α <.6), in some studies (see Boyd, 1999; Grisso, personal communication). This raises questions about the utility of the appreciation measure with adolescents, at least in research that investigates the developmental immaturity hypothesis.

In our opinion, current investigators cognizant of this limitation are justified in selecting the MacCAT-CA for their research because the field does not have available a comparably validated and normed instrument that is tailored to the juvenile justice context. This, however, serves to illuminate a gap in the field that future investigators will have to fill. Whether modeled on the MacCAT-CA or developed *de novo*, a measure assessing the competence-related abilities of youth, suitable for both research and clinical applications in the juvenile justice context, is badly needed.

THE COMPETENCE-RELATED ABILITIES OF YOUTH IN CRIMINAL COURT

As noted above, over the past decade many adolescents, whose antisocial behavior would historically have been dealt with in the rehabilitation-oriented confines of delinquency proceedings in juvenile court, have been transferred in drastically increasing numbers to adult criminal court for disposition of their cases. Historically the mechanism for transfer to adult court has been through a waiver hearing in the juvenile court. In recent years many states have supplemented the discretionary waiver process by enacting legislation that (a) mandates the transfer of youth to adult court for certain severe offenses, and (b) provides for direct filing of charges in adult court at the sole discretion of the state attorney for other specific offenses (or for youth who are chronic offenders) (Heilbrun, Leheny, Thomas, & Huneycutt, 1997). Due to parallel reductions in the statutory age limit for criminal court jurisdiction, youth as young as eleven years of age and charged with serious crimes (i.e., murder) have been subjected to prosecution in adult court.

These changes in policy have occurred in the absence of information about the functional legal abilities of adolescents, and a natural extension of the research described above is the examination of those abilities in youth waived or direct filed into criminal court. Boyd (1999) reported findings from a preliminary study of 88 adolescent males ages 13 to 17 who were charged with felony offenses in criminal court in North Carolina. For purpose of analysis she divided her subjects into three age groups: 15 and younger ($n = 28$), 16 ($n = 30$), and 17 ($n = 17$). The mean scores on the understanding, reasoning, and appreciation measures of the MacCAT-CA were compared among these groups and with the mean scores of 30 adult defendants (age < 40) randomly selected from the Jail Unscreened (JU) sample of the MacCAT-CA norming study (Chapter 5).

Contrary to the developmental hypothesis, which would predict a linear relationship between age and MacCAT-CA performance, Boyd found no significant differences among the groups' mean scores on MacCAT-CA measures; the performance of youth at all age brackets was comparable to that of the adult defendants. These results provide perhaps some comfort that most youth in criminal court have capacities (at least those measured by the MacCAT-CA) comparable to those of adults. There are two noteworthy limitations to this research, however. First, Boyd had relatively few younger adolescents as research participants (for her youngest group, the mean age was 15.1 years, $SD = 9.47$ months). If, as previous research suggests, the age at which youths' capacities become comparable with those of adult is around age 15, then her findings are not informative regarding the competence-related abilities of younger defendants who commit serious offenses and are tried as adults. Second, overall the MacCAT-CA did not perform well in this study. Although interrater reliability was good (intraclass correlations range .88 to .90 for the three MacCAT-CA measures), internal consistencies (alphas range = .33 to .54) and mean inter-item correlations (range = .07 to .13) were well below acceptable levels.

The MacArthur Juvenile Justice Network's adjudicative competence study will also employ the MacCAT-CA to investigate the competence-related abilities of youth in adult court. Data collection is currently underway and it is anticipated that about 150 youth will be recruited into this research sample. Although it is fortunate that few very young adolescents (age < 14) are committing serious offenses and are being tried in adult court in the jurisdictions where data are being collected, once again the paucity of such youth in the research sample will limit what will be learned about the capacities of such defendants. The Network's study, however will provide more information about the utility of the MacCAT-CA with this population and the relationship between developmental factors (e.g., judgment, risk-taking) and legal capacities in older adolescents tried as adults.

THE MacCAT-CA AND DEFENDANTS WITH MENTAL RETARDATION

Another topic ripe for exploration is the utility of the MacCAT-CA with defendants who are mentally retarded. Mentally retarded individuals were excluded from participation in the MacArthur field studies (Chapter 3) and MacCAT-CA norming study (Chapter 5). However, it would be interesting to compare the performance of the MacCAT-CA with other measures designed for the assessment of competence-related abilities in this population, such as the CAST:MR (Everington & Luckasson,

1992). Interestingly, such research might be more critical with adolescent defendant populations, as mental retardation is a frequently occurring diagnosis among youth adjudicated incompetent (McGaha et al., 2001).

COMPETENCE ASSESSMENT IN OTHER COUNTRIES

As noted in Chapters 3 and 5, the MacCAT-CA was crafted specifically to assess competence-related abilities relevant to the criteria for adjudicative competence in the United States (see Table 3.1). However, the U.S. shares a common legal heritage with other countries (Australia, Canada, England) and at least some components of the MacCAT-CA, if not the instrument in its entirety, might prove useful in competence assessments in some of those countries.

Such research has been underway in London for the past several years, where Akinkunmi and colleagues (2001) have made minor modifications to the MacCAT-CA in order to adapt the instrument to the legal criteria for "fitness to stand trial" in England and Wales. These criteria, established in *R. v. Pritchard* (1836), focus on "whether he [the defendant] can plead to the indictment or not ... whether he is of sufficient intellect to comprehend the course of proceedings of the trial ... [and] to know that he might challenge (jurors) to who whom he may object and to comprehend the details of the evidence." The British research version of the instrument is called the MacArthur Competence Assessment Tool – Fitness to Plead (MacCAT-FP) and retains the general structure of the MacCAT-CA, yielding separate scores on measures of understanding, reasoning, and appreciation.

Initial research using the MacCAT-FP has compared the performance of two groups of criminal defendants. The hospital group ($n = 45$) included 41 men and 4 women charged with criminal offenses, who had been admitted to one of three London Forensic Psychiatric Units having been judged in need of urgent hospital treatment under provisions of Sections 48/49 of the Mental Health Act of 1983. The comparison group consisted of 60 pretrial defendants (all males) randomly selected from a London prison. All participants completed the MacCAT-FP, and for each participant in the hospital group a global opinion regarding competence (four point rating scale) was obtained from the senior treating forensic psychiatrist, who was blind to the participants' scores on the MacCAT-FP. The MacCAT-FP was readministered to the hospital group a month after the initial administration.

The results from this initial study suggest that the MacCAT-FP has considerable potential as a research and clinical measure in England and

Wales. Good internal consistency was obtained for each measure, with Cronbach's alphas ranging from .74 (understanding) to .85 (reasoning). For each MacCAT-FP measure, the mean score of the hospital group was significantly lower than the mean of the prison/control group, providing support for the construct validity for the MacCAT-FP. Evidence for the concurrent validity of the MacCAT-FP was examined by comparing mean scores of the hospital group participants judged to be "fit" ($n = 30$) by the treating forensic psychiatrist with those of the hospital group judged to be "unfit" ($n = 15$). For each measure the mean scores of the fit group were higher than those of the unfit group, with the mean differences being statistically different for the reasoning and appreciation measures. Similarly, as the hospital group's psychopathology levels were reduced over a one-month period of treatment (as indicated by significantly lower scores on the Brief Psychiatric Rating Scale), so too did their scores on all three MacCAT-FP measures improve (significantly so for understanding and reasoning).

In summary, this preliminary research by Akinkunmi and colleagues suggests that the MacCAT-CA, with modifications that are sensitive to nuances in the explicit criteria for adjudicative competence (or "fitness"), may prove to be a useful research and/or clinical measure in other countries which share a common legal heritage with the U.S.

The MacCAT-CA has also been employed in adjudicative competence research in Canada, where Zapf and Roesch (2001) compared the performance of the MacCAT-CA with that of the Fitness Interview Test (FIT; Roesch, Zapf, Eaves & Webster, 1998), an interview-based measure constructed to assess the Canadian criteria for adjudicative competence. As in England, the criteria for fitness to proceed in Canada date historically to *Regina v. Pritchard* (1836), although a 1992 amendment to the Criminal Code of Canada (1985) codified the criteria for being "unfit to stand trial." In Canada, a defendant is unfit if he or she is

> Unable on account of mental disorder to conduct a defence at any stage of the proceedings before a verdict is rendered or to instruct counsel to do so, and, in particular, unable on account of mental disorder to (a) understand the nature or object of the proceedings, (b) understand the possible consequences of the proceedings, or (c) communicate with counsel (C.C.C., S.2, 1992).

Zapf and Roesch (2001) compared the functional legal abilities articulated in *Dusky v. United States* (1960) with the Canadian standard and determined that the test in the United States is a stricter test of competence (i.e., is more demanding). In particular, they noted that there is no explicit reference in Canadian law to the "rationality" of the defendant, while the *Dusky* test requires that a defendant have a "rational... understanding of the proceedings." From this analysis they hypothesized that assessments of Canadian defendants that employed the MacCAT-CA would result in more determinations of "unfit" than would assessments using the FIT, which is tailored more precisely to the criteria in Canadian law.

To test this hypothesis both the MacCAT-CA and the FIT were administered to 100 male defendants remanded to the Forensic Psychiatric Institute (FPI) in Port Coquitlam, British Columbia. Experimental criteria for classifying each defendant as unimpaired or impaired on each of these measures were established, and a contingency table was constructed for recording these classifications. The classification agreement for these two measures was quite good, even when corrected for chance agreement ($\kappa = .513$). As predicted, however, a greater proportion of defendants met experimental criteria for being impaired using the MacCAT-CA (48%) than met impairment criteria using the FIT (32%). These results suggest that it would be possible, perhaps even likely, for some individuals to be found incompetent with respect to U.S. standards but "fit" to proceed to adjudication if charged and prosecuted in Canada.

CONCLUSION

In this book, we have reported the first epidemiological studies of attorney-client decision making, argued for advances in the conceptualization and measurement of adjudicative competence, and presented empirical findings regarding the relationships between specific diagnoses and competence. Most importantly, we have developed a structured and nationally norm-referenced clinical measure of diverse competence-related abilities. We have also described ongoing and exciting extensions of this work to youthful defendants in juvenile and criminal court, to people with mental retardation, and to criminal defendants in countries other than the United States.

The study of "competence to stand trial" has changed in the almost 40 years since the publication of Robey's (1965) "checklist for psychiatrists." Only a decade ago, Grisso could say that "without an objective measure of the legally relevant abilities, development of a research foundation for the field of [competence to stand trial] will continue to be limited" (1992, p. 367). Our hope is that the MacArthur Competence Assessment Tool-Criminal Adjudication (MacCAT-CA),[2] documented here, will provide the "objective measure" that will facilitate further progress in the field.

[2] The MacCAT-CA can be obtained from Psychological Assessment Resources, at www.parinc.com. Further developments in research on this instrument will be found at http://macarthur.virginia.edu

References

Adams v. United States *ex rel.* McCann, 317 U.S. 269, 275 (1942).
Akinkunmi, A., Cumbley, L., Goodman, G., Hever, T., Vine, J., Smith, S., & Blizard, R. (2001). The MacArthur Competence Assessment Tool—Fitness to Plead: A research instrument for assessing fitness to plead in England and Wales. In R. Roesch, R. Corrado, & R. Dempster (Eds.), *Psychology in the courts: International advances in knowledge*. London: Routledge.
Allard v. Hellgemoe, 572 F. 2d 1 (1st Cir, 1978).
American Bar Association. (1986). *Association standards for the administration of criminal justice*. Boston: Little Brown.
American Bar Association. (2001). *Model rules of professional conduct*. Chicago: American Bar Association.
American Psychiatric Association. (1994). *Diagnostic and statistical manual of mental disorders* (4th edition). Washington, DC: American Psychiatric Association.
Appelbaum, P., & Grisso, T. (1988). Assessing patients' capacities to consent to treatment. *New England Journal of Medicine, 319*, 1635–1638.
Appelbaum, P.S., Mirkin, S.A., & Bateman, A.L. (1981). Empirical assessment of competency to consent to psychiatric hospitalization. *American Journal of Psychiatry, 138*, 1170–1176.
Argersinger v. Hamlin, 407 U.S. 25 (1972).
Bagby, R.M., Nicholson, R.A., Rogers, R., & Nussbaum, D. (1992). Domains of competency to stand trial: A factor analytic study. *Law and Human Behavior, 16*, 491–508.
Berman, L. M., & Osborne, Y. H. (1987). Attorneys' referrals for competency to stand trial evaluations: Comparisons of referred and nonreferred clients. *Behavioral Sciences and the Law, 5*, 373–380.
Blackstone, W. (1765–69). *Commentaries on the laws of England* (Univ. of Chicago Press, 1979).

Bonnie, R. (1990). The competence of criminal defendants with mental retardation to participate in their own defense. *Journal of Criminal Law and Criminology, 81*, 419–446.

Bonnie, R. (1992). The competence of criminal defendants: A theoretical reformulation. *Behavioral Sciences and the Law, 10*, 291–316.

Bonnie, R. (1993). The competence of criminal defendants: Beyond *Dusky* and *Drope*. *University of Miami Law Review, 46*, 539–601.

Boyd, J.C. (1999, July). The MacCAT-CA and juvenile criminal defendants. Paper presented at the First Annual Psychology and Law: International Conference, Dublin, Ireland.

Boykin v. Alabama, 395 U.S. 238 (1969).

Brakel, J. (1974). Presumption, bias, and incompetency in the criminal process. *Wisconsin Law Review, 1974*, 1105–1130.

Brookhart v. Janis, 384 U.S. 1, 7–8 (1966).

Bukatman, B., Foy, J.L., & DeGrazia, E. (1971). What is competency to stand trial? *American Journal of Psychiatry, 127*, 145–149.

Callahan, L. A., Steadman, H. J., McGreevy, M. A, & Robbins, P. C. (1991). The volume and characteristics of insanity pleas: An eight-state study. *Bulletin of the American Academy of Psychiatry and the Law, 19*, 331–338.

Cascardi, M., & Poythress, N. (1996). Voluntary psychiatric hospitalization: An empirical study of mentally ill persons' capacity to consent. Paper presented at the Annual Convention of the American Public Health Association, New York.

Cauffman, E., & Steinberg, L. (1996). The cognitive and affective influences on adolescent decision-making. *Temple Law Review, 68*, 1763–1789.

Cauffman, E., Woolard, J., & Reppucci, N.D. (1999). Justice for juveniles: New perspectives on adolescents' competence and culpability. *QLR: Quinnipiac College Law Review, 18*, 403–419.

Cocozza, Joseph. Personal communication.

Cohen, J. (1988). *Statistical power analysis for the behavioral sciences* (2nd ed.). New York: Erlbaum.

Cooper, D.K. (1997). Juveniles' understanding of trial-related information: Are they competent defendants? *Behavioral Science and the Law, 15*, 167–180.

Cowden, V.L., & McKee, G.R. (1995). Competence to stand trial in juvenile delinquency proceedings: Cognitive maturity and the attorney-client relationship. *Journal of Family Law, 33*, 629–660.

Criminal Code of Canada (1985). R. S. C., C-46.

Drope v. Missouri, 420 U.S. 162 (1975).

Dusky v. U.S., 362 US 402 (1960).

Edens, J.F., Poythress, N.G., Otto, R.K., & Nicholson, R.A. (1999). Effects of state organizational structure and forensic examiner training on pre-trial competence assessments. *Journal of Behavioral Health and Services Research, 26*, 140–150.

Everett, M. (1996). Training psychologists to function as competent scientists in criminal forensics. In E.P. Benedek (Ed.), *New directions for mental health services* (pp. 49–57). New York: Jossey-Bass.

Everington, C.T., & Luckasson, R. (1992). *Competence assessment for standing trial for defendants with mental retardation (CAST-MR)*. Worthington, OH: International Diagnostic Systems.

Fagan, J., & Zimring, F.E. (Eds.). (2000). *The changing borders of juvenile justice: Transfer of adolescents to the criminal court.* Chicago: University of Chicago Press.

Faretta v. California, 422 U.S. 806, 823 (1975).

Farkas, G.M., DeLeon, P.H., & Newman, R. (1997). Sanity examiner certification: An evolving national agenda. *Professional Psychology: Research and Practice, 28*, 73–76.

Feinberg, J. (1986). *Harm to self: The moral limits of the criminal law*. NY: Oxford UP.

Fiske, D.W. (1971). *Measuring the concepts of personality*. Chicago: Aldine.

Frendak v. United States, 408 A.2d 364 (D.C., 1979).
Gideon v. Wainwright, 372 U.S. 335 (1963).
Godinez v. Moran, 509 U.S. 389, 398 (1993).
Golding, S., Roesch, R. & Schreiber, J. (1984). Assessment and conceptualization of competency to stand trial: Preliminary data on the Interdisciplinary Fitness Interview. *Law and Human Behavior, 8*, 321–334.
Grisso, T. G. (1986). *Evaluating competencies: Forensic assessments and instruments*. New York: Plenum.
Grisso, T. (1987). The economic and scientific future of forensic psychological assessment. *American Psychologist, 42*, 831–839.
Grisso, T. (1991). Clinical assessments for legal decision-making: Research recommendations. In S. Shah & B.D. Sales (Eds.), *Law and mental health: Major developments and research needs* (pp. 49–80). Rockville, MD: Department of Health and Human Services Publication No (ADM) 91-1875.
Grisso, T. (1992). Five year research update (1986–1990): Evaluations of competence to stand trial. *Behavioral Sciences and the Law, 10*, 353–369.
Grisso, T. (1997a). Juveniles' competence to stand trial: New questions for an era of punitive juvenile justice reform. *Criminal Justice, 12*, 5–11.
Grisso, T. (1997b). The competence of adolescents as trial defendants. *Psychology, Public Policy, and Law, 3*, 3–32.
Grisso, T., Cocozza, J., Steadman, H.J., Fisher, W., & Greer, A. (1994). The organization of pretrial forensic evaluation services: A national profile. *Law and Human Behavior, 18*, 377–394.
Grisso, T., & Appelbaum, P.S. (1995). The MacArthur Treatment Competence Study, III: Abilities of patients to consent to psychiatric and medical treatments. *Law and Human Behavior, 19*, 149–174.
Grisso, T., Appelbaum, P.S., & Hill-Fotouhi, C. (1997). The MacCAT-T: A clinical tool to assess patients' capacities to make treatment decisions. *Psychiatric Services, 48*, 1415–1419.
Grisso, T., Appelbaum, P.S., Mulvey, E.P., & Fletcher, K. (1995). The MacArthur Treatment Competence Study, II: Measures of abilities related to competence to consent to treatment. *Law and Human Behavior, 19*, 126–148.
Grisso, T., & Schwartz, R.G. (Eds). (2000). *Youth on trial: A developmental perspective on juvenile justice*. Chicago: University of Chicago Press.
Hagan, J., & Albonetti, C. (1982). Race, class, and the perception of injustice in America. *American Journal of Sociology, 88*, 329–355.
Harkness, A.R., McNulty, J.L., & Ben-Porath, Y.S. (1995). The personality psychopathology five (PSY-5): Constructs and MMPI-2 scales. *Psychological Assessment, 7*, 104–114.
Hart, S., & Hare, R. (1992). Predicting fitness to stand trial: The relative power of demographic, criminal and clinical variables. *Forensic Reports, 5*, 53–66.
Harvard Law Review. (1967). Incompetency to stand trial. *Harvard Law Review, 81*, 454–473.
Heilbrun, K., Leheny, C., Thomas, L., & Huncycutt, D. (1997). A national survey of U.S. statutes on juvenile transfer: Implications for policy and practice. *Behavioral Sciences and the Law, 15*, 125–149.
Hendricks v. Colorado, 10 P.3d 1231 (Colo. 2000).
Hess, J.H., & Thomas, H.E. (1963). Incompetence to stand trial: Procedures, results, and problems. *American Journal of Psychiatry, 119*, 713–720.
Hoge, S., Bonnie, R., Poythress, N., & Monahan, J. (1992). Attorney-client decision-making in criminal cases: Client competence and participation as perceived by their attorneys. *Behavioral Sciences and the Law, 10*, 385–394.
Hoge, S.K., Poythress, N., Bonnie, R., Eisenberg, M., Monahan, J., Feucht-Haviar, T., & Oberlander, L. (1996). Mentally ill and non-mentally ill defendants' abilities to understand

information relevant to adjudication: A preliminary study. *Bulletin of the American Academy of Psychiatry and the Law, 24,* 187–197

Hollingshead, A.R., & Redlich, F.C. (1958). *Social class and mental illness.* New York: Guilford.

In re Gault, 387 U.S. 1 (1967).

Institute of Law, Psychiatry, and Public Policy. (Unpublished). Virginia Forensic Information Management System Annual Report, 1989–1990.

Jackson v. Indiana, 406 U.S. 715, 738 (1972).

Johnson v. Zerbst, 304 U.S. 458 (1938).

Jones v. Barnes, 463 U.S. 745 (1983).

Kaufman, A., Ishikuma, T., & Kaufman-Packer, J.L. (1991). Amazingly short forms of the WAIS-R. *Journal of Psychoeducational Assessment, 9,* 4–15.

Kent v. U.S., 383 US 541 (1966).

Laboratory of Community Psychiatry, Harvard Medical School. (1973). *Competency to stand trial and mental illness.* Washington, DC: Department of Health, Education, and Welfare Publication No. ADM 77-103.

Landis, J.R., & Koch, G.G. (1977). The measurement of observer agreement for categorical data. *Biometrics, 33,* 159–174.

Langan, P., & Brown, J. (1997). Felony sentences in state courts, 1994. In *Bureau of Justice Statistics Bulletin.* Washington, DC: Bureau of Justice Statistics.

Lipsitt, P., Lelos, D., & McGarry, A.L. (1971). Competency for trial: A screening instrument. *American Journal of Psychiatry, 128,* 105–109.

McGaha, A., Otto, R.K., McClaven, M.D., & Petrila, J. (2001). Juveniles adjudicated incompetent to proceed: A descriptive study of Florida's competence restoration program. *Journal of the American Academy of Psychiatry and the Law, 29,* 427–437.

McGarry, A.L. (1965). Competence for trial and due process via the state hospital. *American Journal of Psychiatry, 122,* 623–631.

McKee, G.R. (1998). Competence to stand trial in pre-adjudicatory juveniles and adults. *Journal of the American Academy of Psychiatry and the Law, 26,* 89–99.

Melton, G., Petrila, J., Poythress, N., & Slobogin, C. (1997). *Psychological evaluations for the courts: A handbook for mental health professionals and lawyers* (2nd ed.). New York: Guilford.

Miller, F.W., Dawson, R.O., Dix, G.E., & Parnas, R.I. (1971). *The mental health process.* Mineola, NY: Foundation Press.

Miller v. Commonwealth, 197 Ky. 703, 247 S.W. 956 (1923).

Model Rules of Professional Conduct and Code of Judicial Conduct. (1983). Chicago: American Bar Association.

Moran v. Godinez, 972 F. 2d 263 (9th Cir, 1992).

Morse, S. (1978). Law and mental health professionals: The limits of expertise. *Professional Psychology, 9,* 389–399.

Nicholson, R.A. (1993, August). Current methods for assessing criminal competencies. Paper presented at the Annual Convention of the American Psychiatric Association, San Francisco.

Nicholson, R., & Kugler, K. (1991). Competent and incompetent defendants: A quantitative review of comparative research, *Psychological Bulletin, 109,* 355–370.

Nicholson, R.A., Briggs, S.R., & Robertson, H.C. (1988). Instruments for assessing competency to stand trial: How do they work? *Professional Psychology: Research and Practice, 19,* 383–394.

Nunnally, J.C. (1978). *Psychometric theory.* New York: McGraw-Hill.

Otto, R.K., & Heilbrun, K. (2002). The future of forensic psychology: A look toward the future in light of the past. *American Psychologist, 57,* 5–18.

Overall, J., & Gorham, D. (1962). The Brief Psychiatric Rating Scale. *Psychological Reports, 10,* 799–812.

Overall, J., & Porterfield, J. (1963). Power vector method of factor analysis. *Psychometrika, 28*, 415–422.
Penry v. Lynaugh, 492 U.S. 302 (1989).
People v. Hunt, 427 N.W.2d 907 (Mich.App. 1988).
People v. Newton, 446 N.W.2d 487 (Mich.App. 1989).
People v. Nyberg, 362 N.W.2d 748 (Mich.App. 1984).
People v. Snyder, 310 N.W.2d 868 (Mich.App. 1981).
People v. Welch, 20 Cal. 4th 701, 976 P.2d 754 (1999).
Poythress, N. (1978). Psychiatric expertise in civil commitment: Training attorneys to cope with expert testimony. *Law and Human Behavior, 2*, 1–23.
Poythress, N., Bonnie, R.J., Hoge, S.K., Monahan, J., & Oberlander, L.B. (1994). Client abilities to assist counsel and make decisions in criminal cases: Findings from three studies. *Law and Human Behavior, 18*, 435–450.
Poythress, N., Otto, R., & Heilbrun, K. (1991). Pretrial evaluations for criminal courts: Contemporary models of service delivery. *Journal of Mental Health Administration, 18*, 198–208.
President's Commission for the Study of Ethical Problems in Medicine and Biomedical and Behavioral Research. (1982). *Making health care decisions: A report on the ethical and legal implications of informed consent in the patient-practitioner relationship.* Vol. I. Washington, DC: Government Printing Office.
R. v. Pritchard, 173 Eng. Rep. 135 (1836).
Reaves, B. (1998). Felony defendants in large urban counties, 1994. In Bureau of Justice Statistics, *Executive Summary*. Washington, DC: Bureau of Justice.
Redding, R.E. (1997). Juveniles transferred to criminal court: Legal reform proposals based on social science research. *Utah Law Review, 1997*, 709–763.
Regina v. Pritchard, 7 Car. & P. 304, 173 E.R. 135 (1836).
Reich, J., & Tookey, L. (1986). Disagreements between court and psychiatrist on competency to stand trial. *Journal of Clinical Psychiatry, 47*, 29–30.
Robey, A. (1965). Criteria for competency to stand trial: A checklist for psychiatrists. *American Journal of Psychiatry, 122*, 616–623.
Rock v. Arkansas, 483 U.S. 44, 52–53 (1987).
Roesch, R., & Golding, S. L. (1980). *Competency to stand trial.* Urbana, IL: University of Illinois Press.
Roesch, R., & Golding, S. L. (1987). Defining and assessing competency to stand trial. In I. B. Weiner & A. K. Hess (Eds.), *Handbook of forensic psychology* (pp. 378–394). New York: Wiley.
Roesch, R., Zapf, P.A., Eaves, D., & Webster, C.D. (1998). *The Fitness Interview Test (revised edition).* Burnaby, BC: Mental Health, Law, & Policy Institute, Simon Fraser University.
Rogers, R., & Ewing, C.P. (1989). Ultimate opinion proscriptions: A cosmetic fix and a plea for empiricism. *Law & Human Behavior, 13*, 357–374.
Rogers, R., Grandjeon, N., Tillbrook, C.E., Vitacco, M.J., & Sewell, K.W. (2001). Recent interview-based measures of competency to stand trial: If critical review augmented with research data. *Behavioral Sciences and the Law, 19*, 503–518.
Rutherford, D.M. (2000). Evaluation of competency to stand trial in a juvenile population. *Dissertation Abstracts International: Section B: The Sciences & Engineering* (US : Univ Microfilms International) Vol 61(2-B), August, 1074.
Savitsky, J.C., & Karras, D. (1984). Competency to stand trial among adolescents. *Adolescence, 19*, 349–359.
Scott, E.S., & Grisso, T. (1997). The evolution of adolescence: A developmental perspective on juvenile justice reform. *The Journal of Criminal Law and Criminology, 88*, 137–189.

Scott, E.S., Reppucci, N.D., & Woolard, J.L. (1995). Evaluating adolescent decision making in legal contexts. *Law & Human Behavior, 19,* 221–244.

Sickmund, M. (1994). *How juveniles get to criminal court.* Office of Juvenile Justice and Delinquency Prevention Update. Washington, DC: Department of Justice.

Sieling v. Eyman, 478 F.2d 211 (9th Cir 1973).

Shrout, P.E., & Fleiss, J.L. (1979). Intraclass correlations: Uses in assessing rater reliability. *Psychological Bulletin, 86,* 420–428.

Skeem, J.L., Golding, S.L.,Cohn, N.B., & Berge, G. (1998). Logic and reliability of evaluations of competence to stand trial. *Law and Human Behavior, 22,* 519–547.

State v. Kaiser, 74 N.J.Super. 257, 181 A.2d 184 (1962).

State v. Wilson, 181 La. 61, 158 So. 621 (1935).

State v. Valentino, 356 N.T.S. 2d 962 (1974).

Steadman, H.J. (1979). *Beating a rap? Defendants found incompetent to stand trial.* Chicago: University of Chicago Press.

Steadman, H.J., & Braff, J. (1975). Crimes of violence and incompetency diversion. *Journal of Criminal Law and Criminology, 66,* 73–78.

Steadman, H. J., & Hartstone, E. (1983). Defendants incompetent to stand trial. In J. Monahan & H.J. Steadman (Eds.), *Mentally disordered offenders: Perspectives from law and social science* (pp. 39–62). New York: Plenum.

Steadman, H., & Monahan, J. (Eds). (1983). *Mentally disordered offenders.* New York: Plenum.

Steinberg, L., & Cauffman, E. (1996). Maturity of judgment in adolescence: Psychosocial factors in adolescent decisionmaking. *Law and Human Behavior, 20,* 249–272.

Treece v. Maryland, 313 Md 665, 547 A.2d 1054 (1988).

United States v. Mooney, 123 F. Supp 2d 442 (ND Ill. 2000).

Van, H., & Morganroth, D. (1964). Psychiatrists and the competence to stand trial. *University of Detroit Law Journal, 42,* 75–85.

Ward v. State, 142 Fla. 238, 194 So. 637 (1940).

Warren, J. I., & Lexcen, F. (2001). The developmental, cognitive, and psychiatric correlates of adjudicative competence in juveniles. Unpublished manuscript, Instiute of Law, Psychiatry and Public Policy, Charlottesville, Virginia.

Weihofen, H. (1954). *Mental disorder as a criminal defense.* Buffalo, NY: Dennis.

Weston v. U.S., 255 F 3d 873, US App. (2001).

Whalem v. United States, 120 U.S. App.D.C. 331, 346 F.2d 812 (enbanc), *cert. denied,* 382 U.S. 862 (1968).

Wildman, R., Batchelor, E., Thompson, L., Nelson, F., Moore, J., Patterson, M., & DeLaosa, M. (1980). *The Georgia Court Competency Test: An attempt to develop a rapid quantitative measure for fitness for trial.* Unpublished manuscript, Forensic Services Division, Central State Hospital, Milledgeville, Georgia.

Wilson v. United States, 391 F.2d 460 (1968).

Winick, B. (1987). Incompetency to stand trial: An assessment of costs and benefits and a proposal for reform. *Rutgers Law Review, 39,* 243–287.

Woerner, M.G., Mannuzza, S., & Kane, J.M. (1988). Anchoring the BPRS: An aid to improved reliability. *Psychopharmacology Bulletin, 24,* 112–118.

Zapf, P.A., & Roesch, R. (2001). A comparison of the MacCAT-CA and the FIT for making determinations of competency to stand trial. *International Journal of Law and Psychiatry, 24,* 81–92.

Index

Adams v. United States ex rel McCann, 46
Adjudicative Competence; *see also*
Competence *and* Incompetence
Plea
assessment tools, 41, 53–56, 151, 153
importance of face validity in legal
context, 57–58
attorneys
professional norms, 10–11
perceptions of clients' capacities and
competence, 5–8, 9–10, 14–15, 18–
19, 21–24, 37, 99
in potential insanity defense cases,
28–31
strategies employed with clients of
doubted competence, 8, 15–16, 19,
24–26, 37
work intensity in cases of doubted
competence, 14, 17
conceptualization
as a unitary construct, 47–49
as two separate constructs, 38, 46–48,
56, 99–104
competence to assist counsel, 46–47
decisional competence, 47–48
contextual nature of, 2, 41–42
defendants' perceptions of own
capacities and competence, 21–22
elements of comprehensive evaluation
of, 144
juveniles' capacities as function of age,
147–150
legal criteria, 1, 39–40, 45, 89
in England and Wales, 152

Adjudicative Competence (*cont.*)
motivations for challenging defendant's
competence, 49–50
prevalence of referrals for evaluation, 50
purposes of, 1, 43–46
relevant psycholegal abilities; *see also*
MacSAC-CD and MacCAT-CA
appreciation, 54, 63–64, 100
reasoning, 54, 63, 100
understanding, 54, 61, 99
youths' capacities; *see* Juvenile Court
Akinkunmi, A., 152
Albonetti, C., 73
Allard v. Hellgemoe, 48
American Bar Association, 26, 41, 42, 46
American Bar Association Ethical Code, 37
American Psychiatric Association, 70
Appelbaum, P.S., 3, 68, 89, 105, 107, 110, 121
Argersinger v. Hamlin, 45

Bagby, R.M, 141
Bateman, A.L., 121
Ben-Porath, Y., 118
Berman, L.M., 3
Blackstone, W., 44
Bonnie, R., 1, 11, 35, 44, 46, 48, 49, 56, 89,
92, 99, 100, 103
Boyd, J., 149
Boykin v. Alabama, 46
Braff, J., 69
Brakel, J., 71
Brief Psychiatric Rating Scale, 73, 118
mean scores in MacSAC-CD field study
(males), 76

Brief Psychiatric Rating Scale (*cont.*)
  mean scores in MacSAC-CD field study
    (females), 84
  mean scores in the MacCAT-CA
    norming study, 123
  correlations with MacCAT-CA scores,
    127
  correlations with MacSAC-CD scores
    (males), 79, 97
  correlations with MacSAC-CD scores
    (females), 86
Briggs, S.R., 55, 141
Brookhart v. Janis, 46
Brown, J., 50
Bukatman, B., 53

Callahan, L., 5
Cascardi, M., 110
Cauffman, E., 147
Center for Forensic Psychiatry, 12, 26
Civil Commitment, 36, 104
Civil competence
  legal grounds for overriding competent
    treatment refusals, 109
  MacArthur Network's Civil Competence
    Project, 105
  research measures of, 105–107
    performance on, in comparison to
      adjudicative competence, 108
Coccoza, J., 114, 115
Cohen, J., 126
Competence; *see also* Adjudicative
  Competence
  independence of competencies across
    legal contexts, 104, 109
  to assist counsel, 38, 46–47
  to consent to treatment, 2–3, 104–110
  to decide whether to pursue an available
    insanity defense, 31–34
  to plead guilty, 2
    requirement of client autonomy, 7
    attorneys' perceptions of clients'
      involvement in decision, 7, 15, 19, 22
  to waive Fifth Amendment right and
    testify at trial, 22
    attorneys' perceptions of clients'
      involvement in decision, 19, 22
  to waive trial by jury, 19, 22
    attorneys' perceptions of clients'
      involvement in decision, 19

Competence to Stand Trial Assessment
  Instrument (CAI), 54, 55
Competency Screening Test (CST), 53, 55,
  141
Cooper, D.K., 147
Cowden, V.L., 147
Criminal Code of Canada, 153
Criminal court
  direct file or transfer of youth to, 146,
    150
  lowered age for jurisdiction of, 146, 150

Dawson, R.O., 54
Decisional Competence, 47–48; *see also*
  Competence (for specific
  decisions)
  as fundamental component of
    adjudicative competence, 38
  autonomous client involvement, 38, 41,
    43, 45–46
  capacities implied by, 48
  case law, 2
  encompassed by the *Dusky* standard, 48
  proposals for surrogate decision-making,
    38, 49
Degrazia, E., 53
DeLeon, P., 114
Dix, G., 54
Drope v. Missouri, 40, 44, 45
Dusky v. United States, 1, 40, 45, 46, 48, 49,
  50, 54, 60, 103, 104, 112

Eaves, D., 153
Edens, J.F., 125
Everett, M., 114
Everington, C., 151
Ewing, C., 144

Fagan, J., 146
Faretta v. California, 45
Farkas, G., 114
Feinberg, J., 37
Fisher, W., 114
Fitness Interview Test, 153
Fleiss, J.L., 124
Fletcher, K., 105
Forensic evaluations
  forensic examiner training requirements,
    114–115
  influences on professional practice, 144

INDEX

Forensic evaluations (*cont.*)
   service delivery systems, 114
Foy, J.L., 53
Frendak v. United States, 34

Georgia Court Competency Test (GCCT), 54, 55, 141
Gideon v. Wainwright, 45
Godinez v. Moran, 2, 40, 47–49
Golding, S., v, 2, 10, 41, 42, 54, 70
Gorham, D., 73
Greer, A., 114
Grisso, T., v, 2, 3, 11, 41, 56, 57, 68, 70, 89, 105, 106, 107, 110, 114, 115, 121, 144, 146, 147, 154
Guardianship, 104

Hagan, J., 73
Hare, R.D., 42
Harkness, A., 118
Hart, S.D., 42
Hartstone, E., 2
Harvard Law Review, 44
Heilbrun, K., 25, 114, 150
Hendricks v. Colorado, 49
Hess, J.H., 54
Hill-Fotouhi, C., 121
Hoge, S.K., 68
Hollingshead, A.R., 122
Honeycutt, D., 150

Incompetence for adjudication
   as surrogate for civil commitment, 50
   consequences of finding of incompetence, 50–51
   constitutional bar to adjudication, 40, 45
   developmental immaturity as basis for youths' incompetence, 147
   distinguished from legal insanity, 51
   history of the plea, 39–40
   predicate mental condition for, 51, 147
   prevalence of, 50
   relationship to mental disorder, 92, 98
   values served by incompetence diversion, 43–46
In re Gault, 146
Insanity Defense
   attorneys'
      obligations when clients refuse to plead insanity, 26

Incompetence for adjudication (*cont.*)
   perceptions of clients' competence, 28–31, 36
   preempting client involvement in pursuing an insanity defense, 31–33, 36
   case outcomes and disposition, 29–30
   defendants' attitudes toward, 30
   distinguished from incompetence to proceed, 51
   entered over defendant's objection, 49
   legal norms, 34–36
Interdisciplinary Fitness Interview (IFI), 54, 55
Involuntary hospitalization; *see* Civil commitment
Ishikuma, T., 118

Jackson v. Indiana, 51
Johnson v. Zerbst, 46
Jones v. Barnes, 46
Juvenile court
   increased salience of adjudicative competence in, 146
   juveniles' capacities as function of age, 147–150
   waiver of juveniles to adult court, 146, 150
Juveniles
   competence-related abilities, 146–150
   developmental immaturity hypothesis, 147

Kane, J.M, 73, 118
Karras, D., 147
Kaufman, A., 118
Kaufman-Packer, J.L., 118
Kent v. U.S., 146
Koch, G.G., 88
Kugler, K., 69, 70, 91

Laboratory of Community Psychiatry, 54
Landis, J.R., 88
Langan, P., 50
Leheny, C., 150
Lelos, D., 53, 72, 141
Lexcen, F., 148
Lipsitt, P., 53, 72, 141
Luckasson, R., 151

MacArthur Foundation Research Network on Adolescent Development and Juvenile Justice, 148–149, 151
MacArthur Foundation Research Network on Mental Health and the Law, v, 43, 53, 105, 145
  Adjudicative competence clinical measure, *see* MacCAT-CA
  Adjudicative competence research agenda, 56–57
  Adjudicative competence research measure, *see* MacSAC-CD
  Civil competence project, 105, 110
MacCAT-CA, 60, 111–144
  adapted for use in England and Wales, 152–153
  cautions for clinical use, 143–144
  component measures and items assessing
    appreciation, 113, 149
    reasoning, 113
    understanding, 113
  derived from the MacSAC-CD, 112–113
  use of vignette methodology, 112
  NIMH norming study
    classification utility of MacCAT-CA, 128–131, 137–139, 142
    interpretive norms for the MacCAT-CA
      Appreciation measure, 135–137
      Reasoning measure, 133–135
      Understanding measure, 133–135
    psychometric properties of the MacCAT-CA, 123–124
    validity data for the MacCAT-CA, 124–131
    study sites and participants, 114–118, 120–123
  limitations on use with juveniles, 149
  not a measure of legal competence per se, 143
  structural features of, 145
MacCAT-FP, 152–153
  psychometric properties, 153
  scores' correspondence with clinical judgments, 153
MacSAC-CD, 57–67, 111–112
  component measures, 59–67
    of competence to assist counsel, 61–65
    of decisional competence, 65–67

MacSAC-CD (*cont.*)
  component measures (*cont.*)
    and performance in comparison to civil (treatment) competence, 108–109
    and psychiatric diagnosis, 92–98
  construct validity
    male defendants, 78–82
    female defendants, 85–87
  field studies, 68–89
  limitations of, 89
  pilot study results, 67–68
  psychometric properties
    male defendants, 77–78
    female defendants, 84–85
  use of vignette methodology, 58
Mannuzza, S., 73, 118
McClaren, M., 152
McGaha, A., 152
McGarry, A.L., v, 54, 72, 141
McGreevy, M.A., 5
McKee, G., 147
McNulty, J.L., 118
Melton, G.B., 1, 10, 11, 50, 104, 141
Mental retardation
  among incompetent adolescent defendants, 152
  assessing competence in mentally retarded persons, 151
Miller, F.W., 54
Miller v. Commonwealth, 51
Mirkin, S.A., 121
MMPI PSY-5 Psychoticism Scale, 118–119
  mean scores in the MacCAT-CA norming study, 123
  correlations with MacCAT-CA measures, 127
Model Rules of Professional Conduct, 37, 46
Monahan, J., 50
Moran v. Godinez, 48
Morganroth, D., 54
Morse, S., 143
Mulvey, E., 105

Newman, R., 114
Nicholson, R.A., 55, 69, 70, 91, 125, 141, 141
NIMH norming study: *see* MacCAT-CA
Nunnally, 77
Nussbaum, D., 141

INDEX

Osborne, Y.H., 3
Otto, R.K., 25, 114, 125, 152
Overall, J.E., 73

Parnas, R.I., 54
Paternalism
  in civil commitment, 36
  in insanity defense cases, 36–37
  "soft" paternalism, 48
People v. Hunt, 36
People v. Newton, 35
People v. Nyberg, 36
People v. Snyder, 36
Penry v. Lynaugh, 42
Perceived Criminal Injustice Scale, 73
Petrila, J., 1, 152
Porterfield, J., 73
Poythress, N.G., 1, 25, 36, 110, 125
President's Commission, 3, 10, 11

R. v. Pritcfhard, 39, 40, 152
Reaves, B., 50
Redding, R., 146
Redlich, F.C., 122
Regina v. Pritchard, 153
Reich, J., 42
Reppucci, N.D., 147
Robbins, P.C., 5
Robertson, H., 55, 141
Robey, A., v, 53, 154
Rock v. Arkansas, 46
Roesch, R., v, 2, 10, 41, 54, 70, 153
Rogers, R., 141, 144
Rutherford, D., 147

Savitsky, J.C., 147
Schreiber, J., 54
Scott, E., 147
Seiling v. Eyman, 48

Shrout, P.E., 124
Sickmund, , 146
Slobogin, C., 1
State v. Kaiser, 51
State v. Valentino, 89
State v. Wilson, 51
Steadman, H.J., v, 2, 5, 50, 69
Steinberg, L., 147
Swartz, R., 146

Thomas, H.E., 54
Thomas, L, 150
Tookey, L., 42
Treatment competence; see Civil
    competence
Treece v. Maryland, 26, 35

Ultimate issue, 42, 144
United States v. Mooney, 46

Van, H., 54

Waiver of constitutional rights, 46; see also
    Competence, Decisional
    Competence
Ward v. State, 51
Warren, J., 148
Webster, C., 153
Weihofen, H., 44
Weston v. United States, 109
Whalem v. United States, 34
Wildman, R., 54
Wilson v. United States, 89
Winick, B., 45
Woerner, M.G., 73, 118
Woolard, J., 147

Zapf, P., 153
Zimring, F., 146

Augsburg College
Lindell Library
Minneapolis, MN 55454